Fabric Decorating for the Home

Janet E. Roda

Oxmoor House, Inc. • Birmingham

Fabric Decorating for the Home

ISBN: 0-8487-0422-3
Library of Congress Catalog Card Number: 76-14112
Printed in the United States of America
Copyright ©1976 by Oxmoor House, Inc.
P.O. Box 2463, Birmingham, Alabama 35202
First Edition

Oxmoor House, Inc., is the Book Division of
The Progressive Farmer Company:

Eugene Butler *Chairman of the Board and Editor-in-Chief*
Emory Cunningham *President and Publisher*
Vernon Owens, Jr. *Senior Executive Vice President*
Roger McGuire *Executive Vice President*
Leslie B. Adams, Jr. *Vice President and Director of Book Division*

Conceived, edited and published by Oxmoor House, Inc.,
under the direction of:

John Logue *Editor-in-Chief*
Candace Conard Franklin *Editor*
Robert L. Nance *Production Manager*
Keith Kohler and Eileen Boudreaux *Illustrators*

Contents

Acknowledgments

My sincere thanks to my close friends and family for their continuing support and patience, and to Mary Anne Symons Brown for her invaluable assistance. In addition, special thanks go to the following manufacturers for their generous contributions of supplies for the model projects: American Thread, Stacy Fabrics, WestPoint Pepperell, and the William E. Wright Co.

Introduction

A house becomes a home only when it is filled with visible expressions of love and of you as an individual. Take a moment to look around you right now. How many items in the room are covered with or made of fabric? Probably quite a few. Fabrics—their colors, textures, and designs—are part of our everyday living, whether you define your life-style as formal, casual, trendy, or just plain comfortable. The full-color room illustrations are designed to stimulate your own creativity and imagination and to show you how to decorate with the fabrics and colors you love to live with.

Many items in the home are *purchased* simply because you feel you lack either the time or the know-how to *make* them. I have written *Fabric Decorating for the Home* to help resolve this dilemma and to respond to the thousands of questions about decorating that I have received while traveling throughout the United States. This book is designed to encourage and help you make your home a more charming and inviting place in which to live.

The projects range from the largest (fabric covered walls, slipcovers, braided rugs, etc.), to the smallest (coasters and cocktail napkins), and in between there are instructions on how to make items for every room of the house. Innumerable accessories are also included, such as pillows, place mats, napkins, tablecloths, wastebaskets, covered boxes, lampshades, dust ruffles and many, many more.

Not all of the projects in this book require a sewing machine or even a needle and thread; some items call for glue, and some require staples. But no matter which ideas you choose to try, patience is the key to success. Even though some projects take very little time to complete, try not to rush through them; you will achieve more professional results and discover that items will be finished faster when you do not have to redo a mistake.

All of the projects appearing in *Fabric Decorating for the Home* are rated as to their degree of difficulty. The easiest projects are keyed with one spool of thread while the most difficult ones bear five spools. Do not let a project's rating stop you from trying it. But if you are a beginner to the make-it-yourself game, consider starting with the simpler items and working up.

The 30 room settings offer different concepts in interior decorating; they include ideas for designing or rearranging your own rooms, and the how-to projects in each room illustrate how the item fits into a decorating scheme. However, all projects can be adapted to almost any type of room setting you may have, simply by changing the fabric.

Color is a very important part of interior decorating, and the best color spectrum to choose from is nature itself; flowering plants can be more vibrant than any "green" developed in a laboratory. Even all-green plants have a series of tonal color dimensions few fabrics can achieve. Color should surround your home and be an integral part of your decorating moods. To create an atmosphere of cool serenity, select blues; for a feeling of warm friendliness, choose yellows to reds; and for an aura of cozy casualness, design your room around nature's neutrals. Light colors make rooms appear larger, while dark colors bring in a room and make it feel smaller.

Color plays a very important part in your own psychological moods as well. And the colors you favor tell a bit about what type of an individual you are. If you like red, you probably have a strong, energetic personality—you are a doer, one who does not like to sit on the sidelines. If your favorite color is yellow, you are probably a spontaneous, idealistic individual—one who is innovative, creative, and artistic. Blues probably mean you are a very trusting and conservative person with an inquiring mind—one who seeks serenity and peace in all things.

When selecting color for any area, always carry an exact color swatch or chip with you. No one can carry color tones accurately in his mind. Purchase a yard or more of whatever fabric or paper you'd like to work with. Take the sample home, tack it up in the area to be covered, and live with it for a week. Each time you pass the swatch it should appeal to you again, so that by the end of the week you will know if it is what you really wish to live with. In this way you avoid costly mistakes, and the yard you purchased can always be used for a small project such as a pillow, picture frame, lampshade, book cover, or whatever.

Another basic part of decorating is *room arrangement.* Knowing how and where to place a piece of furniture in a room can change that room from an ordinary functional area to one which is interesting and inviting. An inviting room takes advantage of a view or the most interesting architectural point, or a work of art such as a piece of sculpture or your favorite painting or wall hanging.

As you rearrange or add pieces of furniture to any room, work out a floor plan on paper to make sure the decor remains balanced. If your couch is placed to enjoy a window view, place a similarly heavy piece of furniture near the window, such as a desk, which will also take advantage of the natural lighting. If your couch is in front of the fireplace, balance it by adding chairs or bookcases to each side along the wall. Never crowd furniture into a room just for the sake of filling up space. It is better to have one or two good pieces which will make a strong statement than to have a lot of insignificant pieces of furniture. Keep arrangements uncluttered, especially near windows and passage ways.

Fabric Decorating for the Home deals primarily with *fabrics*—fabrics of practically every type. The great barrier that once existed between "decorator" fabrics and "dressmaker" fabrics is gone. Today, because of the myriad life-styles in the United States, there is a wide range of fabrics to choose from to decorate your home.

It is rather comforting to know that "straight laced" decorating is a thing of the past. As the rule of white wine with fish/fowl

Fabric Weights

Sheer to Lightweight	*Medium-Weight*	*Heavyweight*
Batiste	Chintz	Brocade
Casement Cloth	Corduroy, pinwale	Brocatelle
Gauze	Flannel	Canvas
Dotted Swiss	Moiré	Corduroy, wide wale
Gingham	Muslin	Damask
Leno	Percale	Denim
Marquisette	Piqué	Duck
Ninon	Poplin	Frieze
Organdy	Pongee	Matelassé
	Sheeting	Monk's Cloth
	Toile	Satin
	Union Cloth	Shantung
		Ticking
		Velvet
		Velour
		(Felt is in this group but does not adapt to most decorating projects)

and red wine with beef has diminished in importance, so has the rule of using dark toned, heavyweight fabrics for rough wear areas and light toned and textured fabric for low wear and accent areas. Roles are being reversed all the time, and this seems to be especially true in home decorating. Fabrics are designed with *you* in mind; they are made to create, complement, and enhance individual life-styles. The hard part is knowing what you want and then finding the right fabrics.

Before purchasing fabric for home decorating, check it for construction (tightness of weave), strength, wrinkle resistance, sunfastness, and launderability. Preshrink the fabric if it is washable and if you plan to wash it. Always add extra yardage to your measurements if you are working with a fabric that has a repeating pattern. One extra repeat should be enough to allow for exact matching of the design to give a professional look when finished.

If you decide to use some of the experimental home decorating fabrics, such as the heavyweight upholstery knits, be certain to check for the manufacturer's guarantee as to their wear and performance. Some fabrics are not designed to withstand the wear of decorator projects; become "content conscious" and never buy on the chance it will last forever.

Floor covering is a topic of great concern when decorating a room. In many instances, you as the decorator may begin from the bottom up, working a theme around the colors in your hardwood floor, carpet, or rug. Floors should not dominate a room but should be a natural extension of the walls, draperies, and furniture coverings. It is the one area that can "pull a room together" by its color, tone, texture, or pattern.

Always select a floor covering suited to the styles of the room and the wear it will receive. In a heavily trafficked area, it is best to have a covering that is very durable, easy to care for, and that will not show dirt easily. Select carpets which are thick and dense; they will wear better and longer.

Carpeting comes in many shapes, colors, textures, and patterns. It not only helps soundproof a room, but it can add a feeling of spaciousness and luxury when used wall-to-wall. A solid color carpet gives an illusion of enlarging the room; a patterned carpet creates a smaller, cozier feeling. The bolder and brighter the pattern, the more the rug will dominate the room.

No matter how thick your carpet is, it should always have a pad underneath it. This not only absorbs the sound but helps to lengthen the life of the carpet. An experienced carpet salesperson will know which padding is appropriate for the carpet you purchase.

Area rugs are often treated as works of art, especially when they have a dramatic and unusual design. Small area rugs can even be hung on the wall. Make sure all area rugs have nonskid backings.

All new rugs, carpets, and carpeting, will shed during their first few months of use; frequent vacuuming will help control the shedding. Wipe all spills promptly, and avoid getting the carpet too wet. All carpeting should be professionally cleaned once a year to ensure its longevity.

Floor coverings of vinyl, brick, slate, marble, and other materials are all excellent for heavily trafficked areas. These add an informal atmosphere to any room and usually take a minimum amount of care. Wood floors can be stained, painted, or left bare with simply a clear varnish and a wax finish depending upon the mood you wish to create.

When basic decorating essentials are all together, accessorizing comes into play. This is a pastime for your leisure hours and can range from roaming around flea markets, to browsing through elegant antique shops. Through accessories you can add to your central theme or accent a special feeling. Never be afraid to blend cultures; most have elements which complement each other. But remember, to maintain a unified look if your basic room decor is formal, your accessories should also be formal. If your room is informal, so should be the accessories.

Collections of any sort make wonderful room accents as well as a way of displaying your personal interests and talents. Paintings, shells, rocks, plants—whatever—all add dimension to your home and help make it a living, personal extension of yourself.

Williamsburg Living Room

Williamsburg Living Room

Craftsmen coming from England in the 18th century and settling in the Colonies brought with them the designs which were to be used in the more luxurious dwellings. The colonials wanted to follow the fashions of the times, and furniture was purchased for its grace of design as well as for its function. Mahogany, walnut, rosewood, pine, and other woods were used to execute copies and adaptations of Queen Anne, Chippendale, Georgian, and other styles.

Our Williamsburg Living Room exudes a feeling of history and a soft elegance. Step into it and you are soothed and comforted by the patina of rich-toned, wood wall paneling and the luster of deeper toned and highly polished wood floor.

The colors are soft and somewhat muted or dusty in feeling—natural extensions of the richness of the wood. The rust and gold to yellow tones of the fabrics are all brought into play in the delicate but definite tones of the oriental rug.

The textures also lend a soothing, warm atmosphere to this room with the mixture of satin draperies set off by delicate sheers; a velvet couch accented with needlepoint pillows; the velvet wing chair; the crewel embroidered afghan on the velvet bench cushion; and the satin table skirt with appliquéd velvet bands of ribbon.

The floor-length table skirt adds instant glamour to even the smallest of tables. The skirt here touches the floor, but whether it flows elegantly onto the floor, touches the floor, or rests ½″ (1.3cm) or 1″ (2.5cm) above the floor is simply a matter of personal preference. To keep the top of the table free of smudges you might consider having it covered with a piece of inexpensive glass cut to fit.

The couch and chair here have both been professionally upholstered and treated with a soil-retardant spray. If you enjoy living with light colors, have the diligence to give them that bit of extra care and cleaning they require to keep them at their best.

The lined draperies with sheer curtains behind them are crowned by fabric covered cornices. The window fashions are designed to extend beyond the width and height of the windows to achieve a gracious, open feeling in the room and to add majesty to small and otherwise uninteresting windows. For added drama and color the cornices may be trimmed with an exotic brocade ribbon to accent the graceful curves.

Lined Draperies on a Traverse Rod

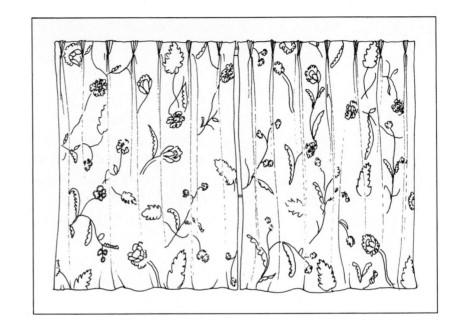

These traditional-style draperies are made in exactly the same manner as the draperies in the *Early American Living Room;* except, for a traverse rod, simply omit the wooden rings and wooden pole, and hang the draperies on a traverse rod with metal drapery hooks.

For a more formal look, crown your draperies with a covered cornice and add matching or contrasting tiebacks at either side.

Before beginning this project, refer to Techniques, Window Treatments.

Fabric Covered Cornice

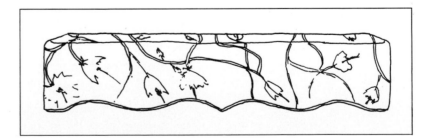

A fabric covered cornice is an effective finishing touch to any window treatment. Whether used alone, with a simple shade, or coordinated with your drapery fabric, cornices serve as excellent camouflage for window frames, rods, hooks, and rollers.

The directions given apply to any shape cornice for any size window.

Materials

- ½″ (1.3cm) plywood
- tape measure
- lead pencil, #2
- jigsaw
- nails
- tailor's chalk
- polyester fleece padding
- fabric shears
- staple gun and staples
- cable cord, ¼″ (6mm) thick
- T-pins
- light- to medium-weight fabric
- 1″ (2.5cm) angle irons and screws

Method

Step 1:

To determine the exact size of the cornice needed to cover your curtain or drapery rod and yet allow the draperies to move freely, measure: (See fig. 1.)

Width: the distance from left to right of the rod. Add 4″ to 6″ (10.2cm to 15.2cm) to provide 2″ to 3″ (5cm to 7.6cm) on each side of the rod when the cornice is mounted.

Length: the distance from 2″ to 3″ (5cm to 7.6cm) above the rod to at least 8″ (20.3cm) below it. A cornice may be 7″ to 11″ (17.8cm to 27.9cm) long, depending on its shape, the location of the rod in relation to the ceiling, and the type of curtains or draperies used.

Depth: the distance from the wall to the front of the cornice. As a rule, the cornice should project 2½″ to 3″ (6.4cm to 7.6cm) in front of the rod. A cornice may be 6″ to 7″ (15.2cm to 17.8cm) deep if two curtain or drapery rods are used.

Step 2:

To make the cornice frame, draw a rectangle the exact width and length of the front section on ½″ (1.3cm) plywood. If desired, draw a curved line along the bottom edge of the

rectangle in any design you desire. Make certain your design is symmetrical and centered correctly. (See fig. 2.)

On another section of the plywood, draw a rectangle for the top of the cornice which is 1″ (2.5cm) less in width and depth than the measurements for the front panel. When the cornice is completed, this section will fit behind the top and inside the side panels; thus the need to subtract 1″ (2.5cm) to allow for the thickness of the plywood.

Draw two side panels on the plywood, the same length as the front section, but subtract ½″ (1.3cm) from the measured depth of the cornice to allow for the thickness of the plywood in the front section. (See fig. 3.) You may wish to draw curved lines along the bottom edges of the sides to correspond with the design of the bottom front of the cornice.

Cut out all pieces with a jigsaw and nail together through the front. (See fig. 4.)

(Continued)

Figure 1

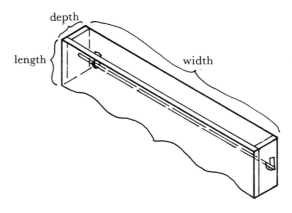

Figure 2

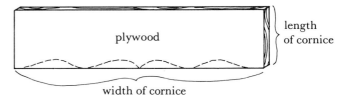

Figure 3

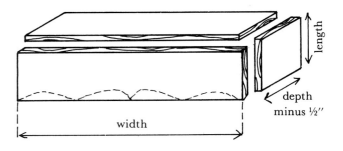

Figure 4

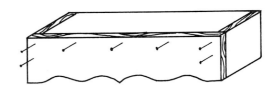

Step 3:
Measure, mark with tailor's chalk, and cut out a section of polyester fleece padding large enough to completely cover the cornice and wrap about ½″ (1.3 cm) to the underside of the back of the top and sides, and around to the underside of the bottom front and sides.

With a staple gun fasten the padding ½″ (1.3cm) from the edge along the underside of the top section. Pull firmly over the top and down the front section, and staple padding to the underside of the center front. (See fig. 5.)

Clip padding along curved edges as necessary to conform to the shape of the cornice. Staple in place. Continue working, mitering corners as you go, until cornice is completely covered with padding. (See fig. 6.)

Step 4:
Measure distance of the bottom edges of the cornice, including curves and sides. To make piping, cover a corresponding length of cable cord with 1½″ (3.8cm) wide bias strips in either a matching or contrasting fabric. (See Techniques, Bias Trim.)

Using T-pins, tack the fabric with the design centered on top of the padded cornice. (See fig. 7.) Keep the fabric smooth and taut as you work.

Pin-baste the piping along the bottom front curved edge and the bottom sides. The line of stitching which attached the bias strips around the piping should rest exactly on the edge of the cornice. (See fig. 8.)

Carefully remove T-pins, and lift the fabric and pin-basted piping from the cornice. Stitch piping in place.

Step 5:
Prepare a 2½″ (6.4cm) wide bias strip from your main fabric. (See Techniques, Bias Trim.) Place the strip, right side down, along the raw edges of the piping. Sew the bias strip to the piping. (See fig. 9.) When the cornice is finished, this strip will cover the bottom edge just behind the piping, thus giving the cornice a nicer, finished appearance.

Trim and clip the seam allowances of the piping, fabric, and bias strip.

Step 6:
Fit the fabric section, with piping and bias strip attached, over the padded cornice. Secure with T-pins. (See fig. 10.)

Following the same procedure used to attach the padding, pull the fabric firmly to the underside of the back of the top and sides and bottom front and sides, and staple in place. Make sure the piping rests exactly on the cornice edge before stapling.

Clip the bias strip as necessary along the bottom edge so that the fabric lies flat along the curved sections when stapled in place.

Step 7:
Attach angle irons to the top edges of the sides. Follow angle iron package directions to mount on the wall.

Figure 5

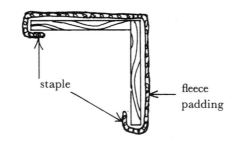

staple

fleece padding

Figure 6

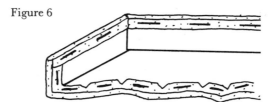

Figure 7

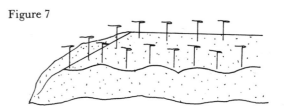

Figure 8

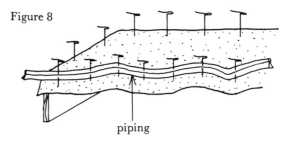

piping

Figure 9

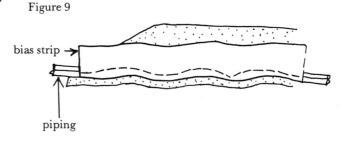

bias strip →

piping

Figure 10

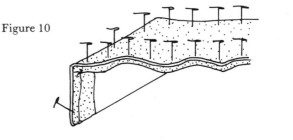

Sheer Curtains

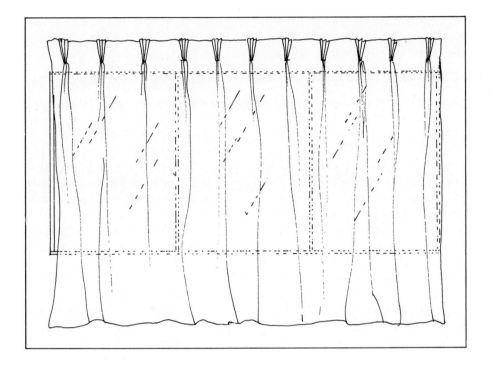

Sheers add a soft feeling to windows and may be hung alone or behind draperies. These curtains are usually three times the width of your window. The top may be pleated or shirred (gathered), depending upon the effect you wish to achieve. Here the curtains are pleated to correspond with the draperies.

The method for making sheers is the same as the method for making draperies except for the fact that they are unlined. The directions given apply to any unlined, pleated curtain or drapery.

Before beginning this project, refer to Techniques, Window Treatments.

Materials
- lightweight, sheer fabric
- tape measure
- tailor's chalk
- fabric shears
- T-pins
- dressmaker's pins
- nonwoven interfacing, 4" (10.2cm) wide
- thread to match
- metal drapery hooks

Method
Step 1:
Press fabric.

Measure, mark with tailor's chalk, and cut fabric lengths 16" (40.6cm) longer than the desired finished length.

Step 2:
Place right sides of fabric together. Using ½" (1.3cm) seams, stitch fabric lengths together to make a panel 3 times plus 10" (25.4cm) wider than the width of the window. (See fig. 1.) Flat-felled seams or French seams may be used. (See Techniques, Seams.) This will give you enough fullness for pleating and seams. It may be necessary to cut a lengthwise strip off one side of the panel to obtain the exact width.

To prevent the finished curtain from puckering if regular seams are used, clip ¼" (6mm) into the selvages along the seam allowances every 4" (10.2cm). Steam-press seams open.

(Continued)

Figure 1

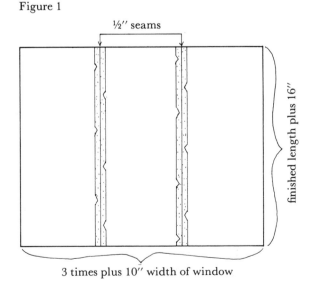

½" seams

finished length plus 16"

3 times plus 10" width of window

Step 3:
To make double hems along both side edges, turn raw edges under 2″ (5cm) and press. Turn under 2″ (5cm) again and press. Machine-stitch in place ¼″ (6mm) in from the inside fold edge; press.

Step 4:
To make the heading, measure and cut a length of nonwoven interfacing to equal the width of the panel plus 6″ (15.2cm).

Fold one end of the interfacing back on itself 3″ (7.6cm). Finger-press to make a sharp crease. (See fig. 2.)

Pin-baste interfacing across the top about ½″ (1.3cm) below the raw edge of the panel. Fold excess interfacing back on itself at opposite side of the panel. Fold top raw edge of fabric down over interfacing.

Stitch across the panel as close as possible to the top edge of the interfacing. Do not stitch across the bottom edge of the interfacing. (See fig. 2.)

Clip top corners to remove excess fabric. Turn top edge under the width of the interfacing and pin to hold in place. (See fig. 3.)

Step 5:
To make a double bottom hem, measure, mark, and turn up the bottom of the curtain panel 4″ (10.2cm); press. Turn bottom up 4″ (10.2cm) again and press. Machine-stitch across the width of the panel. (See fig. 4.) Press.

Step 6:
To measure the top for pleating, place the panel on a large flat surface, right side up. Mark off the areas to be pleated by measuring from each side toward the center.

With a T-pin, mark off 4″ (10.2cm) on each side. Next, mark a 5″ (12.7cm) area for pleats. Working toward the center, alternate 4″ (10.2cm) spaces and 5″ (12.7cm) areas for pleats. (See fig. 5.)

After the entire panel has been marked, check to make certain the pleats are evenly spaced at 4″ (10.2cm) intervals. If not, correct by adjusting the 5″ pleat allowances.

Step 7:
Once you have determined where each pleated area should begin and end, fold each pleat allowance in half, wrong side to the inside, to make one large pleat approximately 2½″ (6.4cm) deep. (See fig. 6.)

Stitch a straight line from the top edge of the curtain panel to the bottom of the interfacing to secure each pleated section. (See fig. 6.)

Pinch each pleated area as illustrated in figure 7 to form three separate small pleats. Tack the pleats in place with several short overcast stitches through the base of the interfacing. (See fig. 7.)

Slip metal drapery hooks into the back of each set of pleats, 1″ (2.5cm) below the top edge at each stitching line. (See fig. 8.)

Place a metal drapery hook ½″ (1.3cm) in from each side edge.

Remove basting stitches from heading. Hang finished curtain on rod.

Figure 3

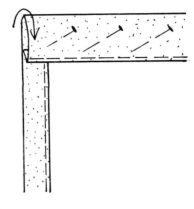

Figure 4

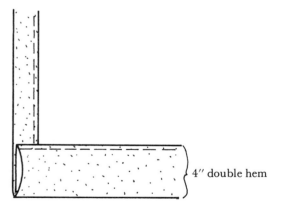

4″ double hem

Figure 2

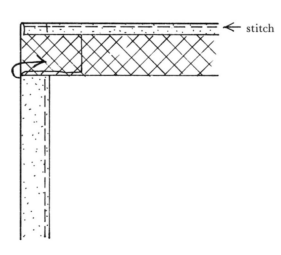

← stitch

Figure 5

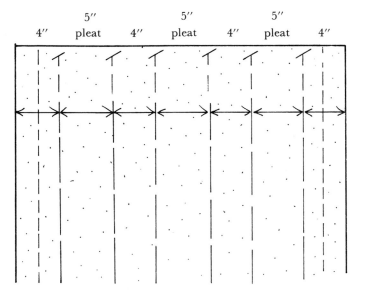

| 4″ | 5″ pleat | 4″ | 5″ pleat | 4″ | 5″ pleat | 4″ |

Figure 7

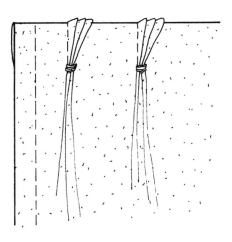

Figure 6

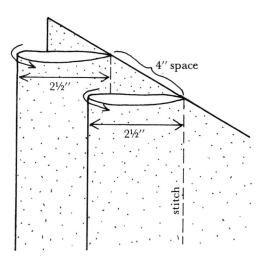

4″ space

2½″

2½″

stitch

Figure 8

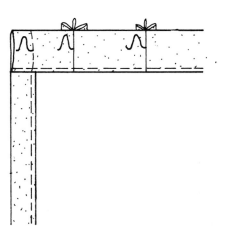

Round, Floor-Length Tablecloth with Ribbon Trim

Before beginning this project, refer to Techniques, Tablecloths. The materials and directions given are for a 90″ (228.6cm) diameter round tablecloth.

Materials
- 5 yards (4.6m) medium- to heavyweight fabric, 48″ to 52″ (121.9cm to 132cm) wide
- 10 yards (9m) ribbon trim, 1½″ (3.8cm) wide
- tape measure
- string
- tailor's chalk
- fabric shears
- dressmaker's pins
- thread to match

Method
Step 1:
Press fabric.

Divide fabric into two equal lengths, 2½ yards (2.3m) each. Cut one piece of fabric in half lengthwise. (See fig. 1.)

With right sides together and using ½″ (1.3cm) seams, pin-baste; then stitch the selvage side of each half width to the selvages of the full width piece. Press seams open. You now have one large piece of fabric.

Step 2:
Fold the large piece of fabric into quarters and pin to hold in place. Press.

Use a length of string with tailor's chalk tied to the end to measure an arc 45″

(114.3cm) plus ½″ (1.3cm) from the folded point. Mark with tailor's chalk. Cut along the arc to form a circle 91″ (231cm) in diameter. (See fig. 2.)

Step 3:
Measure and stitch around the circle ¼″ (6mm) in from the outer edge. Trim to ⅛″ (3mm).

Turn fabric under along stitching line, and turn under once again to form a finished hem. Topstitch ¼″ (6mm) in from the folded edge.

Step 4:
Cut ribbon into two equal lengths, 5 yards (4.6m) each. Overlap and stitch ribbon strips together to form one wide strip, approximately 3″ (7.6cm) across. (See fig. 3.)

Cut wide ribbon strip into two equal lengths, 2½ yards (2.3m) each.

Using the fold marks on the cloth as a guide, pin-baste ribbons in place on the right side of the fabric, extending them perpendicularly across the diameter of the cloth, crossing at the center point. (See fig. 4.)

Topstitch ribbons in place, stitching to within 4″ (10.2cm) of the outer edge of the cloth.

Trim, and fold under ends of ribbons to form mitered points approximately 2″ (5cm) in from the outer edge of the cloth. (See fig. 5.) Topstitch mitered points in place.

Figure 1

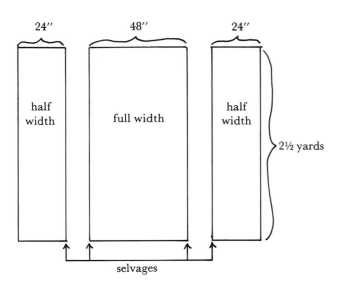

24″ 48″ 24″

half width full width half width

2½ yards

selvages

Figure 3

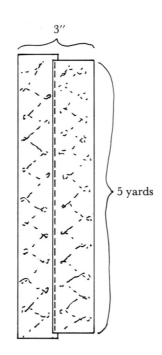

3″

5 yards

Figure 5

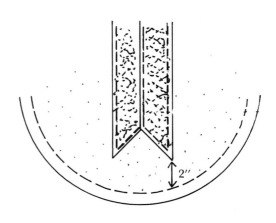

2″

Figure 2

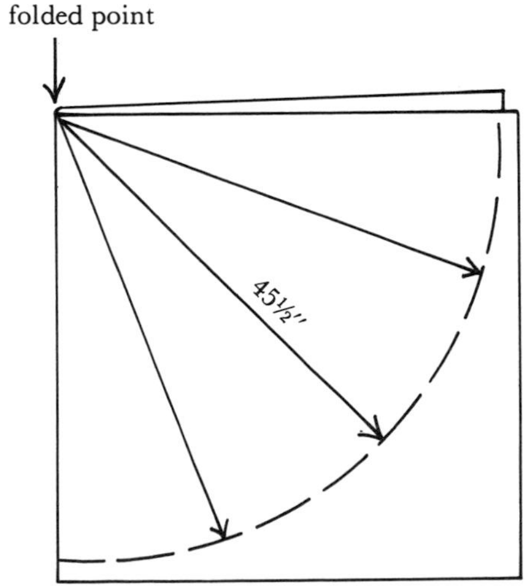

folded point

45½″

Figure 4

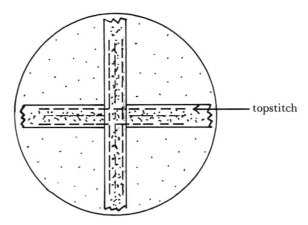

topstitch

Early American Living Room

Early American Living Room

Casual warmth blends with durability to create this Early American living room. Originally all of this style furniture was handmade of such woods as maple, oak, and pine, and was allowed to acquire a deep, natural color and patina through use and time. Today, even though originals are greatly sought after, adaptations offer a wide selection in this distinctive furniture styling.

A hardwood floor greatly enhances this decor, especially if the floor is stained a shade or two darker or lighter than the furniture itself.

The braided rug adds comfortable, rural personality to the room, at the same time establishing the color mood. Bright, sunny yellow is a cheerful room brightener in any language and is especially practical when you wish to create the illusion of a light, lively and happy atmosphere in rooms where sunlight is limited. Instead of using the traditional rags to make a braided rug, execute it with new fabric, treated for soil resistance, and then measured and cut into strips for braiding.

The solid color, yellow pleated draperies add a tailored note to the room. Both the long and short draperies are made in an identical manner and are lined to protect against sun-fading. Draperies hung in this manner give the effect of being café curtains and offer both privacy and light.

The window seat cushion extends the bold plaid to another area of the room. Instructions for the cushion may be easily adapted from the Rectangular Pillow with Boxing in the Mr. Bedroom.

The array of pillows on the couch display accent colors, assorted designs, and individual creativity. Made in varied sizes, shapes, and patterns, pillows always add warmth and dimension to any seating arrangement.

A wall grouping of your "favorite things" adds the final touch of color and visual interest to this already inviting room. When arranging a wall grouping, make it interesting by mixing pictures with mirrors, baskets, plants or other art objects; the grouping should tell a story.

The textures and colors, as well as the furniture style, are geared for easy living—a natural extension of a life-style and a personality.

Lined Draperies on a Wooden Pole

Before beginning this project, refer to Techniques, Window Treatments.

If the drapery fabric requires matching for a large repeat pattern, be sure to purchase extra yardage. A salesperson can help you estimate yardage for a particular fabric design.

The materials and directions given are for two 60″ x 90″ (152.4cm x 228.6cm) curtain panels.

Materials
- 18 yards (16.5m) light- to medium-weight drapery fabric, 48″ (121.9cm) wide
- tape measure
- tailor's chalk
- fabric shears
- 18 yards (16.5m) lining fabric, 48″ (121.9cm) wide
- T-pins
- 10 yards (9m) buckram, 4″ (10.2cm) wide
- thread to match
- 36 metal drapery hooks
- 36 wooden curtain rings, 1¾″ (4.4cm) in diameter
- wooden drapery pole, 1½″ (3.8cm) thick, cut to window's width
- 2 wooden drapery pole brackets

Method
Step 1:
Press drapery fabric.

Measure, mark with tailor's chalk, and cut drapery fabric into lengths 7″ (17.8cm) longer than the desired finished length. (See fig.1.)

Place right sides of drapery fabric together. Using ½″ (1.3cm) seams, stitch fabric lengths together to make two panels, each 2½ times *plus 2″* (5cm) wider than the width of the window. (See fig. 2.) This will give you enough fullness for pleating and seams. It may be necessary to cut a lengthwise strip off one side of the drapery panels to obtain the exact width.

To prevent the finished drapery from puckering, clip ½″ (1.3cm) into the selvages along the seam allowances every 4″ (10.2cm). (See fig. 2.) Press seams open.

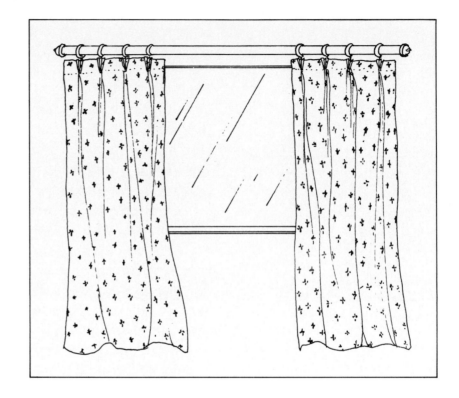

Figure 1

48″

finished length

plus 7″

Step 2:
Press lining fabric. Measure, mark with tailor's chalk, and cut lining fabric into lengths 2″ (5cm) shorter than the drapery panels. (See fig. 3.)

Place right sides of lining fabric together. Using ½″ (1.3cm) seams, stitch lining fabric lengths together to make two panels, each the width of the drapery panel *minus 2″* (5cm). (See fig. 4.) It may be necessary to cut a lengthwise strip off one of the lining panels to obtain the exact width.

To prevent the finished lining from puckering, clip ¼″ (6mm) into the selvages along the seam allowances every 4″ (10.2cm). (See fig. 4.)

Step 3:
Place right sides of drapery fabric and lining panels together, aligning top edges. Using ½″ (1.3cm) seams, pin-baste, then stitch sides together, beginning at the top and stitching to within 10″ (25.4cm) of the bottom of the lining.

Step 4:
Lay panel on a large flat surface with wrong side of lining fabric up and centered so that there is a 1″ (2.5cm) margin of drapery fabric on each side. (See fig. 5.)

Using T-pins, pin-baste lining fabric to the drapery fabric across the top edge.

Press seam allowances in toward the center of the panel.

Step 5:
Measure and cut a length of buckram to equal the width of the drapery panel *plus 6″* (15.2cm). Fold one end back on itself 3″ (7.6cm). Finger-press to make a sharp crease.

Pin-baste buckram to the lining across the top and about ½″ (1.3cm) below the raw edges. Fold excess buckram back on itself at opposite side of the panel. (See fig. 6.)

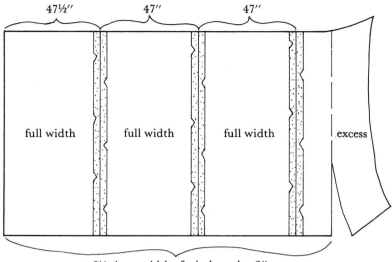

Figure 2

47½″   47″   47″

full width   full width   full width   excess

2½ times width of window plus 2″

Stitch across the panel as close as possible to the top edge of the buckram. *Do not* stitch across the bottom edge of the buckram.

Trim corners to remove excess fabric. Turn panel right side out. Press with lining up, always moving the iron away from the top of the panel.

Step 6:
The lining and the drapery fabric must be hemmed separately.

To hem the lining, turn up 3″ (7.6cm) twice to make a double hem. Machine-stitch across the width of the lining panel. Press. (See fig. 7.)

To hem the drapery fabric, turn up 3″ (7.6cm) twice to make a double hem. Before stitching, miter the corners. (See Techniques, Mitered Corners.) Hand-stitch corners in place.

Finally, hand-stitch the hem, using a slant hemming stitch. (See Techniques, Hand Stitches.)

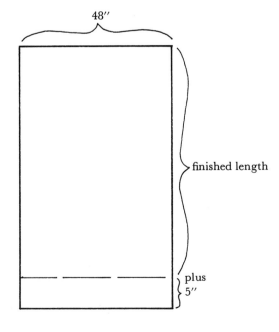

Figure 3

48″

finished length

plus 5″

(Continued)

Step 7:

To measure the top for pleating, place the panel on a large flat surface, drapery fabric up. Mark off the areas to be pleated by measuring from each side toward the center.

With a T-pin, mark off 4″ (10.2cm) on each side. Next, mark a 5″ (12.7cm) area for pleats. Working toward the center, alternate 4″ (10.2cm) spaces and 5″ (12.7cm) areas for pleats. (See fig. 8.)

After the entire panel has been marked, check to make certain the pleats are evenly spaced at 4″ (10.2cm) intervals. If not, correct by adjusting the 5″ (12.7cm) pleat allowances.

Step 8:

Once you have determined where each pleated area should begin and end, fold each pleat allowance in half, lining to the inside, to make one large pleat approximately 2½″ (6.4cm) deep. (See fig. 9.)

Stitch a straight line from the top edge of the drapery panel to the bottom of the buckram to secure each pleated section. (See fig. 10.)

Pinch each pleated area as illustrated in figure 10 to form three separate small pleats. Tack the pleats in place with several short overcast stitches through the lower edge of the buckram.

Step 9:

Slip metal drapery hooks into the back of each set of pleats, 1″ (2.5cm) below the top edge, at each stitching line. Place a metal drapery hook ½″ (1.3cm) in from each side edge. (See fig. 11.)

Attach a wooden drapery ring to each drapery hook. Slip wooden rings onto the wooden drapery pole, and place the pole in the brackets.

Figure 4

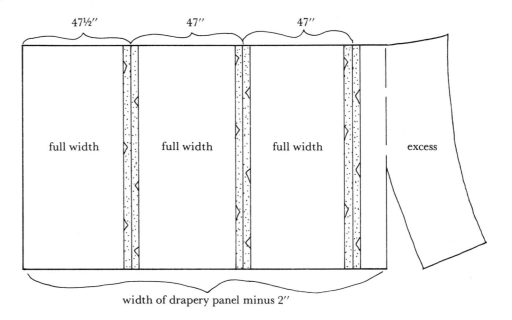

width of drapery panel minus 2″

Figure 5

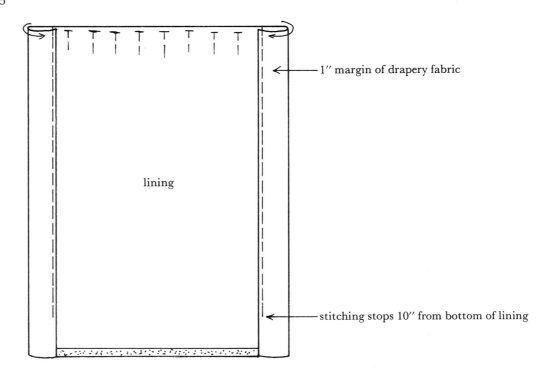

1″ margin of drapery fabric

stitching stops 10″ from bottom of lining

Figure 6

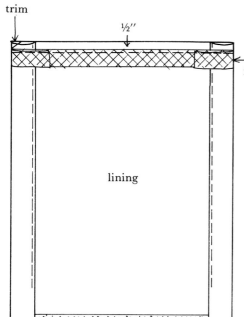

trim

½″

lining

excess buckram
folded toward center

Figure 7

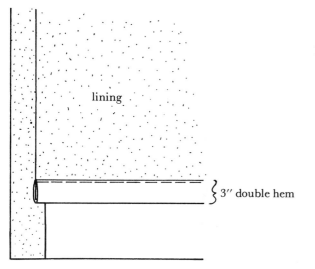

lining

} 3″ double hem

Figure 8

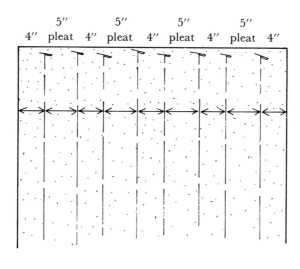

| 5″ | | 5″ | | 5″ | | 5″ | |
| 4″ | pleat | 4″ | pleat | 4″ | pleat | 4″ | pleat | 4″ |

Figure 9

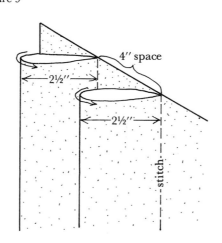

4″ space

2½″

2½″

stitch

Figure 10

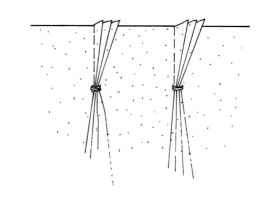

Figure 11

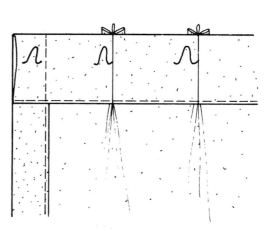

Ruffle Border Pillow

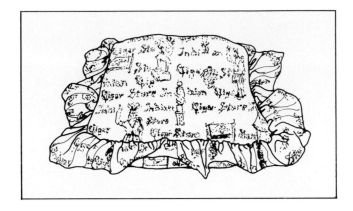

The materials and directions given are for a 16″ (40.6cm) square pillow.

Materials
- 1½ yards (1.4m) light- to medium-weight fabric, 44″ (111.8cm) wide
- 2 yards (1.8m) cable cord, ¼″ (6mm) thick
- polyurethane pillow form, 16″ (40.6cm) square
- tape measure
- tailor's chalk
- fabric shears
- dressmaker's pins
- small safety pin
- thread to match

Method
Step 1:
Press fabric.

Measure, mark with tailor's chalk, and cut out four strips of fabric, each 8″ x 44″ (20.3cm x 111.8cm).

If using a print, plan cutting lines to follow the pattern, since printed fabric may be slightly off grain.

Step 2:
Place strips end to end, right sides together. Using ½″ (1.3cm) seams, pin-baste, then stitch strip ends together. Press seams open. Fold joined strips in half lengthwise, right sides out, and press. You now have a strip of fabric 173″ (4.3m) long and 4″ (10.2cm) wide.

Figure 1

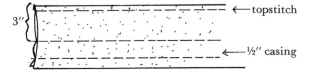

Step 3:
Topstitch along edge of fold. Measure, mark, and stitch a ½″ (1.3cm) casing 3″ (7.6cm) in from fold. (See fig. 1.)

Attach cording to a safety pin and thread it through the casing. Gather fabric to make a ruffle 64″ (162.6cm) long.

Step 4:
With remaining fabric, measure, mark with tailor's chalk, and cut out two 18″ (45.7cm) squares.

Beginning in the middle of one side, pin-baste the ruffle to the right side of one square with the raw edges of the ruffle even with the raw edges of the fabric square. (See fig. 2.) Continue pin-basting until both ends of the ruffle meet. Overlap them to form a narrow, flat-felled seam. (See Techniques, Seams.)

Stitch on top of both sides of the casing stitching to attach ruffle around the entire square. Remove cording from casing.

Step 5:
With right sides facing, place remaining fabric square on top of ruffled square. Pin-baste and stitch in place exactly on top of the inside ruffle stitching, leaving a 12″

Figure 2

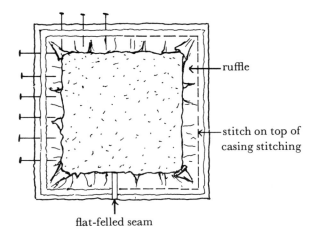

(30.5cm) opening in the center of one side for turning and stuffing.

Trim seam allowances to ¼″ (6mm) and clip as necessary to release fullness. Turn right side out and press.

Insert pillow form. Turn in raw edges and slip-stitch opening closed.

Patchwork Insert Pillow

The materials and directions given are for a 14″ x 24″ (35.6cm x 61cm) rectangular pillow.

Materials
- 1 yard (91.4cm) medium-weight fabric, 42″ to 45″ (106.7cm to 114.3cm) wide
- ¼ yard (22.9cm) of each of three patterned, lightweight fabrics, 42″ to 45″ (106.7cm to 114.3cm) wide
- tape measure
- tailor's chalk
- fabric shears
- dressmaker's pins
- polyester fiber fill
- thread to match

Method

Step 1:
Press fabric.

Measure, mark with tailor's chalk, and cut out 18 triangles (six from each of the three lightweight fabrics). Each triangle should measure 4½″ (11.4cm) at the base, 4½″ (11.4cm) in height and 5″ (12.7cm) on each side. (See fig. 1.)

Arrange the patterned triangles according to fig. 2, cutting four triangles in half to form the ends of the patchwork insert.

Step 2:
With right sides together, and using ¼″ (6mm) seams, stitch triangles together to create the patchwork insert of pillow. Press all seams open. Turn under raw edges of patchwork insert ¼″ (6mm) and press in place.

Step 3:
Measure, mark with tailor's chalk, and cut out two 15″ x 25″ (38cm x 63.5cm) rectangles from the medium-weight fabric.

Center patchwork insert, right side up, on the right side of one rectangle. Pin-baste; then baste in position. Topstitch around perimeter of patchwork section as close to the edge as possible. (See fig. 2.)

Place right sides of two rectangles together. Using ½″ (1.3cm) seams, stitch rectangles together leaving a 6″ (15.2cm) opening in the center of one side for turning and stuffing.

Turn right side out and press. Stuff with polyester fiber fill, packing the corners firmly. Turn in raw edges and slip-stitch opening closed.

Figure 1

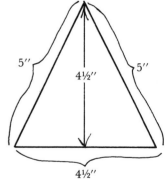

Figure 2

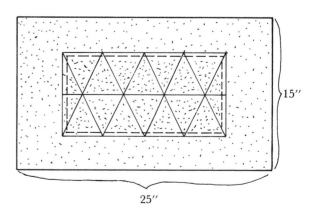

Ribbon Front Pillow

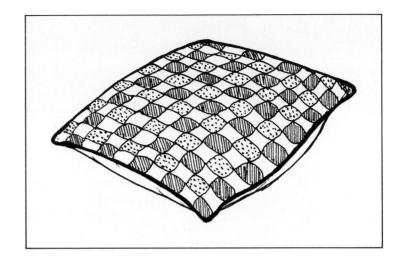

The materials and directions given are for a 16″ (40.6cm) square pillow.

Materials

- 12 yards (11m) grosgrain ribbon, 1½″ (3.8cm) wide—3 yards (2.7m) each of four colors
- tape measure
- tailor's chalk
- fabric shears
- dressmaker's pins
- ½ yard (45.7m) fusible interfacing
- 2 yards (1.8m) cable cord, ¼″ (6mm) thick
- ½ yard (45.7m) light- to medium-weight fabric, 45″ to 60″ (114.8cm to 152.4cm) wide
- polyurethane pillow form, 16″ (40.6cm) square
- thread to match

Method

Step 1:

Press ribbons. Measure, mark with tailor's chalk, and cut ribbons into twenty-four 18″ (45.7cm) lengths.

Working on an ironing board, arrange ribbons in a plaid pattern, 12 across and 12 down, by weaving them in and out of each other. (See fig. 1.) Make sure all sides of ribbons touch with no overlaps or spaces.

When all ribbons are arranged, carefully center interfacing on top of the ribbon plaid and fuse into position.

Step 2:

Press fabric. Measure, mark with tailor's chalk, and cut out an 18″ (45.7cm) square of fabric.

From remaining fabric prepare 2 yards (1.8m) continuous bias strip 2½″ (6.4cm) wide. (See Techniques, Bias Trim.) Cover cable cord with the bias strip as directed to make piping.

Step 3:

Beginning in the middle of one side of the square of fabric, pin-baste piping to the right side of the ribbon panel 1″ (2.5cm) in from outer edges with raw edges of piping even with the raw edges of the ribbons. Using a zipper foot attachment, stitch piping in place. (See fig. 2.)

For a smooth finish where ends of piping overlap, pull cording out of covering and clip cord so that the cut ends of both sides meet. Stitch ends in place. (See fig. 3.)

Step 4:

With right sides together, place fabric square on top of woven ribbon square. Pin-baste,

Figure 1

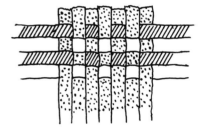

Figure 2

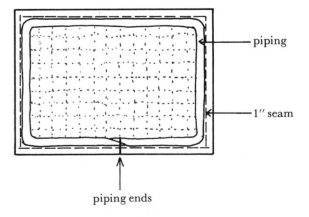

piping

1″ seam

piping ends

and using a zipper foot attachment, stitch in place exactly on top of piping stitching leaving a 12″ (30.5cm) opening for turning and stuffing.

Trim seam allowances to ¼″ (6mm) and clip as necessary to release fullness. Turn right side out and press. Insert pillow form. Turn in raw edges and slip-stitch opening closed.

Figure 3

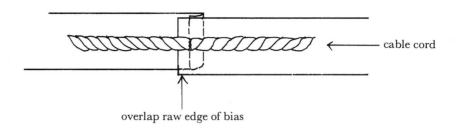

← cable cord

overlap raw edge of bias

Braided Round Rug

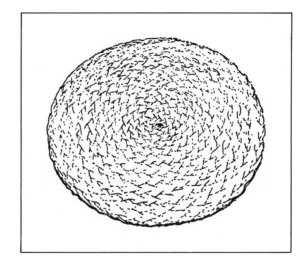

This rug can be as small or as large as you wish, depending on the amount of fabric you have to use. It can also be a growing rug, increasing in size as you gather more scraps.

Materials
- fabric scraps of silk, cotton, wool, or synthetic prints or solids
- tape measure
- fabric shears
- spindle-back chair
- heavy-duty thread

Method
Step 1:
Press all fabric scraps.

Cut scraps into 2″ (5cm) wide strips. Because you are using scraps, the strips will probably all be of different lengths.

Using ½″ (1.3cm) seams and a double row of stitching, sew all strips together end to end, making three strips, each about 5′ (1.5m) long. Press seams open.

Fold raw edges under ¼″ (6mm) and press in place. (See fig. 1.)

(Continued)

Figure 1

¼″

Step 2:

Tie three strips separately to back spindles of a chair or to a suitcase handle. (See fig. 2.) Have someone sit in the chair to weight it (make sure the suitcase is also weighted). Braid the strips together, being careful to keep strips right side up and flat. Do not braid too tightly. Pin ends to hold in place.

Repeat braiding procedure until all fabric strips are used. To make one long braided rope, sew braided strips together by hand, end to end, using ½″ (1.3cm) seams and a double row of stitching. Press seams open. (See fig. 3.) Lay the braid on the floor, and wind it loosely into a circle, making sure it lies flat. As you wind, sew the braids together on the underside with heavy-duty thread, making stitches as invisible as possible. (See fig. 4.)

Figure 2

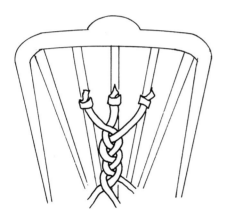

Figure 3

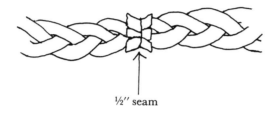

½″ seam

Figure 4

Piped Round Pillow

This project can be executed with or without the center button. The materials and directions given are for a 16″ (40.6cm) round pillow.

Materials
- 1 yard (91.4cm) light- to medium-weight fabric, 44″ (111.8cm) wide
- 2 yards (1.8m) cable cord, ¼″ (6mm) thick
- polyurethane pillow form, 16″ (40.6cm) in diameter
- tape measure
- tailor's chalk
- fabric shears
- dressmaker's pins
- thread to match
- 2 buttons to be covered, each 1½″ (3.8cm) in diameter
- fishing line

Method
Step 1:
Press fabric.

Measure, mark with tailor's chalk, and cut out two 20″ (50.8cm) squares of fabric.

Step 2:
Fold each square into quarters and press. Measure and mark an arc 9″ (22.9cm) from the folded point. Cut along arc to make an 18″ (45.7cm) circle. (See fig. 1.)

From remaining fabric prepare 2 yards (1.8m) continuous bias strip 2½″ (6.4cm) wide. (See Techniques, Bias Trim.) Cover cable cord with the bias strip as directed to make piping.

Step 3:
Pin-baste piping to the right side of one circle 1″ (2.5cm) in from outer edge with the raw edges of piping even with the raw edge of circle. (See fig. 2.) Using a zipper foot attachment, stitch piping in place as close to the cording as possible.

For a smooth finish where ends of the piping overlap, pull cording out of covering and clip cord so that the cut ends of both sides meet. Stitch ends in place.

Step 4:
With right sides together, place remaining circle on top of piped circle. Pin-baste together, and using a zipper foot attachment stitch in place exactly on top of piping stitching leaving a 12″ (30.5cm) opening for turning and stuffing.

Trim seam allowances to ¼″ (6mm) and clip as necessary to release fullness. Turn right side out. Insert pillow form. Turn in raw edges and slip-stitch opening closed.

Step 5:
Cover buttons following directions on the button package.

Thread a large needle with a double strand of fishing line. Double knot end securely.

Locate and mark with tailor's chalk the center of the pillow, draw fishing line through it and pull tightly. Repeat this procedure several times to secure fishing line and to pull both sides of the pillow together in the center.

Pass fishing line through one button and then through center. Pass fishing line through second button on the opposite side. Wind fishing line around both buttons to secure.

Figure 1

folded point →

9″

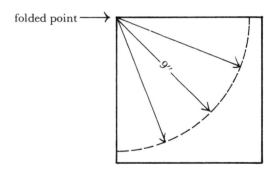

Figure 2

piping

1″ seam

Country French Living Room

Country French Living Room

Country French offers a native type of styling which is less costly to produce than the more elaborate forms of French period furniture. The wood's own beauty is usually stressed; the fine natural finishes of fruit woods, chestnut, pine, and oak. Little embellishment is ever used upon the woods, and the style offers a bucolic feeling which adapts equally well to country or city living.

Our living room is a modified version of the Country French—comfortable, informal, and very livable. A shirred fabric wall is the focal point, adding warmth and bright color to an otherwise cool and pale room. Shirring simply means gathering. This technique of covering walls is marvelous for hiding lumps and cracks, or even doors and cupboards not in use. It tends to draw in a large room and make it acoustically smaller. If you have a small room and would like to try this method of wall covering, treat only one wall with your favorite fabric, and cover the other walls with one of the four flat fabric applications found elsewhere in this book; or else paint the adjoining walls, bringing out one of the colors from the fabric.

Because of the smallness of this room, the shirring technique was used on only one wall. However, the fabric was used again as shirred window curtains so that the color continues to take your eye around the room. White casement curtains behind the shirred ones offer privacy and conceal a window extending to the floor. The side shutters, even though white, add depth and textural interest to the room.

A traditionally styled couch lends inviting comfort, and the display of many brightly colored pillows picks up all of the colors of the shirred fabric wall.

The French provincial-style chair in the foreground, executed in the same fabric as the shirred wall and the window curtains, continues to carry the eye. As a decorative surprise, the back of the chair is covered in a bold plaid containing colors compatible and/or matching the colors of the predominant fabric.

In contrast to the brightly colored fabric, the pale, celery colored tile floor and glass-topped coffee table create a feeling of spaciousness in what otherwise might seem to be cramped quarters. Add a luscious wool area rug in accent colors for cool winter months.

Knife-Edge Pillow with Silk Cord Trim

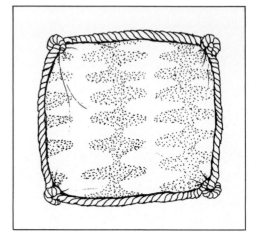

This is an elegant way to trim a pillow, especially when you don't have enough fabric to make piping. The materials and directions given are for an 18″ (45.7cm) square pillow.

Materials
- ¾ yard (68.6cm) medium- to heavyweight fabric, 42″ to 45″ (106.7cm to 114.3cm) wide
- tape measure
- tailor's chalk
- fabric shears
- dressmaker's pins
- polyester fiber fill
- thread to match
- sewing needle
- 2½ yards (2.3m) silk cording, ¼″ (6mm) thick

Method
Step 1:
Press fabric.

Measure, mark with tailor's chalk, and cut out two 19″ (48.3cm) squares of fabric.

Place right sides together. Using ½″ (1.3cm) seams, pin-baste; then stitch squares in place leaving a 6″ (15.2cm) opening in the center of one side for turning and stuffing.

Step 2:
Trim corners. (See fig. 1.) Turn pillow right side out, press, and stuff firmly with polyester fiber fill.

Turn in raw edges and slip-stitch opening closed.

Step 3:
To trim pillow, sew silk cording by hand directly on top of seam. As you come to a corner, poke it into the pillow a bit, tie a knot in the cord, and sew it in place. (See fig. 2.) This gives the pillow a more rounded effect.

Figure 1

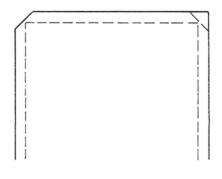

Figure 2

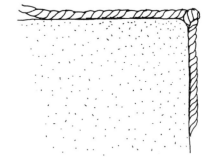

Casement Curtains

This window treatment is particularly practical when windows open into or out of a room, or where glass or French doors are used.

Before beginning this project, refer to Techniques, Window Treatments. The directions given apply to any size casement.

Materials
- fabric, light- to medium-weight
- tape measure
- tailor's chalk
- fabric shears
- dressmaker's pins
- thread to match
- 2 café curtain rods and brackets

Method
Step 1:
Mount café curtain rods according to the manufacturer's directions. Remember to place bottom rod brackets upside down.

Step 2:
Press fabric.

Measure, mark with tailor's chalk, and cut fabric into lengths 10″ (25.4cm) longer than the desired finished length.

Step 3:
Place right sides of fabric together. Using ½″ (1.3cm) seams, stitch fabric lengths together to make a panel 2½ times *plus* 4″ (10.2cm) wider than the width of the window. (See fig. 1.) This will give you enough fullness for gathering and seams. It may be necessary to

cut a lengthwise strip off one side of the panel to obtain the exact width. Flat-felled seams or French seams may be used. (See Techniques, Seams.)

To prevent the finished curtain from puckering, clip ¼″ (6mm) into the selvages along the seam allowances every 4″ (10.2cm). (See fig. 1.) Press seams open.

Step 4:
To make double hems along both side edges, turn raw edges under 1″ (2.5cm) and press. Turn under 1″ (2.5cm) again and press. Machine-stitch in place and press.

Step 5:
To make the top casing, fold down the top raw edge 5″ (12.7cm) onto the wrong side of the fabric. Press.

Measure, mark, and stitch across the curtain panel 2″ (5cm) below the fold. Turn raw edge under ½″ (1.3cm) and press. Stitch across panel again 2½″ (6.4cm) below first stitching line, securing raw edge as you do so. (See fig. 2.) Top and bottom headings and casings may vary in size depending upon the thickness of the café rod.

To make the bottom casing, repeat the procedure outlined in Step 5.

Step 6:
Slide the casement curtain onto the curtain rods and place in brackets. Distribute gathers evenly.

(Continued)

Figure 1

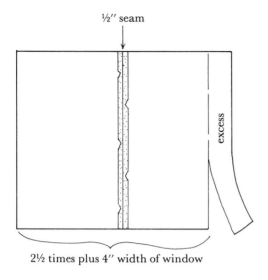

½″ seam

excess

2½ times plus 4″ width of window

Figure 2

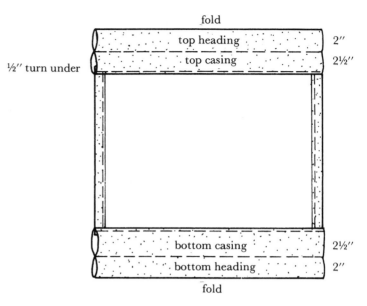

fold

top heading   2″

top casing   2½″

½″ turn under

bottom casing   2½″

bottom heading   2″

fold

Fabric Covered Brick Doorstop

Two covered bricks make attractive book-ends. The directions are easily adapted to fit any size brick.

Materials
- 1 brick, 2½″ x 4½″ x 8½″ (6.4cm x 11.4cm x 21.6cm)
- 1 sheet heavy grade sandpaper, 8½″ x 11″ (21.6cm x 27.9cm)
- tracing paper
- lead pencil, #2
- fabric shears
- ¼ yard (22.9cm) solid color felt
- ¼ yard (22.9cm) contrasting solid color felt
- 6 strands tapestry yarn or embroidery floss
- tapestry or embroidery needle

Method
Step 1:
Sand rough edges and irregularities from brick.

Enlarge and cut your choice of three initials from the alphabet chart. (See fig. 1.) Pin patterns to a small section of felt, and carefully cut out the letters.

Figure 1

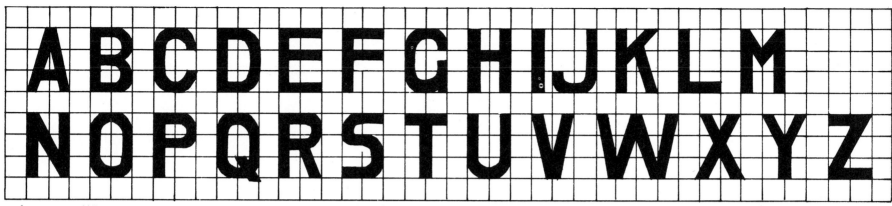

each square = ½″

Step 2:
Measure, mark with pencil, and cut out two sections of contrasting felt ½″ (1.3cm) larger on all sides than top and bottom of the brick. (See fig. 2.)

Center initials on top of contrasting felt and pin in place. Using tapestry yarn or embroidery floss, whipstitch letters to the felt. (See Techniques, Hand Stitches.) (See fig. 3.)

Step 3:
Measure, mark with pencil, and cut out two sections of contrasting felt ½″ (1.3cm) larger on all sides than the sum of the lengths of one long and one short side of the brick. (See fig. 4.)

Pin-baste felt sections together around brick, tucking in ½″ (1.3cm) seam allowances as you do so.

Using tapestry yarn or embroidery floss slip-stitch seams together. (See Techniques, Hand Stitches.)

Figure 2

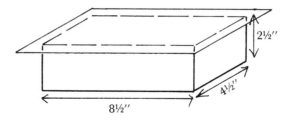

Figure 4

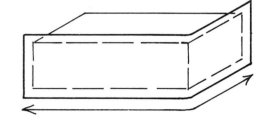

Figure 3

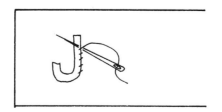

Fabric Covered Walls—Shirred

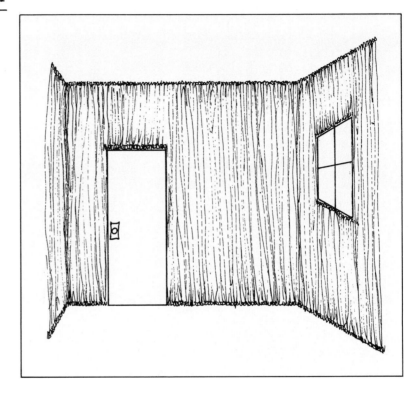

Before beginning this project, refer to Techniques, Fabric Covered Walls. This method of applying fabric to a wall is often preferred to other methods because the shirred fabric is easily hung and easily removed for cleaning. However, the shirred fabric covered wall requires much more material than other methods, and therefore tends to be more expensive. Shirred walls make a room feel acoustically smaller. If your room is already small, do just one wall shirred, and cover the remaining walls with fabric using one of the flat methods explained elsewhere in this book. The results will be as effective as if the entire room were covered with shirred fabric.

Materials
- fabric, cut to size 2½ to 3 times wider and a yard or two longer than the wall area to be covered
- tape measure
- tailor's chalk
- fabric shears
- dressmaker's pins
- thread to match
- café curtain rods cut to size
- rod brackets and nails

Method
Step 1:
Measure the width of the wall area to be covered. Have café curtain rods cut to that width.

Rods and brackets are needed for ceiling and floor areas. If the area is very wide, you will need nails to support the rods in between the brackets.

Attach top brackets so that the rod will rest 1½″ (3.8 cm) from the ceiling or molding. Attach bottom brackets in an upside down position so that the rod will be 1½″ (3.8cm) up from the floor or molding. If windows or doors are on the wall, rods must also be positioned 1½″ (3.8cm) above and below the windows and 1½″ (3.8 cm) above the doors. (See fig. 1.)

Step 2:
Measure the height and width of each wall section. (See fig. 1.)

Cut fabric panels 2½ to 3 times wider than the section. Sections around door and window areas should be measured and cut separately. Add 6″ (15.2cm) for top and bottom hem allowances to the measured length of each panel. Add an additional 1″ (2.5 cm) because shirring takes up about that much in tautness. (See fig. 2.) The extra yard or two of fabric listed in Materials for this project allows for any measuring errors.

The heading will account for 1½″ (3.8cm) and the casing 1″ (2.5cm) at the top and bottom. (See fig. 2.)

Step 3:
Press fabric.

Cut fabric to correct lengths, matching

repeats if necessary. Turn selvages to wrong side of fabric and press.

Turn fabric under 3″ (7.6cm) at the top and bottom for hems. Press in place. Turn raw edges under ½″ (1.3cm) and stitch top and bottom hems. Stitch casing seam 1″ (2.5cm) toward the fold from the hem stitching. This leaves a 1½″ (3.8cm) heading. (See fig. 3.) It is important not to allow the heading to be over 2″ (5cm) because the weight of the fabric will eventually make the taller heading flop over.

After stitching, press fabric panels thoroughly.

Step 4:
Thread panels onto café curtain rods through top casing. (See fig. 4.) Place rods in brackets and distribute gathers evenly, making sure brackets are covered. Thread panels onto café curtain rods through bottom casing and pull taut. Place rods in bottom brackets. Distribute gathers evenly, making sure brackets are covered.

To cover brackets, cut a slit in back of the casing exactly where the bracket is positioned after fabric has been gathered onto café rods. Slip bracket through hole and arrange gathers to cover.

If light switches are on the wall, simply make a tiny slit in the fabric exactly where the switch is after the fabric is correctly distributed onto the café rods. Whipstitch raw edges to prevent raveling.

Variation: If you do not wish to use café curtain rods, shirr fabric onto cording, distribute gathers evenly, and staple fabric along top and bottom casings to wood stripping on wall.

Figure 1

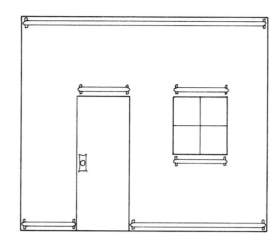

Figure 2

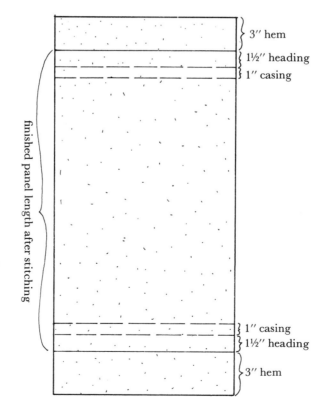

finished panel length after stitching

3″ hem
1½″ heading
1″ casing

1″ casing
1½″ heading
3″ hem

Figure 3

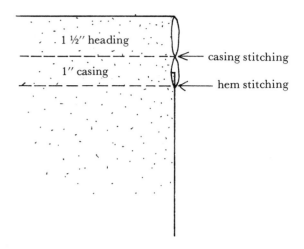

1 ½″ heading
1″ casing

casing stitching
hem stitching

Figure 4

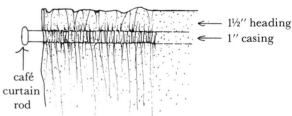

1½″ heading
1″ casing

café curtain rod

Eclectic Living Room

Eclectic Living Room

Creating an eclectic room is probably the most difficult type of decorating to execute effectively. One must be discerning enough to be able to select the best styled pieces from several periods and not only make those pieces interrelate with each other but with the modern pieces of today's furnishings as well.

Here, space, light, pattern on pattern, and mixed pieces of furniture all work together to offer a sophistication and easy living style. The mood is rather casual, and the colors, varying from yellow to off-white, are accented with rich red-toned russets and browns.

With large, comfortable pieces of furniture, such as the ones in this Eclectic Living Room, few others are needed. Printed floor cushions extend the seating area and give a dimensional quality to the solid color carpeting. The nice thing about floor cushions is that they are very seldom a large investment, they can be easily recovered and/or refurbished, and they may be moved from room to room or stored out of sight.

The reversible, floor-length table skirt is a differently designed fabric print from the fabric used on the club chair. However, the colors are the same in both prints.

Slipcovers for the couch may be made by adapting the instructions for Slipcovered Club Chair. The measuring instructions and tips on fabric selection for slipcovers are found in Techniques, Slipcovers.

The window shades, shown here in white, would be very effective in a printed fabric and are easily adapted from the instructions appearing in the Mr. Bedroom. In addition, you may wish to cover the pleated lampshade in a smart accent color. Directions for covering the shade appear in the Den/Guest Room.

Slipcovered Club Chair

For general instructions on fabric selection, measuring, preparation of the furniture piece, and the basic steps involved in making any slipcover, refer to Techniques, Slipcovers, before beginning this project.

The materials and directions given are for a medium-size club chair with a corner pleated skirt, self-welting, and a loose seat cushion. However, the directions may be adapted to any size club chair or couch with similar styling.

In making any slipcover, you will recognize that each piece of furniture has a distinctive style which must be considered as you work. As a general rule, welting should be sewn along the same seam lines as the welting which appears on the original cover. The instructions given here may not include welting in all areas applying to your chair. Should you wish to insert welting in any seams not included in these instructions, the technique for attaching welting is easily applied to any seam. Be sure to allow enough extra fabric and cable cord to suit your purposes.

In slipcovering some chair styles you can prepare several adjacent fabric sections at a time. On other chairs, you must prepare the closest or most important adjacent section, then remove the cover, sew the welting and seams, return the cover to the chair and repeat the procedure. The rule of thumb is to remove the cover only as often as is necessary to insure a custom fit.

Materials
- 8 to 10 yards (7.3m to 9m) tightly woven, medium-weight fabric, 48″ (121.9cm) or wider
- 15 yards (13.6m) cable cord, ½″ (1.3cm) thick
- 3 spools heavy-duty thread to match
- T-pins
- dressmaker's pins
- tape measure
- tailor's chalk
- fabric shears
- brown wrapping paper
- 2 upholstery zippers
- 4 snaps
- zipper for cushion

Method
Step 1:
Familiarize yourself with the parts of the chair as shown in fig. 1.

Press fabric. Always work with the right side of the fabric facing up and the lengthwise grain running vertically.

Figure 1

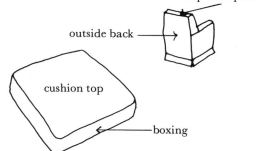

Using T-pins to secure the fabric as you work, place a length of fabric at the top edge of the inside back of the chair so that the design is centered.

The fabric should extend 3″ (7.6cm) above the top back panel, run down and across the full width of the inside back, allowing for a 5″ (12.5cm) deep tuck at the back of the seat, across the seat (not the cushion), and down the front to 5″ (12.7cm) below the apron. (See fig. 2.)

Be generous with the amount of fabric you're working with. You can always trim excess fabric as necessary, but you cannot replace fabric that has been trimmed away too soon.

Once you have pin-basted the fabric to the inside back, seat, and front apron, step back a few feet and check that the fabric is positioned correctly and that the pattern is centered vertically and horizontally. Make any necessary adjustments.

Step 2:
Once the fabric is correctly positioned, use the handle of a pair of scissors to push the fabric as far as possible into the chair crevices down the sides of the inside back and along the seat. This will provide enough fabric to tuck in the finished cover so it will stay securely in place during use. Each time you place the cover on the chair after attaching the various fabric sections, push the fabric into the crevices in the same manner.

Trim the fabric to within 3″ (7.6cm) all around the area you have tucked in.

Step 3:
Cut 15 yards (13.6m) continuous bias, 3″ (7.6cm) wide. (See Techniques, Bias Trim.) Cover cable cord with bias as directed to make welting.

Step 4:
Beginning at the top of one arm and leaving a 1″ (2.5cm) extension of welting, pin-baste welting to the right side of the fabric exactly along the seam lines around the outer edge of the inside back, to the top of the opposite arm, making sure that the rounded part of the welting faces toward the inside of the chair and the raw edges extend outward. (See fig. 3.)

Very carefully remove the fabric from the chair with the welting pin-basted in position. Stitch the welting to the fabric using a zipper foot attachment.

Replace the fabric on the chair, tucking and pinning it into position as before.

Step 5:
Measure and cut out a section of fabric about 3″ (7.6cm) larger on all sides than the inside arm. Pin-baste it in position, wrapping fabric from the outside arm around and down the inside arm. (See fig. 4.) Repeat for remaining arm.

With tailor's chalk, mark seam lines which will attach fabric to the seat. It is often helpful to make a practice of using tailor's chalk to mark all seam lines that do not require welting.

Trim fabric to within 1″ (2.5cm) on all sides of the inside arm sections. For rounded areas such as the front of the arms, you may need to form small gathers or tucks to control the fullness. (See fig. 5.)

Step 6:
As you make slipcovers, it is important to analyze each seam. Some will need to rest exactly on an edge to give a good fit. Other seams will be tucked into the crevices of the chair to hold the cover in place. Some seam allowances may be pin-basted with the raw edges facing upward toward the right side of

(Continued)

Figure 2

Figure 3

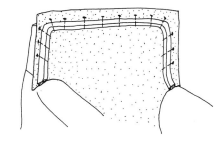

Figure 4

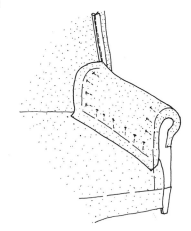

the fabric because it is easier to pin-baste in this manner while the fabric is on the chair. On curved areas, you may need to clip the fabric to release the fullness. (See fig. 6.) Be careful not to clip closer than ¼″ (6mm) from the seam lines.

To reverse the seam allowances and turn them toward the wrong side of the fabric, mark along the pins with tailor's chalk. Remove the pins carefully, and finger-press the seam allowances to the wrong side along the chalked lines. Replace pins to secure the seam and stitch seam using a zipper foot attachment. Follow this procedure for accuracy in joining two sections where the seam must rest exactly on an edge, such as the seam where the inside arm sections meet the inside back and the seat area.

Using the chalked and pressed lines as a guide, pin-baste both inside arm sections to the inside back section.

Carefully remove the cover from the chair. Stitch the inside arm to the inside back.

Return the cover to the chair. Pin it in position along the inside back top edge, arms and seat. Tuck in folds along the base of the inside back and inside arms.

Step 7:
Measure and cut fabric sections for the outside arms and the side back panels. Pin-baste these sections to the cover. (See fig. 7.)

Pin-baste welting around the front of the arms. Carefully remove cover from chair. Stitch outside arms, side back banels, and welting to the cover.

Step 8:
Prepare a pattern for the front arm panels by pinning a piece of brown wrapping paper directly onto the chair. Trace around the front arm panels exactly on the stitching lines used to attach welting. Make a separate paper pattern for each front arm panel. Often one arm will have received more wear than the other and will therefore have a slightly different shape. However, if the difference in shape is too obvious, pad the arm fronts with layers of polyester fleece, hand-basted to the original cover.

Once you have the front arm panel patterns prepared, pin them to the chair to double-check the shapes. Then pin the patterns to the fabric, and cut out the two fabric shapes, allowing a generous 1″ (2.5cm) seam allowance around all sides.

As before, remember to consider the pattern of the fabric. Just as the two inside arm sections must match, so too should the front arm panels match each other. (Refer again to Techniques, Slipcovers.) Pin-baste; then stitch front arm panels to the welting attached in Step 7. (See fig. 8.)

Step 9:
Return the cover to the chair. As before, use T-pins to attach it securely, and tuck in the folds along the crevices at the sides and base of the inside back and seat.

Measure and cut the top back panel and the outside back panel. Pin-baste fabric sections to the cover, marking and finger-pressing seams as before. Pin-baste welting around the bottom of the apron and to the bottom of the outside arm areas so that the welting rests exactly on the bottom edge of the chair. (See fig. 9.) Pin-baste welting along the bottom of the outside back of the cover so that the welting rests exactly on the edge of the chair and continues the line of welting extending from the bottom of the outside arm areas.

Remove the cover and stitch the welting to the cover. Sew top back panel to the inside back and outside back panel along the top edges. Do not sew the side seams joining the side back and outside arm panels to the outside back.

Step 10:
Return the cover to the chair. Insert upholstery zippers in the side seams of the back panel following the package directions for a lapped zipper application. The laps should be facing outward toward the sides of the chair.

For a chair with a corner pleated skirt, use either one zipper which extends from the bottom corner to the top edge of the chair, or use two zippers, one in each back seam. (See fig. 10.) This double zipper method makes the cover easier to remove.

Figure 5

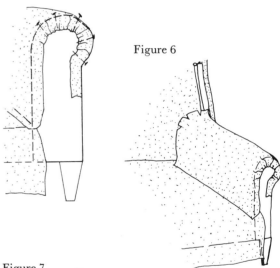

Figure 6

Figure 7

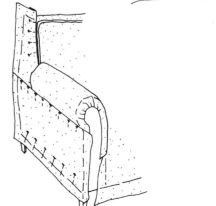

Step 11:

To make a corner pleated skirt, cut pieces of fabric 5″ (12.7cm) longer than the distance from the welting at the base of the chair to the floor, and the full width of the fabric. Stitch several of these strips together, end to end, to make a fabric piece long enough to go around the chair. As a rule for a tailored skirt, make strips 1½ yards (1.4m) longer than the distance around the base of the chair.

Measure carefully. Many chairs are designed so that the back is a bit closer to the floor than the front, or the chair may have a slight slant backward. Because of such possibilities, do not hem the skirt section until it has been attached to the chair cover.

To pin-baste the skirt in place, attach one end of the fabric strip 5″ (12.7cm) beyond one back corner. Wrap fabric around that corner and form one 5″ (12.7cm) deep pleat at the side of the corner. (See fig. 11.) Continue positioning skirt around the chair, forming two 5″ (12.7cm) deep pleats at each front corner. At the opposite back corner, form one 5″ (12.7cm) deep pleat on the side of the corner, and wrap 5″ (12.7cm) around the corner as in the beginning. Cut the skirt strip to end there. Stitch skirt to welting around outside arm section and apron, stopping at the back corners. Do not stitch the 5″ (12.7cm) of wrapped fabric to the back panel.

From the remaining skirt strip, form one 5″ (12.7cm) deep pleat at one back corner, positioning it on top of the 5″ (12.7cm) extension of wrapped fabric. (See fig. 12.) Extend skirt to opposite back corner, forming final 5″ (12.7cm) pleat and pin-basting back skirt section to the bottom of the back panel.

The pleats at the two back corners at the base of the two zippers are left open so that the chair cover can be removed. Stitch the back skirt to the welting at the bottom of the back panel.

Secure each 5″ (12.7cm) wrapped extension to the underside of the two back pleats with snaps.

Mark the hem of the skirt ½″ (1.3cm) above the floor. Stitch a 2″ to 3″ (5cm to 7.6cm) hem with a ½″ (1.3cm) turn-under, using the machine blind stitch.

(Continued)

Figure 8

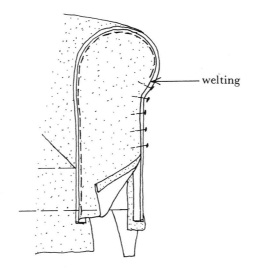

welting

Figure 9

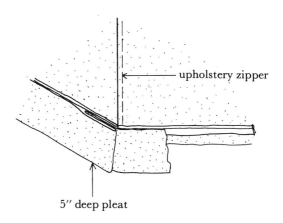

Figure 10

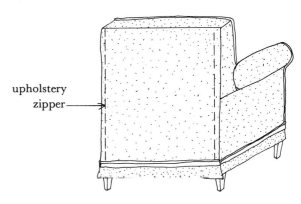

upholstery zipper

Figure 11

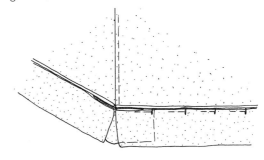

upholstery zipper

5″ deep pleat

Figure 12

Step 12:

To cover the chair cushion, place a piece of fabric on the cushion with the design centered to complement the design on the inside back and the inside arms of the chair when the cushion is in position. Trim fabric, allowing a 1″ (2.5cm) extension on all sides.

Pin-baste welting around the outer edge of the cushion, exactly on top of the seam line of the original cover. Stitch in place using a zipper foot attachment. (See fig. 13.)

Repeat procedure for the other side of the cushion.

Step 13:

To prepare the cushion's boxing, cut two strips of fabric the width of the distance around the cushion and the depth of the cushion, allowing for 1½″ (3.8cm) seams along all sides of the boxing.

Use a lapped zipper application to attach the zipper to the boxing. The zipper should be centered horizontally on the boxing and extend at least the length of one side. You may want to extend the zipper around one corner. (See fig. 14.)

Stitch the zippered boxing to the top and bottom cushion cover sections.

Step 14:

Trim all seam allowances to ½″ (1.3cm) and, where necessary, clip to within ¼″ (6mm) of the seam line to release fullness along curved edges. Press slipcover, smooth onto chair, tucking fabric into crevices, and close zippers. Slip cushion into cover and insert in chair.

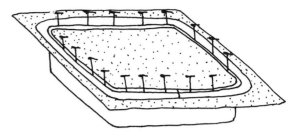

Figure 13

Figure 14

Turkish Corner Floor Pillow

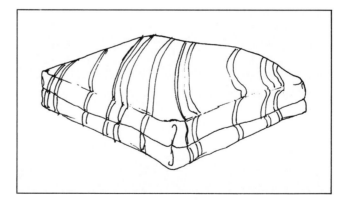

The materials and directions given are for a 30″ (76.2cm) square pillow.

Materials

- 2 yards (1.8m) medium- to heavyweight fabric, 36″ (91.4cm) wide
- tape measure
- tailor's chalk
- fabric shears
- dressmaker's pins
- thread to match
- polyester fiber fill

Method

Step 1:

Press fabric.

Measure, mark with tailor's chalk, and cut out two 31″ (78.7cm) squares of fabric.

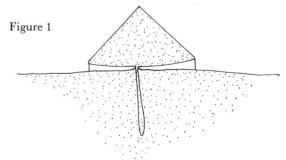

Figure 1

Step 2:
Fold each corner of each square of fabric according to fig. 1. Make sure the edges of the folds touch; then pin-baste in place.

Stitch folds in place across each corner. (See fig. 2.)

Step 3:
When all corners of each square are stitched, place the two fabric pieces together, right sides facing, with stitched corners matched exactly. Using ½″ (1.3cm) seams, pin-baste sections together leaving an 8″ (20.3cm) opening in the middle of one side for turning and stuffing. (See fig. 3.) Stitch in place. Steam-press seams open.

Step 4:
Turn pillow right side out, and stuff with polyester fiber fill. Slip-stitch opening closed.

Figure 2

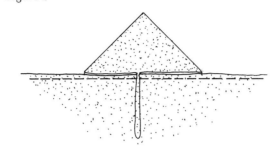

Figure 3

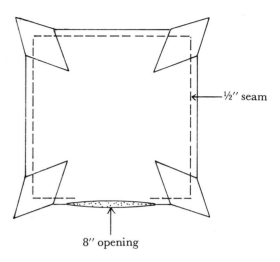

½″ seam

8″ opening

Fringed Cocktail Napkins

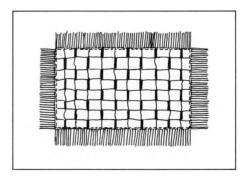

The directions given are easily adapted to make any size napkin. Change your fabric selection and make guest towels for the bathroom. The materials and directions given are for six 6″ x 9″ (15.2cm x 22.9cm) rectangular napkins.

Materials
- ½ yard (45.7cm) medium-weight fabric, 50″ (127cm) wide
- cardboard
- lead pencil, #2
- ruler
- fabric shears
- thread to match

Method
Step 1:
Draw a 6″ x 9″ (15.2cm x 22.9cm) rectangle on a piece of cardboard and cut it out. This will be your pattern for the napkins.

Step 2:
Press fabric.

Place cardboard pattern on top of wrong side of fabric, making sure the pattern is on the straight grain. Trace and cut out six rectangles of fabric.

Step 3:
To fringe the napkins, unravel them along the crosswise and lengthwise edges until one thread can be pulled from edge to edge. Pull threads to make fringe as deep or as narrow as you wish. If necessary, trim fringe to even off sides.

Machine-stitch in matching thread around the perimeter of the napkins just inside the fringe. This will prevent the napkins from unraveling any farther.

Reversible, Floor-Length, Round Tablecloth

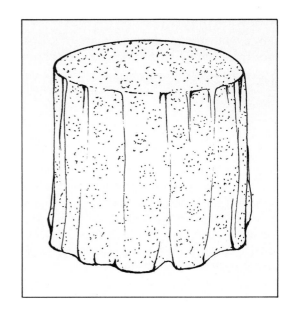

Before beginning this project, refer to Techniques, Tablecloths. The materials and directions given are for a 72" (182.9cm) round tablecloth.

Materials
- 4¼ yards (3.9m) light- to medium-weight fabric, 48" to 52" (121.9cm to 132cm) wide
- 4¼ yards (3.9m) light- to medium-weight contrasting fabric, 48" to 52" (121.9cm to 132cm) wide
- yardstick
- tape measure
- tailor's chalk
- fabric shears
- thread to match

Method
Step 1:
Press fabric.

Divide one 4¼ yard (3.9m) piece of fabric into two equal lengths, 2⅛ yards (1.9m) each. Take one 2⅛ yard (1.9m) piece of fabric and cut it in half lengthwise, making two equal strips.

With right sides together and using ½" (1.3cm) seams, pin-baste, then stitch the selvage side of each half width to the selvages of the full width piece of fabric. Press seams open.

Step 2:
Fold the large piece of fabric into quarters and pin to hold in place.

Using a yardstick, measure an arc 36½" (92.7cm) from the folded point. (See fig. 1.) Mark with tailor's chalk and cut along the arc to form a circle 73" (185.4cm) in diameter.

Repeat Steps 1 and 2 to make another 73" (185.4cm) circle from the contrasting fabric.

Step 3:
Pin-baste the two circles, right sides together, so that one circle extends 1/16" (1.5mm) beyond the other. This will prevent the contrasting fabric from rolling out along the hem edge of the finished tablecloth.

Using ½" (1.3cm) seams, stitch the circles together, leaving an 8" (20.3cm) opening for turning.

Notch seam allowances around the tablecloth every inch or so to within ⅛" (3mm) of the stitching line. (See fig. 2.) Turn the tablecloth right side out and press.

Step 4:
Turn and pin-baste raw edges of the 8" (20.3cm) opening inside the tablecloth to form a finished edge.

Topstitch about ⅛" (3mm) inside the outer edge of the tablecloth to hold it in place during use and to close the opening.

If the fabric rolls out along the hem edge of the finished tablecloth when in use, re-stitch around the cloth 1" (2.5cm) in from the outside edge.

Figure 1

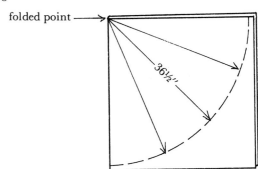

folded point

36½"

Figure 2

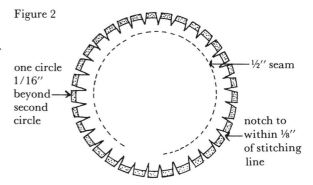

one circle 1/16" beyond second circle

½" seam

notch to within ⅛" of stitching line

Kissing Corners Pillow

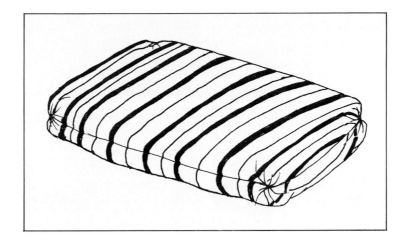

The materials and directions given are for a 16" x 10" (40.6cm x 25.4cm) rectangular pillow but can easily apply to a square pillow.

Materials
- ⅓ yard (30.5cm) light- to medium-weight fabric, 42" to 45" (106.7cm to 114.3cm) wide
- tape measure
- tailor's chalk
- fabric shears
- dressmaker's pins
- dental floss
- thread to match
- polyester fiber fill

Method
Step 1:
Press fabric.

Measure, mark with tailor's chalk, and cut out two 17" x 11" (43.2cm x 27.9cm) rectangles of fabric.

Step 2:
Place right sides of rectangles together. Using ½" (1.3cm) seams, pin-baste, then stitch around pillow leaving a 6" (15.2cm) opening in the center of one side for turning and stuffing. Turn right side out and press.

Step 3:
Turn pillow cover wrong side out. Measure and mark 2" (5cm) in from each corner point, wrap along mark with dental floss, and tie securely. (See fig. 1.)

Turn pillow right side out, and stuff with polyester fiber fill until firm. Turn in raw edges and slip-stitch opening closed.

Figure 1

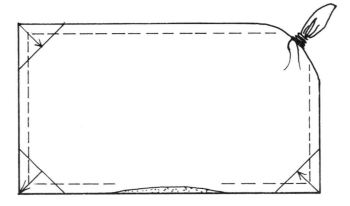

Williamsburg Dining Room

Williamsburg Dining Room

Dining in simple yet traditional elegance is the theme in the Williamsburg Dining Room.

French doors open onto a terrace, and in some instances, such as here, these doors are left uncovered to take full advantage of the view and to add nature's own atmosphere to your dining. A fabric covered cornice, adapted from instructions in the Williamsburg Living Room, brings color to the ceiling height and conceals a traverse rod for the draperies. The draperies may be closed when necessary to add color drama to the room and to insulate against cold weather in winter.

The gracious sideboard adds practicality to the room as a serving center for buffets or a tea. Candlelight is used throughout the room in hurricane globes, wall sconces, and candlesticks, adding an aura of romance and elegance.

The rich golden color enveloping the room appears in small items such as a tea cozy, napkins, and coasters, and in larger items such as the chair slip seats and draperies.

The pale washed walls of the period do not detract from the lovely pieces of furniture, and an impressionistic oil painting of the tropics lends a modern note of style and brightness.

Finally the oriental rug in tones of yellow and off-white draws color, texture, and furniture together in what is sure to be a haven of dining pleasures.

Oval Tablecloth

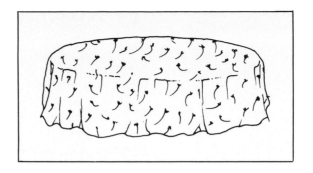

Before beginning this project, refer to Techniques, Tablecloths. The materials and directions given are for an approximate 70″ x 90″ (177.8cm x 228.6cm) oval tablecloth.

Materials
- 5 yards (4.6cm) medium- to heavyweight fabric, 48″ to 52″ (121.9cm to 132cm) wide
- 6 to 8 heavy books
- tape measure
- tailor's chalk
- fabric shears
- dressmaker's pins
- thread to match

Method
Step 1:
Press fabric.

Measure, mark with tailor's chalk, and divide fabric into two equal lengths, 2½ yards (2.3m) each.

Cut one piece in half lengthwise.

With right sides together and using ½″ (1.3cm) seams, pin-baste, then stitch the selvage side of each half width to the selvages of the full width piece. (See fig. 1.) Press seams open. You now have one large piece of fabric.

Step 2:
Place fabric right side up on top of an oval table. The middle section of the fabric should be centered across the widest part of the table so that the seams run along the sides. (See fig. 2.)

Carefully place weights on top of the fabric in the center and evenly around the edge of the table to hold the fabric in place during measuring and cutting.

Measure around fabric and place pins approximately 12″ below the table edge at 3″ intervals. (See fig. 2.) Cut along the pinned line. Remove weights and fabric from table.

Step 3:
Machine-stitch around the oval ¼″ (6mm) in from the outer edge. Trim to ⅛″ (3mm).

Turn fabric under along stitching line. Turn under once again to form a finished hem. Topstitch ¼″ (6mm) in from the folded edge. Press.

Figure 1

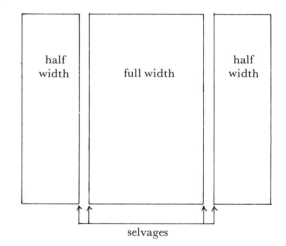

Figure 2

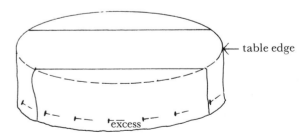

Fabric Covered Slip Seats

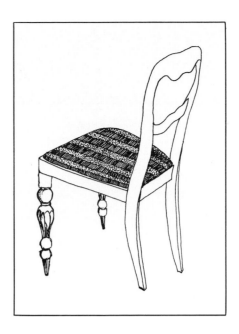

A slip seat is the removable, upholstered wooden seat that slips into the framework of a chair. Covering a slip seat is easy as well as adaptable to any size chair or stool. If the fabric you are using has a repeat pattern, add the length of one repeat to your calculations.

The materials and directions given are for four 17″ x 20″ (43.2cm x 50.8cm) slip seats.

Materials
- 1¼ yards (1.1m) fabric, 54″ (137.2cm) wide
- tape measure
- fabric shears
- staple gun and staples

Method

Step 1:
Remove slip seats from chairs. Remove old fabric from seats only if there is a muslin covering underneath. If not, do not remove the old fabric, but cover it with the new material.

Step 2:
Press fabric.

Working with one seat at a time, place it upside down on top of the wrong side of the fabric. If the fabric has a design, make sure the seat is centered over the design. Cut fabric 2″ larger on all sides than the seat area. (See fig. 1.)

Holding fabric to the slip seat, flip it right side up to make sure the pattern is centered. Return to upside down position.

Step 3:
Wrap fabric around side edges of slip seat and staple in place. Trim excess fabric from corners. (See fig. 2.)

Wrap fabric around front and back edges of slip seat making sure corners are neatly square. Staple in place. Trim off excess fabric and replace slip seat in chair.

Figure 1

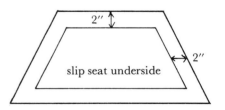

Figure 2

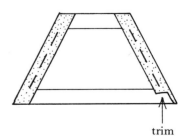

Tea Cozy

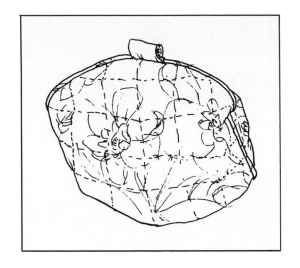

For serious tea drinkers this is a charming and practical accessory to keep tea or any other beverage nice and hot in the pot.

The materials and directions given are for a pot 10″ (25.4cm) wide by 7″ (17.8cm) tall.

Materials
- 1 yard (91.4cm) light- to medium-weight fabric for outside lining, 44″ to 52″ (111.8cm to 132cm) wide
- ¾ yard (68.6cm) polyester batting, any width
- ½ yard (45.7cm) lightweight fabric for backing, 44″ to 52″ (111.8cm to 132cm) wide
- 1 yard cable cord, ¼″ (6mm) thick
- tape measure
- square ruled paper
- lead pencil, #2
- fabric shears
- dressmaker's pins
- thread to match
- 3″ (7.6cm) satin ribbon, 1″ (2.5cm) wide, in an accent color

Method
Step 1:
On square ruled paper, draw a pattern which is 5″ (12.7cm) wider (measuring from the tip of the spout to the handle) and 5″ (12.7cm) taller than your teapot. Cut the upper edges into a dome-shaped curve, starting the curve halfway up from the bottom. (See fig. 1.)

Step 2:
Press fabric.

Using the paper pattern, cut out four shapes from the outside fabric.

Cut out two shapes from the backing fabric.

Cut out four shapes of polyester batting.

Step 3:
Measure and lightly draw horizontal and vertical lines 2″ (5cm) apart on the right side of each outside fabric shape. (See fig. 2.)

Place two pieces of polyester batting between one piece of outside fabric and one piece of backing fabric, right sides out. Pin; then baste along the quilting lines to hold fabric in place. Stitch along all quilting lines beginning with the center vertical line, then the center horizontal line. (See Techniques, Quilting.) (See fig. 2.)

Repeat on remaining half of tea cozy.

Step 4:
From the remaining outside fabric, prepare a bias strip 1½″ (3.8cm) wide by 36″ (91.4cm)

Figure 1

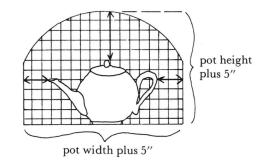

pot height plus 5″

pot width plus 5″

Figure 2

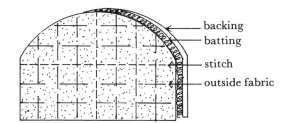

backing
batting
stitch
outside fabric

long. (See Techniques, Bias Trim). Cover the cable cord with the bias strip as directed to make piping.

Using ½″ (1.3cm) seams, pin the piping in between the two quilted halves, right sides together. Raw edges of the piping should be even with the raw edges of the quilted fabric shapes.

Fold the piece of ribbon in half. Position the ribbon in the center top, facing down between the two quilted halves. Using a zipper foot attachment, stitch piping and ribbon in place. Leave the straight bottom edge open. (See fig. 3.) Trim and clip curve.

Step 5:
Place tea cozy over pot to check height and to see if any adjustments are necessary.

Turn bottom edge under ½″ (1.3cm) and slip-stitch in place. (See fig. 4.) Turn right side out and press.

Step 6:
To make a lining, place right sides of remaining two shapes of outside fabric together. Using ½″ (1.3cm) seams, pin-baste; then stitch around the curve, leaving the straight bottom edge open. Trim and clip curve. (See fig. 5.) Press seam open. With wrong sides together, place lining inside the quilted form. (See fig. 6.)

Turn under bottom straight edge of the lining so that it rests ¼″ (6mm) above the quilted form's bottom edge. Pin-baste; then slip-stitch in place to quilted form. Tack lining to quilted form at random points to hold it in place.

Figure 3

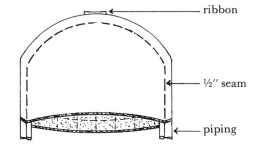

ribbon

½″ seam

piping

Figure 4

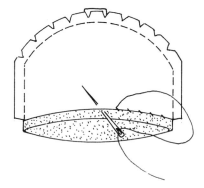

Figure 5

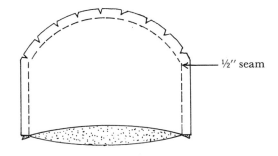

½″ seam

Figure 6

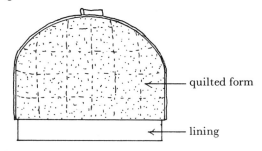

quilted form

lining

Early American Dining Room

Early American Dining Room

What could be more inviting than a simple, functional, and traditionally American dining area? The smooth, polished, warm brown woods offer a nice contrast to the rough texture of the natural brick floor.

The shirred window curtains add warmth and color, trimmed with bright contrasting bands of fabric and threaded onto café curtain rods. When doing only one panel for a window, the fabric looks its best when its fullness is measured two and one-half to three times the width of the curtain rod.

The braided place mats are machine washable and match the window curtains, carrying the cheery bright yellow down into the room. The piped, round breakfast napkins add a flourish to the table top to begin the day on a bright note. The natural basket lined with a sectioned bun warmer completes the setting. To keep rolls warm throughout the meal, bake a tile in the oven while the rolls are baking; then place the tile inside the basket under the liner before serving. Place the basket on a hot mat to avoid scarring your table.

The multicolored braided rug is easily made in many colors from the directions in the Early American Living Room.

For added accents, you may wish to include a bench or chair cushion. Directions for the many choices of cushion styles are found throughout the book. Choose the fabric and design to suit your dining needs.

Curtains with Tiebacks

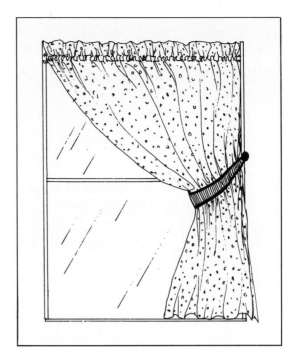

Curtains with tiebacks create a soft effect in any room, and they are one of the simplest curtain styles to make.

Before beginning this project, refer to Techniques, Window Treatments. The materials and directions given apply to any size, double-hung window.

Materials
- light- to medium-weight fabric
- tape measure
- tailor's chalk
- fabric shears
- dressmaker's pins
- thread to match
- 1 café curtain rod with brackets

Method
Step 1:
Mount the café curtain rod according to manufacturer's directions.

Step 2:
Press fabric.

Measure, mark with tailor's chalk, and cut fabric into lengths 11″ (27.9cm) longer than the desired finished length.

Step 3:
Place right sides of fabric lengths together. Using ½″ (1.3cm) seams, stitch fabric lengths together to make a panel 2 times plus 10″ (25.4cm) wider than the width of the window. Flat-felled seams or French seams may

be used. (See Techniques, Seams.) This will give you enough fullness for gathering and seams. It may be necessary to cut a lengthwise strip off one side of the panel to obtain the exact width. (See fig. 1.)

To prevent the finished curtain from puckering if regular seams are used, clip ¼″ (6mm) into the selvages along the seam allowances every 4″ (10.2cm). Press seams open.

Step 4:
To make double hems along both side edges, turn raw edges under 1″ (2.5cm) and press. Turn under 1″ (2.5cm) again and press. Machine-stitch in place ¼″ (6mm) from the inside fold edge; press.

Step 5:
To make the top casing, fold down the top raw edge 5″ (12.7cm) onto the wrong side of the fabric; press.

Measure, mark, and stitch across the curtain panel 2″ (5cm) below the fold. Turn

Figure 1

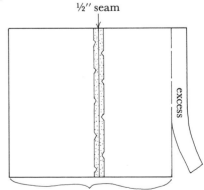

½″ seam

excess

2 times width of window plus 10″

raw edge under ½″ (1.3cm) and press. Stitch across panel again 2½″ (6.4cm) below first stitching line, securing raw edge as you do so. Headings and casings may vary in size depending upon the thickness of the café rod and how deep you wish the heading ruffle to be.

Step 6:
To make a double bottom hem, measure, mark, and turn up the bottom of the panel 3″ (7.6cm) and press. Turn bottom up 3″ (7.6cm) again, and press. Machine-stitch across the width of the panel. (See fig. 2.) Press.

Step 7:
To make the tiebacks, see the Shirred, Floor-Length Shower Curtains with Tiebacks in the Mrs. Bathroom.

Slide the curtain onto the café curtain rod and place in brackets. Distribute gathers evenly across the window, and pull back with tieback positioned in the center of one side of the window.

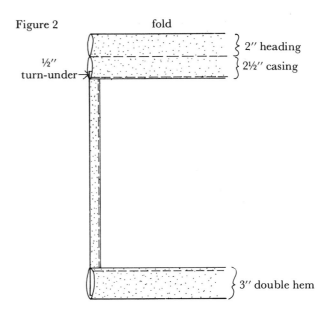

Figure 2

fold

2″ heading

2½″ casing

½″ turn-under→

3″ double hem

Braided Place Mats

For each place mat, follow the directions for the Braided Round Rug in the Early American Living Room, with the following exceptions:
• Use 1″ (2.5cm) wide strips of fabric.
• Wind braid loosely into an oval until it reaches approximately 18″ (45.7cm) in length and 12″ (30.5cm) in width. Your old place mats make excellent size guides.

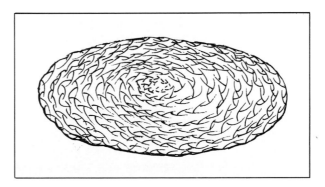

Bun Warmer

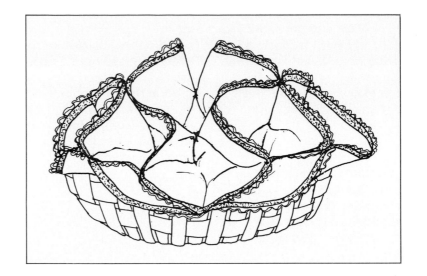

This very useful item can be made as plain or as fancy as you wish. It's an attractive way to keep rolls, buns, or muffins warm in a straw basket.

Materials
- ½ yard (45.7cm) medium-weight fabric, 45″ (114.3cm) wide
- brown wrapping paper
- lead pencil, #2
- ruler
- fabric shears
- tailor's chalk
- 1 package double-fold bias tape
- dressmaker's pins
- 2 small snaps
- thread to match

Method
Step 1:
Cut out a 12″ (30.5 cm) diameter circle from brown paper to use as a pattern for the bun warmer.

Step 2:
Press fabric.

Place paper pattern on top of wrong side of fabric. Trace with lead pencil and cut out three circles.

Step 3:
Cut bias tape into three long pieces, the circumference of each circle plus 1″ (2.5cm). Unfold and pin-baste the tape onto the right side of each circle, overlapping the ends. Stitch in place ¼″ (6mm) from the inside edge.

Whipstitch tape in place on wrong side of each circle. (See Techniques, Hand Stitches.) Press.

Step 4:
With wrong sides together, place one circle (center circle) on top of another circle (bottom circle) and divide into four equal sections with tailor's chalk. Machine-stitch sections together along chalk lines. (See fig. 1.)

Place remaining circle, right side up, on top of other two circles. Pin-baste top two circles together at center of each stitched section. Be careful not to pin through the bottom circle. Stitch top two circles together along pin-basted lines 5″ (12.7cm) toward center of circle. (See fig. 1.) Press.

Step 5:
Sew snaps on top circle, 2″ (5cm) in from the outer edge so that section #1 meets #2, and #3 meets #4. (See fig. 2.)

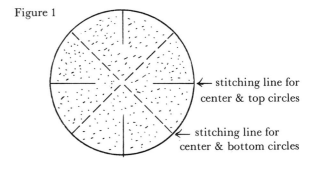

Figure 1

← stitching line for center & top circles

← stitching line for center & bottom circles

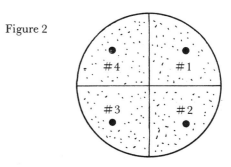

Figure 2

#4 #1 #3 #2

Round Breakfast Napkins

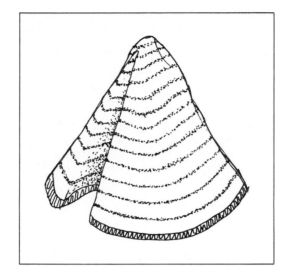

There is no firm rule that a napkin must be square. It may be any shape you desire: square, round, rectangular, triangular, hexagonal, and so on—even circular! These are just right for breakfast or luncheon.

The materials and directions given are for six 16″ (40.6cm) round napkins.

Materials
- 1½ yards (1.4m) light- to medium-weight fabric, 45″ (114.3cm) wide
- brown wrapping paper
- lead pencil, #2
- fabric shears
- ruler
- tailor's chalk
- tape measure
- 2 packages double-fold bias tape
- dressmaker's pins
- thread to match

Method
Step 1:
Cut out a 16″ (40.6cm) diameter circle from brown paper to use as a pattern for the breakfast napkins.

Step 2:
Press fabric.

Fold fabric in half lengthwise, right sides together. Place paper pattern on top of fabric. Trace with pencil and cut through doubled fabric to get six circles.

Step 3:
Cut bias tape into six long pieces, the circumference of each circle plus 1″ (2.5cm). Unfold and pin-baste tape onto right side of each circle, overlapping ends; then stitch in place ¼″ (6mm) from the inside edge. Press.

Whipstitch tape in place on wrong side of each circle. (See Techniques, Hand Stitches.) Press.

Country French Dining Room

Country French Dining Room

The distinctive styling in this dining room is simple and direct in its message. The wood paneling seems reminiscent of more elaborate city dwellings; the three-dimensional effect is achieved by nailing strips of molding on top of flat paneling. The molding and wall here are stained the same rich golden brown, but you might consider accenting the walls by painting the molding strips in a bright, contrasting color. The painted wooden shutters and ladder-back chair add color and textural interest to this pastoral atmosphere.

The color theme is easily carried up to the ceiling with chandelier lampshades covered in fabric to match the shutters. The chandelier cord is covered with a tube of fabric shirred onto the cord, adding a bit of richness to rather austere furnishings.

The rugged table is softened by a bright, multicolored, reversible runner which is machine washable. A hot mat made from a decorative tea towel cushions a hearty stew, and napkins here are actually tea towels—ample protection for the most corpulent of laps.

The tile floor is a practical and easy to care for pearl gray. An interesting area rug might be added for cooler months, along with curtains and accent cushions on the bench and chair.

Fabric Covered Smooth Lampshade

The directions given apply to any size plain, smooth lampshade. If you select a sheer or light colored fabric, make sure the shade you are covering is white or off-white. A dark colored shade will make the fabric appear tinted.

Materials
- light- to medium-weight fabric
- 1 plain, smooth lampshade
- 2 sheets newspaper
- scissors
- dressmaker's pins
- tailor's chalk
- white household glue
- small disposable container
- paintbrush, 2″ (5cm) wide
- narrow braid, rickrack, or ribbon trim (optional)

Method
Step 1:
Depending on the size of the shade to be covered, tape two full sheets of newspaper together and treat them as one. Wrap newspaper around lampshade in funnellike fashion, making sure the outside of the shade is completely covered by one main section of the paper. (See fig. 1.) Trim newspaper around top and bottom rims of shade.

Step 2:
Open newspaper pattern, and place it on the right side of the fabric. If the fabric you are using has a design, center the pattern over the design carefully. Trim one side of the paper pattern in a straight line. (See fig. 2.)

Pin pattern in place. Mark with tailor's chalk, and cut out fabric 1″ (2.5cm) larger on all sides than the newspaper pattern. (See fig. 3.)

Step 3:
Pour glue into a disposable container and dilute with water until it spreads evenly with a paintbrush—approximately two parts glue to one part water.

Brush diluted glue onto the lampshade and wrap fabric around it, right side out. Begin with the slanted edge and allow 1″ (2.5cm) extra fabric at the top and at the bottom of the shade. Carefully smooth fabric in place, making sure the straight edge of the fabric overlaps the slanted edge. (See fig. 4.)

Figure 1

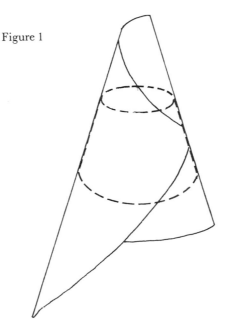

Figure 2

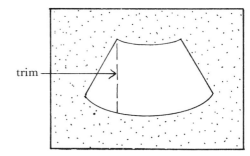

trim →

Figure 3

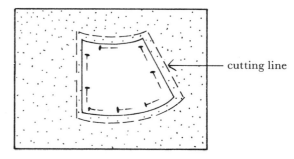

← cutting line

Step 4:
Place untrimmed shade on its base to dry overnight. When thoroughly dry, trim away excess fabric around the top and bottom edges. (See fig. 5.)

Using undiluted glue, trim as desired with narrow braid, rickrack, or ribbon.

Figure 4

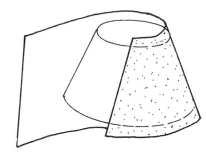

Figure 5

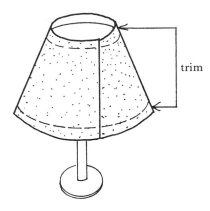

trim

Hot Mat

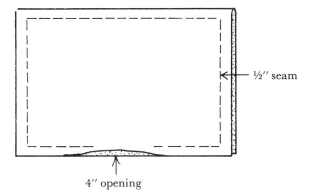

A hot mat can be made to any size. A small version makes a very nice pot holder.

Materials
- 1 tea towel with printed design
- polyester batting
- tape measure
- fabric shears
- thread to match
- sewing needle

Method
Step 1:
Press tea towel.

Fold towel in half horizontally, wrong side out, so that the design is centered. Using ½″ (1.3cm) seams, pin-baste around all four sides and stitch in place, leaving a 4″ (10.2cm) opening in the center of one side for turning and padding. (See fig. 1.)

Step 2:
Turn towel right side out and press.

Measure and cut out a double layer of polyester batting the same size as the stitched towel. Place batting inside mat, making sure all corners are evenly filled.

Turn edges of opening in, and slip-stitch opening closed.

Step 3:
Following design of tea towel, pin-baste; then topstitch around the design to hold the padding in place.

Figure 1

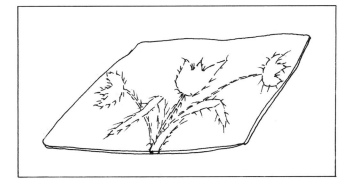

½″ seam

4″ opening

Patchwork Table Runner

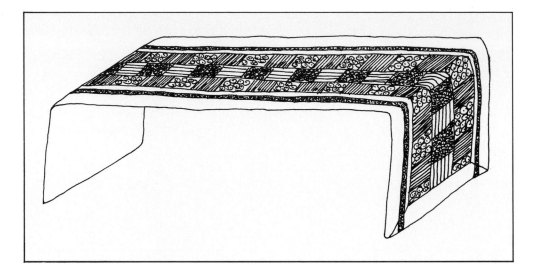

This is a very pretty way to use up any washable scraps of fabric. The materials and directions given are for a 32″ x 88″ (81.3cm x 223.5cm) runner.

Materials
- 2¾ yards (2.5cm) light- to medium-weight washable fabric, 54″ (137.2cm) wide
- 7 assorted, contrasting, ¼ yard (22.9cm) pieces light- to medium-weight washable fabric, 42″ to 45″ (106.7cm to 114.3cm) wide
- tape measure
- tailor's chalk
- fabric shears
- dressmaker's pins
- 6 yards (5.5m) decorative washable braid or ribbon trim, 2″ (5cm) wide
- thread to match

Method

Step 1:
Press fabric.

Measure, mark with tailor's chalk, and cut out forty-two 7″ (17.8cm) squares from the seven ¼ yard (22.9cm) pieces of fabric. You should get six squares from each piece of fabric. (See fig. 1.)

Step 2:
Arrange squares, right sides up, in fourteen rows of three across, placing darker colored squares next to lighter ones for effective design variation.

Using ½″ (1.3cm) seams and with right sides facing, pin-baste; then stitch patchwork squares together to form three long columns. Press seams open.

Step 3:
Using ½″ (1.3cm) seams and with right sides facing, pin-baste; then stitch the three columns together making sure the squares are positioned next to each other at their midpoints. Press all seams open. Trim half-blocks at either end. (See fig. 2.) The patchwork runner should measure approximately 19″ x 81½″ (48.3cm x 207cm).

Step 4:
From the remaining large piece of fabric, measure, mark with tailor's chalk, and cut out a section of fabric 49″ x 98½″ (124.5cm x 250.2cm).

Step 5:
With right sides facing, place patchwork in the center of the long fabric piece, 8½″ (21.6cm) in from each end and 15″ (38cm) in from each side.

Figure 1

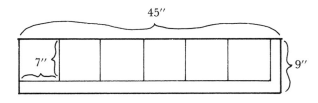

Figure 2

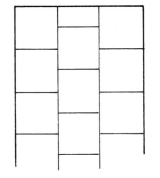

Fold the side margins over to meet the side edges of the patchwork; pin-baste. Press the fold. (See fig. 3.)

Using ½″ (1.3cm) seams, stitch long sides. Press seams open; then turn table runner right side out. Center patchwork and press.

Step 6:
Fold end margins under ½″ (1.3cm) and press. Fold toward patchwork 4″ (10.2cm) to make wide hems. Press. Miter corners. (See Techniques, Mitered Corners.) Pin-baste; then topstitch in place. (See fig. 4.)

Step 7:
Cut trim into two equal lengths. Position trim on each long margin, and pin-baste. Topstitch in place, turning ends under. (See fig. 5.)

Figure 3

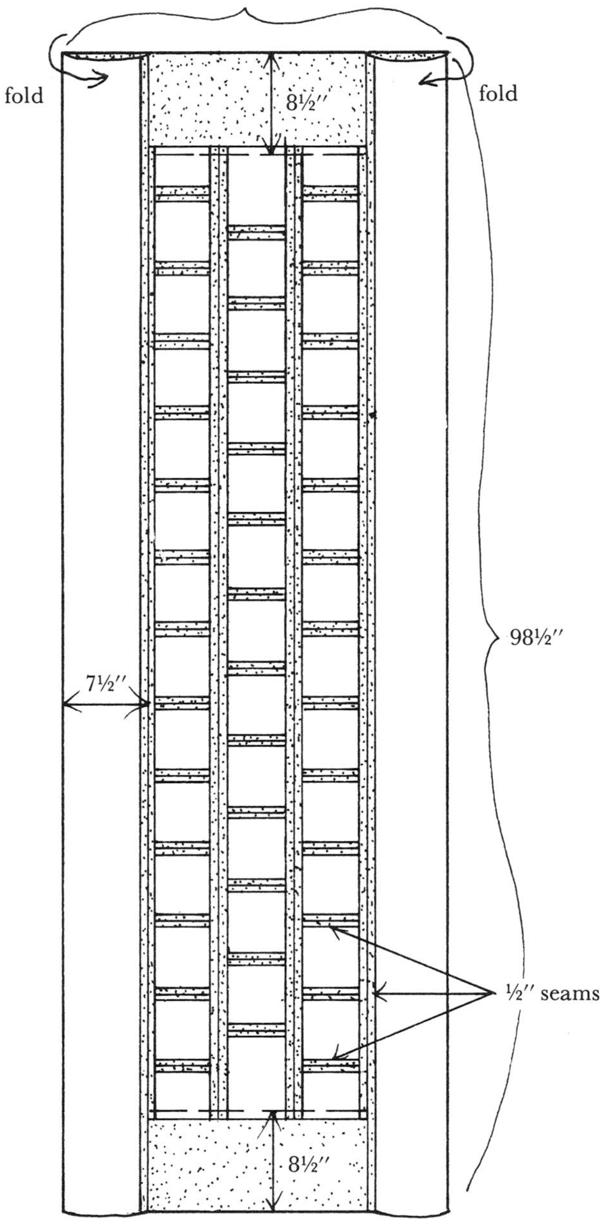

fold   8½″   fold

7½″

98½″

½″ seams

8½″

Figure 4

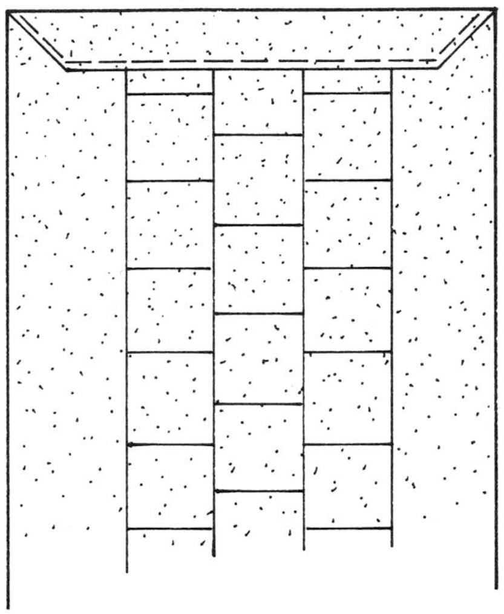

Figure 5

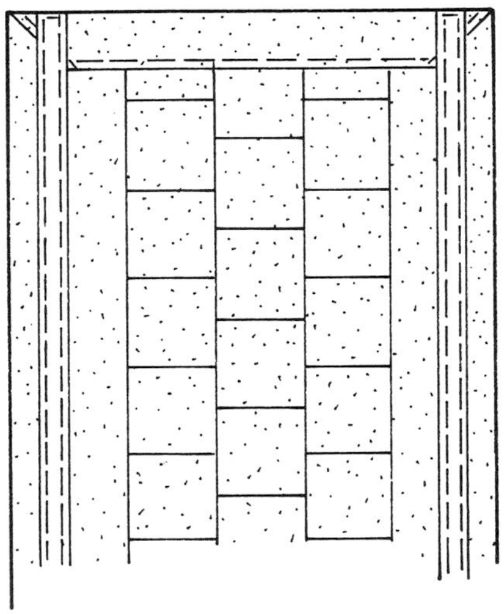

Fabric Covered Chandelier Cord

This is an elegant way to disguise an unattractive chandelier cord or one that is exceptionally low.

Method
Using ½" (1.3cm) seams, make a casing 3 to 4 times longer and 1" (2.5cm) wider than the cord to be covered. Press seams open, and turn casing right side out.

Remove light fixture from the ceiling. Thread casing onto the chandelier cord, and distribute the gathers evenly. Replace fixture.

Napkin Rings

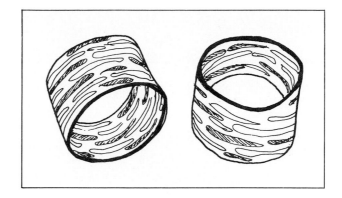

These add a decorative touch to any meal. The materials and directions given are for eight napkin rings.

Materials
- 3 cardboard tubes from bathroom toilet tissue
- ¼ yard (22.9cm) fabric, any width
- single-edged razor blade
- tape measure
- tailor's chalk
- scissors
- white household glue
- small disposable container
- paintbrush, ½″ (1.3cm) wide

Method
Step 1:
Cut cardboard tubes into 1¼″ (3.2cm) sections. (See fig. 1.)

Step 2:
Press fabric.
    Cut fabric into 3″ x 6″ (7.6cm x 15.2cm) strips.

Step 3:
Pour glue into disposable container and dilute with water until it spreads evenly with a paintbrush—approximately two parts glue to one part water.

    For each napkin ring, brush diluted glue onto outside of cardboard. Center fabric so that an even amount extends over each edge.

Brush glue onto inside of ring. Turn raw edges of fabric to inside and smooth in place. (See fig. 2.)

    When fabric is firmly in position, lightly brush diluted glue over entire ring as a protective finish. Allow to dry thoroughly before using.

Figure 1

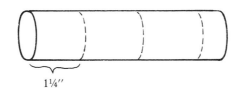

1¼″

Figure 2

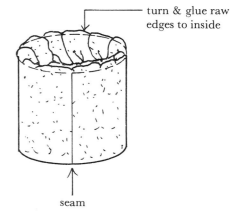

turn & glue raw edges to inside

seam

Eclectic Dining Room

Eclectic Dining Room

Though eclectic in feeling, a more modern trend is indicated in this dining area.

Chrome sawhorses support a thick glass table top. Old chairs from a flea market have been refurbished, cushioned, and painted to set the color tone of the room.

The table setting corresponds to the chairs, creating an even stronger color statement. The place mats and matching napkins are all reversible and machine washable.

The background interest of the room is a wall of mirror panels, creating a feeling of spaciousness and light. The tray slings break the cold expanse and are a decorative answer to storing platters, trays, or rare plate collections.

The floor covering here is a soft, pearl gray wall-to-wall carpeting, again adding to the feeling of spaciousness.

With all of the glass and mirror, warmth is brought into the room in the form of large potted palms and smaller plants. An attractive tablecloth in accent colors of yellows, greens, and blues would add even more warmth to the room as would a colorful painting mounted on the mirrored wall.

Reversible Place Mats

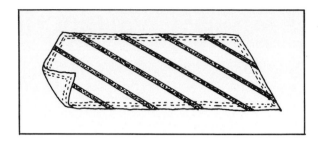

Place mats can be made in many shapes and sizes. For practical purposes these reversible mats are not only pretty but versatile. When not in use as mats themselves, they can be used as table protectors under larger, unlined place mats.

The materials and directions given are for six 12″ x 18″ (30.5cm x 45.7cm) reversible place mats.

Materials
- 1¼ yards (1.1m) fabric, 45″ (114.3cm) wide
- 1¼ yards (1.1m) contrasting fabric, 45″ (114.3cm) wide
- 1 yard (91.4cm) polyester fleece padding, 45″ (114.3cm) wide
- brown wrapping paper
- lead pencil, #2
- fabric shears
- ruler
- tailor's chalk
- tape measure
- dressmaker's pins
- thread to match
- buttonhole twist in a contrasting color for topstitching (optional)

Step 1:
Cut out a 12½″ x 18½″ (31.8cm x 47cm) rectangle from brown paper to use as a pattern for the reversible place mats.

Step 2:
Press fabric.

Fold each piece of fabric in half lengthwise, wrong sides out. Place the paper pattern on top of the fabric. Trace with pencil and cut through the doubled fabric to get six rectangles from each fabric piece.

Step 3:
Place right sides of contrasting rectangles together. Using ¼″ (6mm) seams, pin-baste, then stitch leaving a 6″ (15.2cm) opening in the center of one side. (See fig. 1.) Trim corners. Turn place mats right side out and press.

Step 4:
Cut out a 12″ x 18″ (30.5cm x 45.7cm) rectangle from brown paper to use as a pattern for the polyester fleece padding. Ease the padding into the place mats, making sure that the corners lie flat. Hold padding in place with random pin-basting.

Fold in raw edges of opening ¼″ (6mm) and slip-stitch closed, making stitches as invisible as possible.

Topstitch place mats with regular thread or buttonhole twist, ½″ (1.3cm) in from the outer edges. (See fig. 2.) Topstitch again 1″ (2.5cm) in from the outer edges. Press.

Figure 1

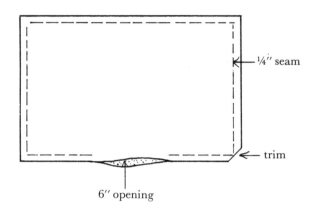

¼″ seam

trim

6″ opening

Figure 2

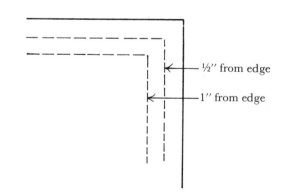

½″ from edge

1″ from edge

Reversible Napkins

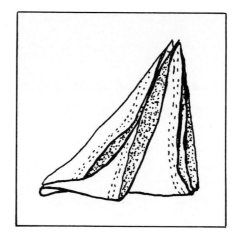

These napkins add a dramatic touch to any table. When making anything reversible, always topstitch the item as a finishing touch. This holds the fabric in place during washing so that one side does not "crawl" onto the other.

Let your imagination be your guide when trimming the finished product: ribbon, piping, braid, fringe—all topstitched in place.

The materials and directions given are for six 20″ (50.8cm) reversible square napkins.

Material

- 1¾ yards (1.6m) fabric, 45″ (114.3cm) wide
- 1¾ yards (1.6m) contrasting fabric, 45″ (114.3cm) wide
- lead pencil, #2
- ruler
- fabric shears
- tailor's chalk
- tape measure
- dressmaker's pins
- thread to match
- buttonhole twist in contrasting color for topstitching (optional)

Method

Step 1:
Cut out a 20½″ (50.8cm) square from brown paper to use as a pattern for the reversible dinner napkins.

Step 2:
Press fabric.

Fold each piece of fabric in half lengthwise, wrong sides out. Place the paper pattern on top of the fabric. Trace with pencil and cut through doubled fabric to get six squares from each fabric piece.

Step 3:
Place right sides of contrasting squares together. Using ¼″ (6mm) seams, pin-baste, then stitch leaving a 6″ (15.2cm) opening in the center of one side. (See fig. 1.) Trim corners. Turn napkins right side out and press.

Fold in raw edges of opening ¼″ (6mm) and slip-stitch closed, making stitches as invisible as possible.

Topstitch napkins with regular thread or buttonhole twist, ¼″ (6mm) in from the outer edges. (See fig. 2.) Topstitch again ½″ (1.3cm) in from the outer edges. Press.

Figure 1

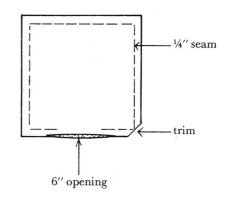

¼″ seam

trim

6″ opening

Figure 2

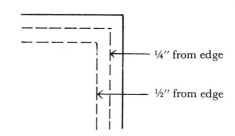

¼″ from edge

½″ from edge

Tray Sling

This handy sling adds a decorative and practical touch to any dining area. It is also a very orderly way to keep your serving trays in place and displayed at the same time.

Materials
- 1 round plastic ring, 3″ (7.6cm) in diameter
- 2⅓ yards (2.1m) woven trim, 2½″ (6.4cm) wide
- tape measure
- fabric shears
- dressmaker's pins
- thread to match

Method
Step 1:
Press trim.
   Thread trim through the plastic ring, forming a double loop as illustrated in fig. 1. Pin-baste to hold trim in place; then stitch ends together. Position ends underneath trim touching the ring.

Step 2:
Spread loops apart where they overlap, and tack with thread to hold in position. (See fig. 2.)
   Hang tray sling on wall.

Figure 1

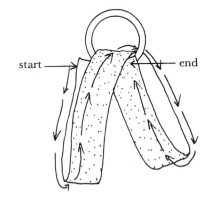

start — end

Figure 2

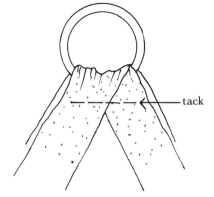

tack

Round Coasters

These practical additions to your table fashions can be made to coordinate with a tablecloth or place mats. They serve as protection under hot or cold beverages anywhere at any time.

The materials and directions given are for six 4″ (10.2cm) round coasters. For very pretty place mats, enlarge the size to 16″ (40.6cm).

Materials
- ¼ yard (22.9cm) fabric, any width
- ⅛ yard (11.4cm) polyester fleece padding, 45″ (114.3cm) wide
- lead pencil, #2
- fabric shears
- ruler
- tailor's chalk
- tape measure
- dressmaker's pins
- 2½ yards (2.3m) matching bias strip, 1″ (2.5cm) wide
- thread to match or contrast

Method
Step 1:
Draw a 4″ (10.2cm) in diameter circle on brown paper, and cut it out. This will be the pattern for the coasters.

Step 2:
Press fabric.

Fold fabric in half with selvages together, wrong side out. Place paper pattern on top of fabric. Trace six circles with pencil, and cut folded fabric to get 12 circles.

Repeat procedure, and cut out six fleece padding circles the same size as the fabric circles.

Step 3:
Place padding between two fabric circles, right sides out. Pin-baste to hold in position.

Firmly holding all three layers together and treating them as one, machine-stitch through the center of the circle four times until the circle is divided into eight pie-shaped sections. (See fig. 1.)

Step 4:
From remaining fabric, make 2½ yards (2.3m) continuous bias strips 1″ (2.5cm) wide. (See Techniques, Bias Trim.)

Cut bias strips into six long pieces the circumference of each circle plus 1″ (2.5cm). Fold strips in half and press. Unfold and pin-baste strips to the top side of each circle overlapping ends. Stitch ¼″ (6mm) in from the outer edge. Press.

Whipstitch bias strip in place on underside of each circle; then press. (See fig. 2.)

Figure 1

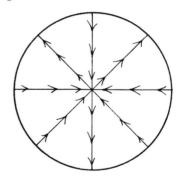

Figure 2

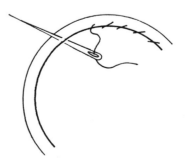

Den/Guest Room

Den/Guest Room

This distinctive den is a room for all seasons and an extra guest or two. The rich dark wood paneling and the lighter toned, freestanding book shelves, cabinets and chest mean ample storage and mobility for future room arrangements.

This is a room to put your feet up in and relax. The studio couches are slip-covered in a washable suede-type fabric; directions for the studio couch covers are found in the Teenager's Bedroom. The belted rolls on the couches serving as back cushions are covered foam pads, which, when opened, afford extra sleeping space and, when rolled closed, give extra storage space for sleeping pillows.

The ottoman can easily take on a more tailored look than is shown here by slip-covering it with thick welting accenting the edges.

The pleated lampshades are easy to cover and add a special decorator touch to any room.

The eye never stops moving as color accents are carried throughout the den by use of paint—the parson's coffee table, and brightly colored and textured fabrics. The luggage rack straps add a note of portable color as do the matching bookmark and the covered books. Even though this room is dark, it is warmly inviting because of the accents of bright color throughout.

Fabric Covered Pleated Lampshade

Pleated lampshades made from "scratch" not only require much more time and trouble than they are worth, but they present a possible fire hazard once completed. It is better to use an existing pleated shade as a base and cover it. If you plan to use a sheer or light colored fabric, be sure to purchase a white or off-white lampshade. A dark colored shade will make the fabric appear tinted.

Materials
- fabric
- 1 pleated lampshade
- white household glue
- small disposable container
- paintbrush, 2″ (5cm) wide
- butter knife
- manicure scissors
- fabric shears

Method
Step 1:
Measure the height of the lampshade and the circumference of its bottom edge. (See fig. 1.)

Step 2:
Press fabric.

Cut a rectangle of fabric the width of the height of the shade plus 2″ (5cm) and the length 3 times the bottom circumference.

Step 3:
Pour glue into a disposable container and dilute with water until it spreads evenly with a paintbrush—approximately two parts glue to one part water.

Beginning at the shade's seam, brush glue onto the shade, three to four pleats at a time. Allowing 1″ (2.5cm) extra fabric at the top and bottom of the shade, place fabric edge on the inside of a pleat. (See fig. 2.) Using your fingers and a butter knife, carefully press fabric deeply into pleats.

Continue brushing glue and attaching fabric to the shade, three to four pleats at a time, until the lampshade is completely covered with fabric. Allow a 1″ (2.5cm) overlap at the seam. When all pleats are covered, place the untrimmed lampshade on its base to dry overnight.

Step 4:
When the shade is thoroughly dry, trim excess fabric with manicure scissors.

Figure 1

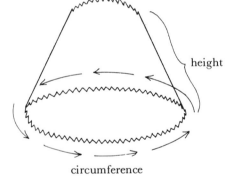

height

circumference

Figure 2

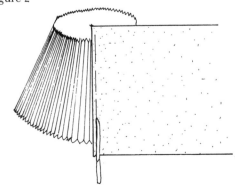

Book Covers

This is an easy way to refurbish old or ugly book covers and to add decorative accents to your book shelves.

Materials
- 1 book
- lightweight fabric
- tape measure
- tailor's chalk
- fabric shears
- pinking shears
- thread to match
- needle

Method
Step 1:
Press fabric.
   Measure, mark with tailor's chalk, and cut out a piece of fabric 2 times the height and 2 times the width of the opened book.

Step 2:
With right sides out, fold fabric so that the long raw edges meet in the center. Press folds. Trim ends with pinking shears. Loosely baste center raw edges together to hold fabric in place.

Step 3:
Center book on top of fabric, and slip front and back covers into the open ends.

Slipcovered Ottoman

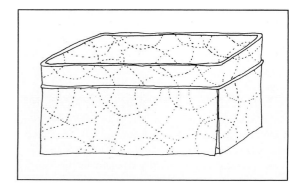

Before beginning this project, refer to Techniques, Slipcovers.
   The materials and directions given are for a standard-size ottoman, 17″ x 23″ x 15″ (43.2cm x 58.4cm x 38cm).

Materials
- 3 to 4 yards (2.7m to 3.7m) tightly woven, medium-weight fabric, 48″ (121.9cm) wide
- 6 to 8 yards (5.5m to 7.3m) cable cord, ½″ (1.3cm) thick
- tape measure
- T-pins
- dressmaker's pins
- tailor's chalk
- fabric shears
- 2 spools heavy-duty thread to match

(Continued)

Method

Step 1:
Following the guidelines given in Techniques, Slipcovers, measure to determine the exact amount of fabric you need to cover the ottoman.

From remaining fabric, cut continuous bias strip 6 to 8 yards (5.5m to 7.3m) long and 3″ (7.6cm) wide. (See Techniques, Bias Trim.) Cover cable cord as directed to make welting.

Step 2:
Press fabric.

Position a section of fabric, right side up, so that the design is centered on top of the ottoman. Trim to size, allowing for 1″ (2.5cm) seams on all four sides. (See fig. 1.)

Step 3:
Carefully pin-baste welting around the outer edge of the top section of the ottoman, raw edges of welting facing in the same direction as the raw edges of the fabric. (See fig. 2.)

Remove fabric from ottoman, and stitch welting in place using a zipper foot attachment. The line of stitching which attaches the welting to the fabric should rest exactly on top of the welting on the original cover.

For a smooth finish where the ends of the welting overlap, pull cable cord out of its cover about 1″ (2.5cm) and cut off. Repeat on other cording end. Smooth out the casings, and overlap them at an angle. Stitch in place. (See fig. 3.)

Step 4:
Replace fabric, with welting attached, on the ottoman. Measure, mark with tailor's chalk, and cut out a strip of fabric to cover the top side section, allowing 1″ (2.5cm) seams along the top and bottom edges and a 1″ (2.5cm) seam where the short ends meet.

Pin-baste fabric into position. (See fig. 4.)

Remove cover, and stitch to first row of welting using the zipper foot attachment. Press; then stitch 1″ (2.5cm) seam where short ends meet.

Step 5:
Replace cover on ottoman. Follow same procedure as above and pin-baste a second row of welting around the lower edge of the ottoman's top side section, raw edges of the welting facing in the same direction as the raw edges of the fabric. (See fig. 4.) Remove cover, and stitch welting in place.

Place cover on ottoman.

Step 6:
Measure distance from the second row of welting to the floor and add 3½″ (8.9cm). Cut out strips of fabric this length and the full width of the fabric. You'll need to stitch several of these strips together, end to end to make a fabric piece long enough to wrap around the ottoman. As a rule, make the strip 1½ yards (1.4m) longer than the distance around the ottoman to allow enough fabric to make pleats at each corner for a professional-looking cover.

Step 7:
Press long strip of fabric to form a ½″ (1.3cm) turn-under and a 2″ (5cm) hem. Stitch hem in place using the sewing machine's blind stitch, or blind stitch by hand.

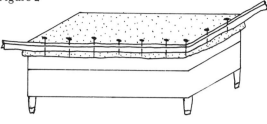

Figure 2

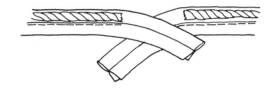

Figure 3

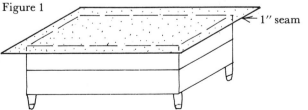

Figure 4

first welting

top side section

second welting

Figure 1

1″ seam

Step 8:
Starting 5″ (12.7cm) from one corner, pin-baste long strip of fabric to second row of welting so that the hem rests ½″ (1.3cm) above the floor. Make 5″ (12.7cm) deep pleats facing each other at each corner. (See fig. 5.) Overlap pleats about ⅛″ (3mm) at the welting so that they meet exactly on the finished cover.

Note: The top seam allowance of the skirt section may vary from ½″ (1.3cm) to 1″ (2.5cm) because the ottoman may be worn so that some sections of it are closer to the floor than others.

Remove ottoman cover with skirt pin-basted in position. Stitch skirt to welting.

Stitch seam where ends meet under the last pleat by machine or by hand. Press slip-cover.

Figure 5

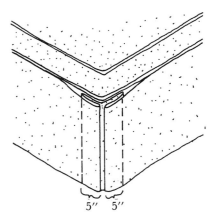

Luggage Rack Straps

Materials
- ½ yard (45.7cm) medium-weight fabric, 42″ to 45″ (106.7cm to 114.3cm) wide
- 1¾ yards (1.6m) trim, 2½″ (6.4cm) wide
- tape measure
- tailor's chalk
- dressmaker's pins
- fabric shears
- thread to match
- staple gun and staples

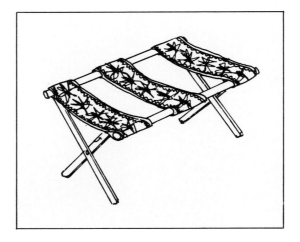

Method
Step 1:
Press fabric

Measure, mark with tailor's chalk, and cut out three strips of fabric, each 19″ x 6″ (48.3cm x 15.2cm)

Step 2:
Fold each strip in half lengthwise, wrong side out. Using ½″ (1.3cm) seams, stitch each strip to form a tube. Center seams and press.

Turn tubes right side out. Center seams again and press.

Turn in raw edges at ends ½″ (1.3cm) and press.

Step 3:
Press woven trim. Measure and cut trim into 19″ (48.3cm) strips.

Center trim on top of fabric tubes, seam sides up. Make sure trim extends ½″ (1.3cm) inside the tube end openings.

Step 4:
Topstitch around perimeter of trim.

Evenly space, then staple, finished straps to luggage rack.

Study

Study

A place for everything and everything in its place, this den is a dream room you can put in your home now.

This room holds inspiration for anyone—as an inviting haven for an aspiring writer, as a secluded spot for office overtime, as a hideaway for paying bills—a map of the world to encourage adventures in your mind, a shell collection to recall happy, lazy days on sunny beaches, and books for reference on whatever subject you may need.

The oversize wastepaper basket is covered with fabric scraps left over from other projects. The practical bookends are simply bandanas filled with sand! The in/out boxes create a uniform look as well as being practical. The fabric covered wall behind the shelves is easily executed with double-faced carpet tape.

On the table/desk, the typewriter cover certainly dresses up a very functional machine. And to continue the color theme, the desk blotter and pencil cup are covered to match.

Fabric Covered Walls—Double-Faced Carpet Tape

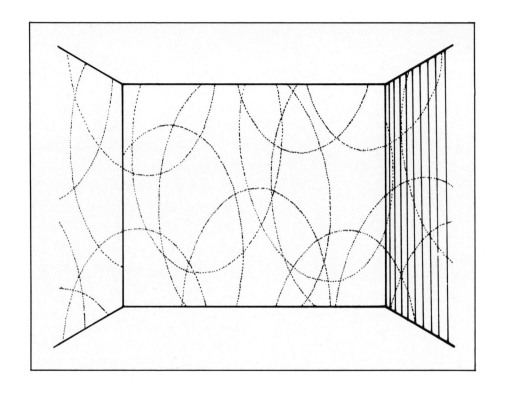

Before beginning this project, refer to Techniques, Walls.

This wall covering method is ideal if you do not wish to mar your existing walls and need to do a small area in a hurry. However, the carpet tape method is not recommended for large areas because it is not very strong and it tends to show ridges unless you use a dark colored, all-over print.

Materials
- fabric
- tape measure
- tailor's chalk
- fabric shears
- double-faced carpet tape
- ribbon
- white household glue

Method
Step 1:
To calculate the exact amount of fabric needed, measure the height and width of each area to be covered. If the fabric you select has a repeat design, add one extra repeat in length to your calculations. It may be necessary to seam several lengths of fabric together to obtain the exact width needed. If this is the case, be sure to match the design at the seam.

Step 2:
Place double-faced carpet tape around the perimeter of the area to be covered. You may wish to add a few extra strips of tape down the center of the area for reinforcement. (See fig. 1.)

Smooth fabric into place on top of the double-faced carpet tape. If desired, trim the raw edges with ribbon glued directly to the fabric.

Figure 1

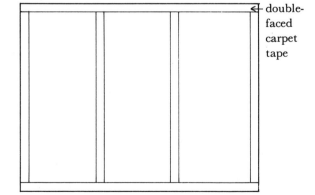

double-faced carpet tape

Fabric Covered Desk Pad with Blotter

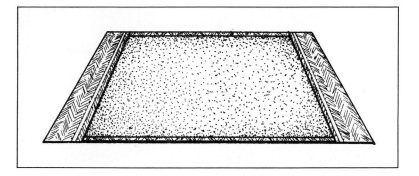

Materials

- 1 desk pad with blotter, 19″ x 24″ (48.3cm x 61cm)
- ¾ yard (68.6cm) light- to medium-weight fabric, 42″ to 45″ (106.7cm x 114.3cm) wide
- tape measure
- tailor's chalk
- fabric shears
- white household glue
- small disposable container
- paintbrush, 1″ (2.5cm) wide
- 24 nonrusting, 2″ (5cm) paper clips
- 1½ yards (1.4m) narrow ribbon or braid

Method

Step 1:
Press fabric.

Center desk pad on top of wrong side of fabric.

Measure, mark with tailor's chalk, and cut out a section of fabric to extend 1″ (2.5cm) beyond top and bottom of the pad, and 4″ (10.2cm) beyond each side. (See fig. 1.)

Remove desk pad from fabric, and remove blotter from desk pad.

Step 2:
Pour glue into disposable container and dilute with water until it spreads evenly with a paintbrush—approximately two parts glue to one part water.

Brush diluted glue onto the back of the desk pad and attach fabric, smoothing out air bubbles and ripples.

Brush diluted glue onto top and bottom edges of desk pad, and smooth fabric around pad to front. Make vertical clips where side panels are joined to pad. (See fig. 2.) Glue 1″ (2.5cm) overlap in place.

Brush diluted glue onto side panels, and smoothly pull fabric over and around outside edges to the front. (See fig. 3.)

Brush diluted glue onto inside edges of side panels, and tuck fabric under. Use paper clips to hold in place. Stand one paper clip on its side to hold inside edge of panel away from desk pad while the glue dries.

Add a bit more water to diluted glue to create a wash, and brush it over covered desk pad.

Step 3:
Using undiluted glue, trim with ribbon or braid as desired, removing and replacing paper clips as you proceed.

Allow desk pad to dry thoroughly before removing paper clips and inserting blotter.

Figure 1

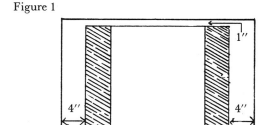

Figure 2

Figure 3

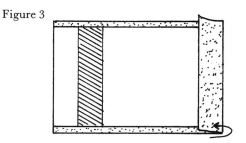

Fabric Covered In/Out Box

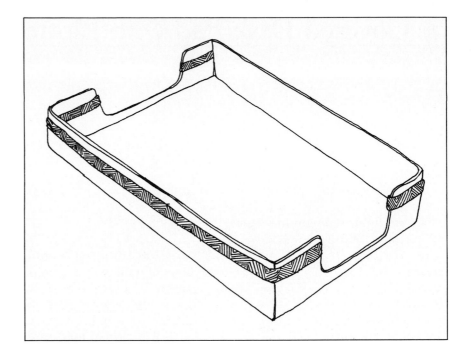

Materials
- 1 in/out box, 9½" x 12" (24cm x 30.5cm)
- ¾ yard (68.6cm) light- to medium-weight fabric, 42" to 45" (106.7cm x 114.3cm) wide
- tape measure
- tailor's chalk
- fabric shears
- white household glue
- small disposable container
- paintbrush, 1" (2.5cm) wide
- 24 nonrusting, 2" (5cm) paper clips
- 1 sheet medium-weight cardboard, 9½" x 12" (24cm x 30.5cm)
- 4 nonrusting paperweights, any size
- 2 yards (1.8m) narrow ribbon or braid

Method
Step 1:
Press fabric.

Measure, mark with tailor's chalk, and cut out a piece of fabric 21" x 24" (53.3cm x 61cm).

Step 2:
Pour glue into disposable container and dilute with water until it spreads evenly with a paintbrush—approximately two parts glue to one part water.

Brush diluted glue onto bottom of in/out box. Center and attach fabric, smoothing out air bubbles and ripples.

Step 3:
Brush diluted glue onto long sides inside and out, and onto bottom of box. Smooth fabric up and over edges to inside of box, extending 1" (2.5cm) onto inside bottom. Clip corners vertically just to the top edge to allow fabric to lie flat. Use paper clips to hold fabric in place. (See fig. 1.)

Clip diagonally from outside corner of fabric to corner of box. (See fig. 1.)

Step 4:
To cover ends of in/out box, brush diluted glue onto ends, inside and out, and wrap fabric around corners toward center of outside end. (See fig. 2.) Smooth fabric up and over edges to inside of box, extending 1" (2.5cm) onto inside bottom.

Following fig. 2, clip fabric flap ¼" (6mm) from fold line and flush with the bottom of box. Fold ¼" (6mm) in as illustrated.

Brush diluted glue onto outside ends, and smoothly wrap fabric over ends. Trim excess fabric from center of end flaps as illustrated in fig. 3.

Figure 1

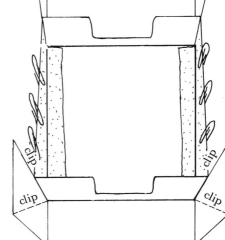

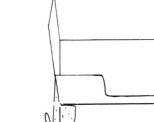

Brush diluted glue onto inside ends and bottom of box, and smoothly wrap fabric over edge of inside of box, extending 1″ (2.5cm) onto inside bottom.

Use paper clips to hold fabric in place until thoroughly dry. (See fig. 4.)

Step 5:
Measure, mark with tailor's chalk, and cut out a piece of fabric 10″ x 13″ (25.4cm x 33cm).

Trim cardboard to fit snugly but easily on inside bottom. Brush diluted glue on cardboard, and cover with fabric, turning edges under and trimming excess from underside corner. (See fig. 5.)

Brush undiluted glue on inside bottom of box. Place covered cardboard, right side up, on bottom. Place paperweights on top of cardboard to hold firmly until dry.

Step 6:
Using undiluted glue, trim with ribbon or braid as desired, removing and replacing paper clips as you proceed.

Allow to dry thoroughly before removing paper clips and weights.

Figure 2

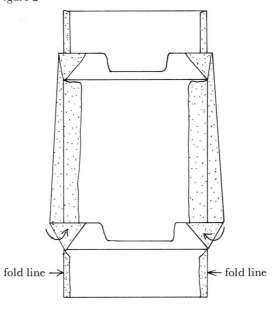

fold line → ← fold line

Figure 4

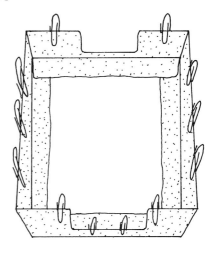

Figure 3

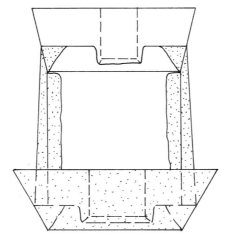

Figure 5

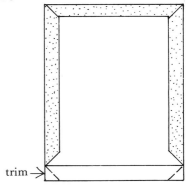

trim →

Typewriter Cover

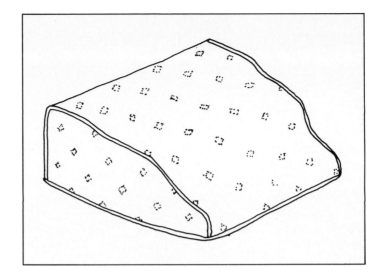

The materials and directions given apply to any portable or standard-size office typewriter.

Materials
- 1 yard (91.4cm) heavyweight fabric, 44″ (111.8cm) wide
- ½ yard (45.7cm) contrasting heavyweight fabric, 44″ (111.8cm) wide
- 4 yards (3.7m) cable cord, ¼″ (6mm) thick
- weights
- tape measure
- tailor's chalk
- fabric shears
- dressmaker's pins
- thread to match

Method
Step 1:
Using the ½ yard (45.7cm) piece of fabric, prepare a 2″ (5cm) wide bias strip. (See Techniques, Bias Trim.) Cover cable cord with the bias strip as directed to make piping.

From the 1 yard (91.4cm) piece of fabric measure, mark with tailor's chalk, and cut out a rectangle 22″ (55.9cm) wide and 36″ (91.4cm) long, and two smaller sections, each approximately 22″ x 10″ (55.9cm x 25.4cm). (See fig. 1.)

Step 2:
Center the long strip, right side up, on top of the typewriter so that it runs from front to back.

Use weights to hold the back and front ends of the fabric strip in place as you work. (See fig. 2.)

Pin-baste piping to the fabric, making sure the raw edges are even. (See fig. 2.)

When you have pin-basted the piping along both outer side edges, measure from the center of the typewriter to each piped edge to be certain that the sides are symmetrical.

Remove fabric from typewriter. Using a zipper foot attachment, stitch piping to fabric strip. Replace fabric on typewriter, and secure again with weights.

Step 3:
Pin-baste remaining two side sections to the piping, right sides out. Trim to the general shape of the typewriter, leaving 1½″ (3.8cm) seam allowances. (See fig. 3.)

Fold under side section seam allowances as you pin-baste them to the piping. When both side sections are completely pinned, remove cover from typewriter.

Figure 1

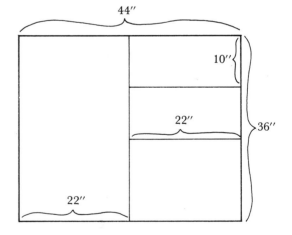

Check to make sure both sides are identical by folding the cover so that one section rests directly on top of the other. If necessary, readjust some of the pins. Before stitching, replace cover on typewriter to be certain the fit is correct.

Once the side sections are pinned from the outside as accurately as possible, transfer the pins to the inside of the cover. Trim excess seam allowance.

Using a zipper foot attachment, attach side sections to cover, stitching directly on top of piping stitching.

Replace cover on typewriter.

Step 4:

Run your fingers along the bottom of the cover, pulling the excess fabric outward.

Position and pin-baste piping to the cover so that the rounded side faces upward and the raw edge rests on top of the excess fabric. (See fig. 4.)

Using a zipper foot attachment, stitch piping in place around bottom edge of typewriter cover.

Trim seam allowances along the bottom of the cover so that when folded under, the raw edges of the piping conceal the raw edges of the fabric.

Turn seam allowances under. Whipstitch bottom edge seam allowances to those of the side sections to keep them from rolling out when the cover is used. (See Techniques, Hand Stitches.)

Figure 2

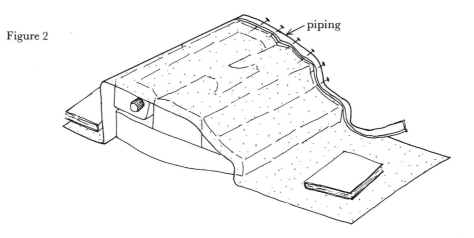

Figure 3

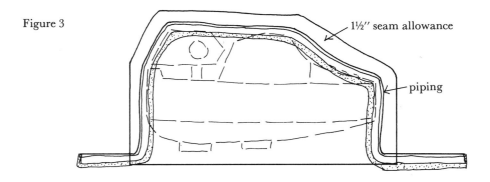

Figure 4

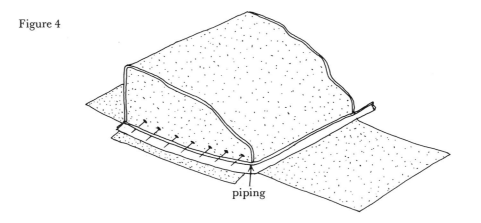

Music Room

Music Room

Plants love good music almost as much as people do. This music room is alive with lush greenery; natures own colors blending with the rich man-made tones.

Here the soft muted tones of dark gold walls are warmly accented with an orange stripe. The walls are easy to change by simply removing the fabric from the fiberboard panels.

A big, soft couch is so nice to sink into when listening to your favorite selections. Notice the welting matches the stripe of the fabric wall, drawing the color accent into the room.

The covered record holder is a very neat and organized way to store and move long playing records.

The planter is covered with old sheet music. You might consider using the same technique to cover books.

The piano bench cushion made of woven ribbons makes practicing more comfortable and may be changed periodically to underline various color schemes. A few floor cushions, as found in the Eclectic Living Room, would increase the seating choices and could bring in a new texture.

Fabric Covered Record Holder

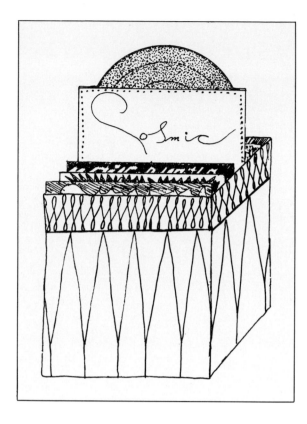

Materials

- 1 cardboard carton, 14″ (35.6cm) wide by 12″ (30.5cm) deep
- 2 yards (1.8m) light- to medium-weight border print fabric for inside lining and outside trim, 44″ to 52″ (111.8cm to 132cm) wide
- 1½ yards (1.4m) medium- to heavy weight fabric for outside, 44″ to 52″ (111.8cm to 132cm) wide
- white household glue
- small disposable container
- paintbrush, 2″ (5cm) wide
- tape measure
- tailor's chalk
- fabric shears
- stainless steel dinner knife

Method

Step 1:

Press fabric.

Measure, mark with tailor's chalk, and cut out a rectangle of border-print fabric 66″ x 9″ (167.6cm x 25.4cm).

Fold strip in half lengthwise, right sides together. Using ½″ (1.3cm) seams, stitch along the long side of the strip to form a tube.

Turn tube right side out. Center the border design and press. Turn raw edges at ends inside and topstitch in place.

Step 2:

From the remaining inside fabric, measure, mark with tailor's chalk, and cut out a strip 42″ x 15″ (106.7cm x 38cm), and two rectangles, each 14″ x 15″ (35.6cm x 38cm).

Step 3:

Pour glue into disposable container and dilute with water until it spreads evenly with a paintbrush—approximately two parts glue to one part water.

Brush diluted glue onto the inside back, bottom, and front of the carton. Press the 42″ x 15″ (106.7cm x 38cm) fabric strip into position covering all of these surfaces, leaving an equal amount of excess at the back and front edges. Using a dinner knife, smooth wrinkles and push fabric into corners of carton. If necessary, pinch corners and trim away excess fabric.

Wrap excess fabric over the rim of the carton and glue to the outside edge. (See fig. 1.)

Step 4:

Brush diluted glue onto the two remaining inside surfaces. Attach each fabric rectangle so that a 14″ (35.6cm) raw edge rests on the bottom and the rest of the piece covers the side, extending over the top edge. Wrap excess fabric over the rim of the carton and glue to the outside edge.

Allow the carton to dry thoroughly before covering the outside.

Figure 1

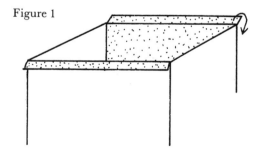

Step 5:

To cover the outside, place the carton, top down, on a flat working surface. Brush diluted glue onto the bottom. Center the uncut piece of outside fabric so that it extends over all of the outside surfaces. Press and smooth in place.

Brush glue onto two opposite sides of the carton and smooth fabric into place. Trim fabric to extend ½″ (1.3cm) from the top rim and 1″ (2.5cm) from the corners of both sides. (See fig. 2.) Glue the 1″ (2.5cm) over-laps to the adjacent sides of the box.

Brush diluted glue onto the remaining two sides of the carton. Smooth fabric into place, trimming it to extend ½″ (1.3cm) from the top rim.

Step 6:

Using undiluted glue, attach the tube of border trim around the outside top of the carton about ¼″ (6mm) below the rim.

Allow to dry thoroughly before using.

Figure 2

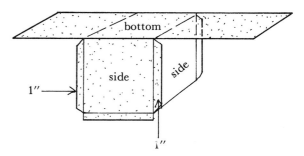

Piano Bench Cushion

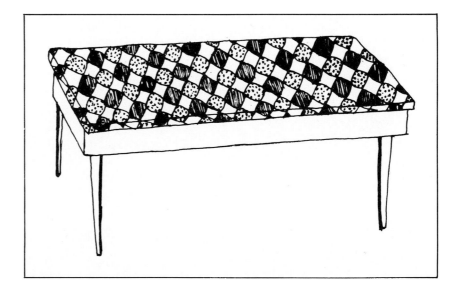

This is a very pretty way to accent any rectangular bench.

Materials
- polyurethane foam pad, 1″ (2.5cm) thick
- three assorted colors of satin ribbon, each 1½″ (3.8cm) wide
- contrasting medium-weight fabric
- tape measure
- fabric shears
- thread to match

Method
Measure the top of your piano bench in order to estimate the correct amount of materials needed.

Follow the directions given for the Ribbon Front Pillow in the Early American Living Room, enlarging the instructions to suit the above dimensions.

Once completed, you may wish to attach narrow elastic bands to the cushion corners to secure it to the piano bench.

Sheet-Music Covered Flower Pot

Materials
- plastic flower pot, any size
- ruler
- old sheet music
- scissors
- white household glue
- small disposable container
- paintbrush, 2″ (5cm) wide
- decoupage wood finish, clear, waterproof, and not soluble in alcohol

Method

Step 1:
Thoroughly clean and dry the flower pot.

Measure and cut sheet music into 2 ½″ x 5″ (6.4cm x 12.7cm) strips. Include as many of the musical notes or titles as possible.

Step 2:
Pour glue into disposable container and dilute with water until it spreads evenly with a paintbrush—approximately two parts glue to one part water.

Brush diluted glue onto backs of the strips of sheet music. Attach strips to the outside of the flower pot (see fig. 1), making sure they extend about ½″ (1.3cm) onto the inside. Overlap strips for an interesting effect.

Step 3:
Coat the covered flower pot with a final layer of diluted glue. Allow to dry several hours or overnight.

Paint or spray with decoupage wood finish. Allow to dry thoroughly before using.

Figure 1

Fabric Covered Walls—Fiberboard

Before beginning this project, refer to Techniques, Walls.

This method of covering walls with fabric works exceptionally well when walls end in open space, such as archways. This is also an excellent method to use whenever you are unable to work directly on the walls. The fiberboard method allows you to take your walls with you when you change residence.

Materials
- fiberboard cut to size of wall, ½″ (1.3cm) thick
- fabric
- tape measure
- tailor's chalk
- fabric shears
- staple gun and staples
- headless nails
- hammer

Method
Step 1:
Carefully measure wall areas to be covered, and have the lumberyard cut fiberboard to exact measurements. If a large area requires several fiberboard panels to fit together, have each panel cut 4″ (10.2cm) smaller than the width of fabric you are using.

Step 2:
To calculate amount of fabric needed, measure the height and width of each fiberboard panel and add 4″ (10.2cm) to each dimension. If the fabric you select has a repeat design, add one repeat extra in length to the calculations.

Press fabric, and cut fabric panels 4″ (10.2cm) longer than the height of the fiberboard panels.

Step 3:
Lay fiberboard panels on the floor, and carefully smooth fabric into position, tightly wrapping all edges around to the back of the board. Staple fabric in place on the wrong side of fiberboard, mitering the corners. (See Techniques, Mitered Corners.) (See fig. 1.) Repeat this procedure for all the fiberboard panels.

Step 4:
Attach covered panels to the walls with headless nails. Carefully push weave of fabric back in place with a straight pin so that the nail holes do not show.

There will be an obvious seam where panels are joined side by side, which is really rather attractive. However, if you wish to camouflage these seams, use undiluted white household glue to attach decorative braid over the seams, or nail painted or fabric-covered molding over the seams.

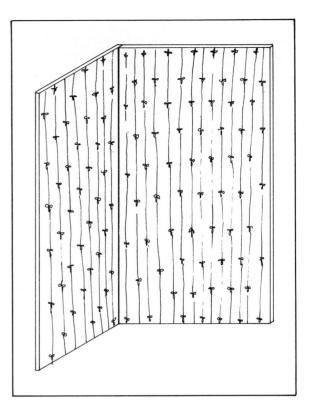

Figure 1

back of fiberboard

Art Studio

Art Studio

Any artist would love to spend hours in this attic room, painting or sculpting (or sewing). The windows are cut right out of the roof to offer all the sunlight possible for those creative hours.

The floor here is easy-to-care-for tile. This is especially practical when cleaning up after a busy day of painting.

The fabric covered panel screen creates a nice backdrop for still life arrangements or as a screen for radiators, sinks, and such. Change the fabric with your moods.

Open spaces and an abundance of sunlight are musts for any artist. The walls in this studio are bare except for a few pieces of art mixed with fabric, a geometric design of satin ribbons, a sculpted piece of fabric on fabric—and fabric simply stretched over a frame—all are expressions of your own creativity.

Ribbon Art

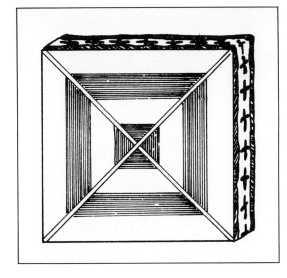

This striking hanging is a bit tricky to construct; the ribbons must be cut precisely. However, the end result is well worth your efforts.

Materials
- 4 wooden, artist's stretcher bars, each 12″ (30.5cm) long
- ½ yard (45.7cm) light- to medium-weight fabric, any width
- 48″ (121.9cm) satin ribbon, 1½″ (3.8cm) wide—color #1
- 38″ (96.5cm) satin ribbon, 1½″ (3.8cm) wide—color #2
- 26″ (66cm) satin ribbon, 1½″ (3.8cm) wide—color #3
- 6″ (15.2cm) satin ribbon, 1½″ (3.8cm) wide—color #4
- 52″ (132cm) satin ribbon, ⅞″ (2cm) wide—color #4
- 38″ (96.5cm) flat braid trim, ¼″ (6mm) wide—color #1
- ½ yard (45.7cm) fusible bonding web, 18″ (45.7cm) wide
- lead pencil, #2
- ruler
- fabric shears
- staple gun and staples
- white household glue

Method

Step 1:
Following manufacturer's instructions, push stretcher bars together to form a 12″ (30.5cm) square frame.

Step 2:
Press fabric.
  Measure, mark, and cut out a section of fabric 4″ (10.2cm) wider and longer than the frame.

Step 3:
Place frame, face side down, on top of right side of fabric and lightly trace around the outside edge with a pencil. Remove frame and draw an X across the square from corner to corner.
  Following the colors indicated in fig. 1, carefully measure, mark with a pencil, and cut ribbons to fit into all four sections of the square.

Figure 1

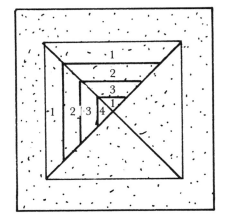

Figure 2

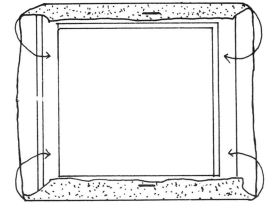

Step 4:
Carefully disassemble ribbon design and cut fusible bonding web to the exact size of the ruled square. Place web between ribbons and fabric. Carefully reassemble ribbons. Place a lightweight scrap of fabric on top of the ribbons; then press lightly with a warm iron. Do not slide the iron.

Step 5:
Center the fused ribbon design on top of the frame. Beginning at the center top, wrap fabric around frame and staple in place on the back. (See fig. 2.)

Wrap tautly and staple center bottom into place, then the center sides. After all center sides are in place, staple toward the corners of the frame, making sure the fabric is smooth and taut.

At the corners, pull fabric down from the corner point toward center of frame and staple in place. (See fig. 3.)

Fold point A down, then point B, and staple in place. (See fig. 4.)

Step 6:
Cut the flat braid trim into two equal lengths. Coat one side of one length of braid with undiluted glue.

Place the braid on top of the ribbons along one diagonal of the X, covering raw edges where the ribbons meet.

Repeat on the remaining diagonal. Allow to dry thoroughly.

Step 7:
To finish the side edges of the frame, cut fusible bonding web into strips ⅞″ (2 cm) wide. Lay web on frame edge, then lay ⅞″ (2cm) wide ribbon on top. Using a scrap of cloth as protection, gently press ribbon and web with a warm iron. (See fig. 5.)

Figure 3

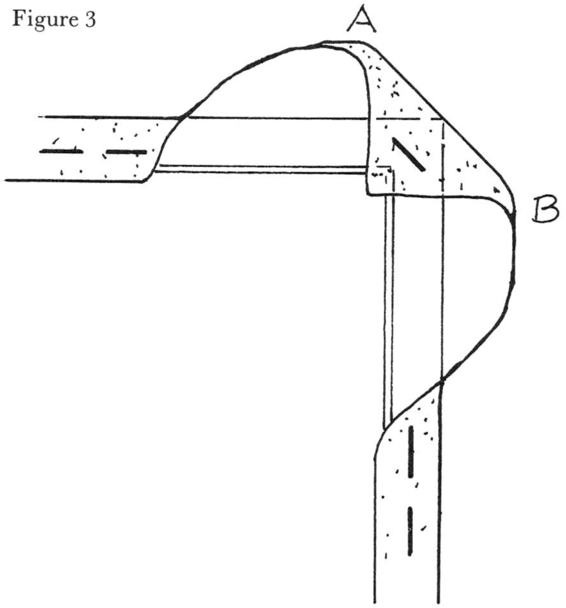

Figure 4

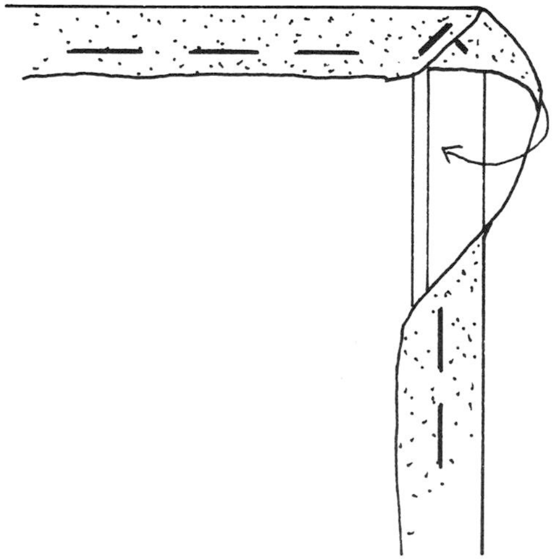

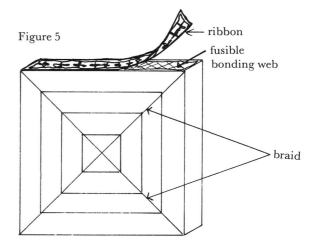

Figure 5

Framed Fabric

This is a simple way to add color and design to a room. Scarves, as well as any favorite printed fabric, make very effective hangings.

Materials
- 4 artist's wooden stretcher bars—any size
- printed fabric
- tape measure
- tailor's chalk
- fabric shears
- push pins
- staple gun and staples

Method
Step 1:
Following manufacturer's instructions, push stretcher bars together to form a frame.

Step 2:
Press fabric.

   Measure, mark with tailor's chalk, and cut out a piece of fabric 4″ (10.2cm) wider and longer than the assembled frame. Make sure the fabric design is centered as you do this.

   Place fabric on top of frame, right side up. Recenter design within perimeter of the frame. Use push pins to hold fabric in place on the face of the frame.

Step 3:
Beginning at the center top, wrap fabric tautly around frame and staple in place on the back. Smooth and staple center bottom in place, then the center sides. After all centers are in place, staple toward the corners of the frame.

   At the corners, pull fabric down from the corner point toward center of frame, and staple in place. (See fig. 1.)

   Fold point A down, then point B, and staple in place. (See fig. 2.)

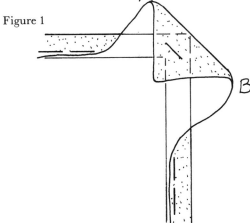

Figure 1

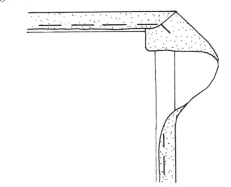

Figure 2

Fabric Art

Bright, bold, contrasting colors or pale monochromatics may be used for an eye-catching wall hanging. Select fabrics which will create an interesting textural statement as well as a color statement. The materials and directions may easily be applied to any size hanging.

Materials
- 4 wooden, artist's stretcher bars, each 12″ (30.5cm) long
- ½ yard (45.7cm) light- to medium-weight solid color fabric, any width
- ½ yard (45.7cm) lightweight contrasting fabric, any width
- 1½ yards (1.4m) ribbon, ⅞″ (2cm) wide
- tape measure
- tailor's chalk
- fabric shears
- staple gun and staples
- white household glue

Method
Step 1:
Following manufacturer's instructions, push stretcher bars together to form a 12″ (30.5cm) square frame.

Step 2:
Press fabric.
    Measure, mark with tailor's chalk, and cut out a square of fabric 4″ (10.2cm) wider and longer than the frame.

Step 3:
Beginning at the center top, wrap fabric around frame and staple in place on the back.
    Wrap tautly and staple center bottom into place, then the center sides.
    Staple toward the corners of the frame, making sure the fabric is smooth and taut.

Step 4:
Measure and cut out a section of contrasting fabric, wider and longer than the covered frame. The exact dimensions depend on the effect desired.
    Pleat, gather—or whatever—the contrasting fabric; any number of creations is possible. Staple design in place.

Step 5:
Using undiluted household glue, trim edges of the frame with ⅞″ (2cm) wide ribbon.

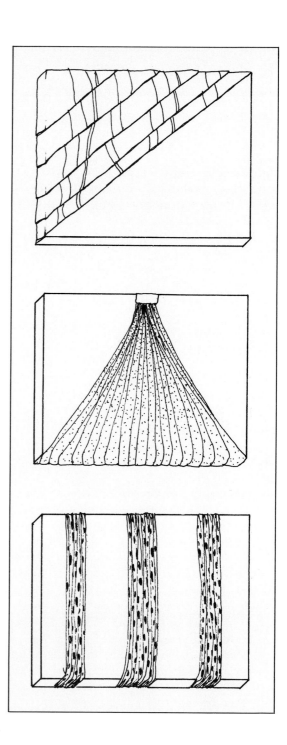

Fabric Covered Folding Screen

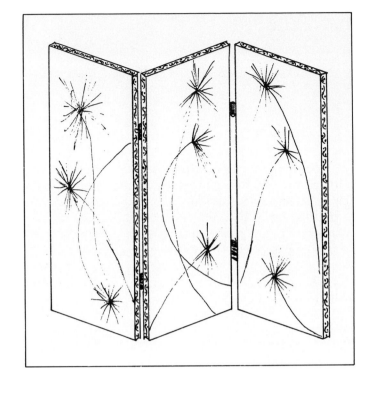

This attractive screen is an ideal way to camouflage radiators or air conditioning units. The directions given apply to any size free-standing, folding screen.

Materials
- light- to medium-weight fabric
- 1″ by 2″ (2.5cm x 5cm) wooden frames, 12″ (30.5cm) wide and any height up to 7′ (210cm)
- tape measure
- fabric shears
- push pins
- staple gun and staples
- decorative braid or ribbon trim, 1″ (2.5cm) wide
- white household glue

Method

Step 1:
Have the local lumberyard construct and join the frames together with bifold hinges. (See fig. 1.) An odd number of panels makes an effective screen.

Step 2:
Press fabric.

Measure, mark with tailor's chalk, and cut out sections of fabric 4″ (10.2cm) longer and wider than each frame.

Working with one frame at a time, align the fabric section, right side out, and hold it in position at the top of the frame with push pins. (See fig. 2.)

Make sure the fabric extends 2″ (5cm) from the frame edges on all four sides.

Step 3:
Pull fabric taut and staple in place along the side edges of the frame, mitering corners. Trim excess fabric. (See fig. 3.)

Staple second fabric section to the other side of the frame following the procedure outlined in Step 3. (See fig. 4.)

Hinges should not be a problem. Simply pull fabric taut, and staple around them.

Step 4:
Using undiluted glue, attach braid or ribbon trim along the side edges to cover the staple heads. (See fig. 5.)

Figure 1

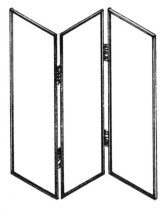

Figure 2

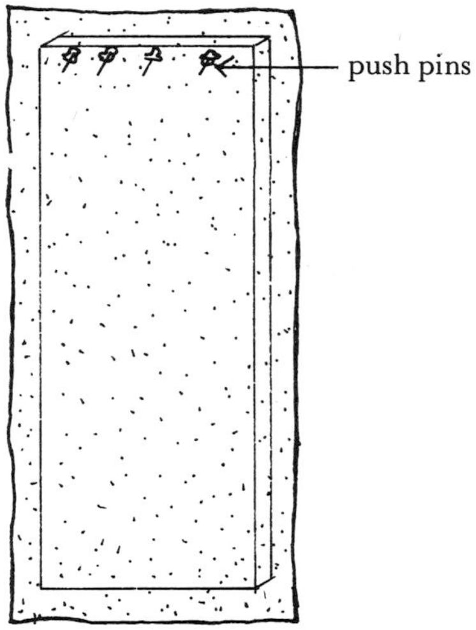

push pins

Figure 4

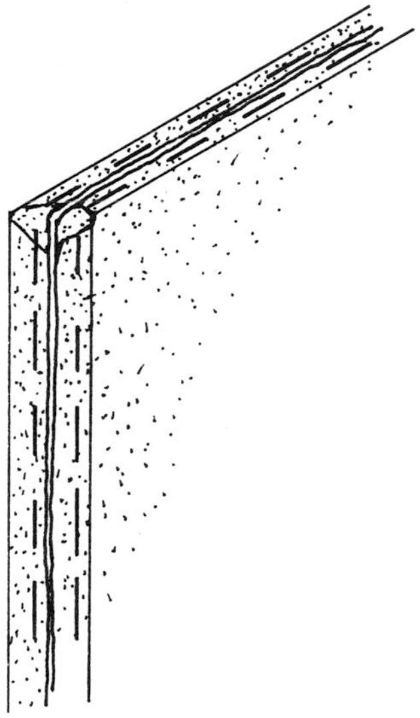

Figure 3

Figure 5

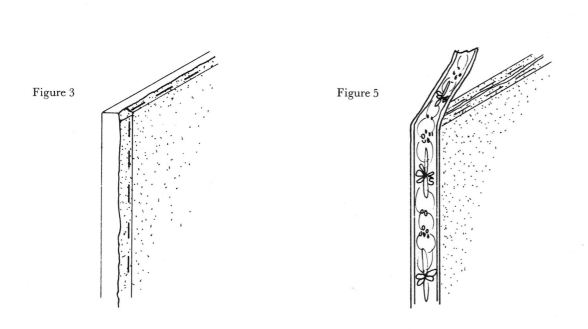

Photography Studio

Photography Studio

If you are a photography buff, you know there must be a niche for everything; neatness is imperative to enable working quickly and efficiently. The mood here is dramatic—ultra violet—the lighting used in a photographer's studio.

No-seam paper is rolled up and out of the way. Freestanding shelves stacked upon chests afford excellent storage space and can be moved at will.

To display some of your better efforts, fabric covered picture frames add a cheerful note, as do the large, hanging covered frames and mirrors.

A covered album, padded or unpadded, is a nice way to dress up an ordinary scrapbook or to camouflage a telephone book.

Padded Album Cover

Materials
- 1 album (3-ring binder) 10¼″ x 12″ (26cm x 30.5cm)
- 1 yard (91.4m) lightweight fabric, 44″ to 52″ (111.8cm to 132cm) wide
- tape measure
- tailor's chalk
- fabric shears
- polyester batting
- dressmaker's pins
- sharp needle
- thread to contrast for quilting
- thread to match

Method
Step 1:
Press fabric.

Measure, mark with tailor's chalk, and cut out two rectangles of fabric, each 43″ x 14″ (109.2cm x 35.6cm).

Measure, mark, and cut out a rectangle of polyester batting 43″ x 14″ (109.2cm x 35.6cm).

Step 2:
Center the open album on right side of one rectangle of fabric. Trace around album with tailor's chalk, and mark fabric at the album spine.

With tailor's chalk draw the desired design between the outside vertical lines and the album spine lines.

Step 3:
Place batting between the two fabric sections, right sides out.

Pin-baste around all raw edges and along vertical chalked lines to hold batting in place. (See fig. 1.)

Using contrasting thread, stitch along spine markings following chalked design, stitching through all three thicknesses. (See fig. 1.)

Stitch vertical parallel lines about 1½″ (3.8cm) apart on remaining side sections of fabric. Stop stitching 1″ (2.5cm) in from end edges. (See fig. 1.)

Trim batting between end edges. Turn raw edges in and slip-stitch in place.

Step 4:
Recenter album on top of right side of quilted fabric. Fold sides of fabric over front and back covers and pin-baste flaps in place along top and bottom edges. Baste in place. Turn cover right side out, and make sure it fits over album. Stitch top and bottom flap edges in place. (See fig. 2.)

Trim excess batting and seam allowances to ½″ (1.3cm). Do not trim unstitched area around spine. (See fig. 3.)

Turn album cover right side out and press. Insert album.

Figure 1

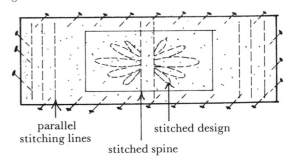

parallel stitching lines · stitched design · stitched spine

Figure 2

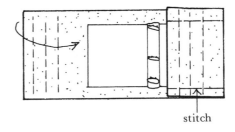

stitch

Figure 3

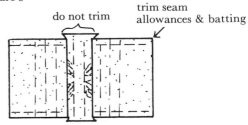

do not trim · trim seam allowances & batting

Unpadded Scrapbook Cover

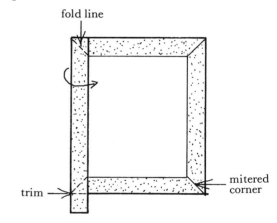

Make sure the fabric you select to cover the album is dark enough to hide the color of the original cover.

Materials

- 1 album or scrapbook with removable covers, approximately 10″ x 12″ (25.4cm x 30.5cm)
- ½ yard (45.7cm) light- to medium-weight fabric, 48″ (121.9cm) or wider
- tape measure
- tailor's chalk
- fabric shears
- white household glue
- small disposable container
- paintbrush, 1″ (2.5cm) wide
- pinking shears
- weight (telephone book)

Method

Step 1:
Press fabric.

Measure, mark with tailor's chalk, and cut out two rectangles of fabric, each 14″ x 16″ (35.6cm x 40.6cm).

Measure, mark, and cut out two additional rectangles of fabric, each 9″ x 11″ (22.9cm x 27.9cm). Pink the edges of the two small rectangles.

Step 2:
Pour glue into disposable container and dilute with water until it spreads evenly with a paintbrush—approximately two parts glue to one part water.

Remove any cord from scrapbook binding.

Working with one side of the album at a time, brush diluted glue onto outside of cover. Center one large piece of fabric over cover, right side up, and smooth in place. Wrap fabric around to inside of cover and glue in place, mitering corners and trimming excess. (See fig. 1.)

Brush diluted glue onto inside of cover. Center one small piece of pinked fabric, right side up, and smooth in place covering raw edge of wrapped fabric. (See fig. 2.) Place a heavy weight on top of each completed cover, and allow to dry thoroughly.

Using the scissors point, pierce front and back covers for cord. Reassemble scrapbook.

Figure 1

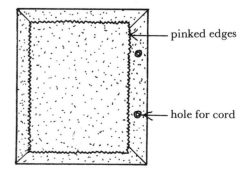

fold line

trim

mitered corner

Figure 2

pinked edges

hole for cord

Fabric Covered Open-Back Picture Frame

Materials
- 1 picture frame with glass
- 4 strips light- to medium-weight fabric
- fabric shears
- white household glue
- small disposable container
- paintbrush, 2″ (5cm) wide
- soutache or similar trim

Method
Step 1:
Remove backing and glass from picture frame.

Measure the circumference of the frame molding, and add ¼″ (6mm). (See fig. 1.)

Step 2:
Press fabric.

Cut four strips of fabric the width of the above measurement, and 1″ (2.5cm) longer than each side of the frame.

Step 3:
Pour glue into disposable container and dilute with water until it spreads evenly with a paintbrush—approximately two parts glue to one part water.

Brush glue onto frame, one side at a time, making sure your brush reaches into every crevice.

Carefully attach fabric to front of frame as illustrated in fig. 2. Trim corner fabric to follow diagonal of frame molding. (See fig. 2.) Wrap and glue excess fabric around to back of frame.

Follow the above procedure for each side of the frame. Allow to dry thoroughly.

Step 4:
Using undiluted glue, attach soutache braid over diagonally cut corners, wrapping it from the inside front of the frame around to the back. (See fig. 3.)

Figure 1

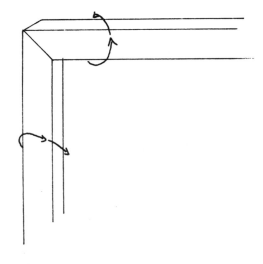

Figure 2

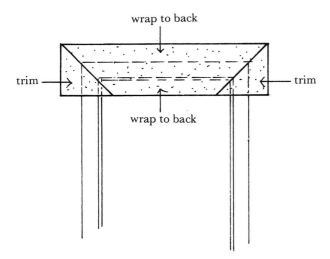

wrap to back

trim →

← trim

wrap to back

Figure 3

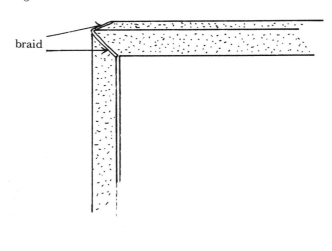

braid

Game Room

Game Room

Bright, cheery, and lively are the colors in a room designed especially for fun and games. All of the fabrics are very durable and completely washable. The basement walls are painted a soft yellow to lighten up a usually dark area. The wall-to-wall carpeting is a thick shag, one that is easy to care for and adds warmth to the cement and concrete surroundings.

The bridge tablecloth is reversible, and the matching chair seat cushions and back covers add a custom touch to ordinary folding chairs.

The felt and ribbon checker/chess board can be toted anywhere as can the bull's-eye floor pillows; they are all constructed of fabrics designed not to show the soil.

The backgammon board, easily cut out of felt and glued into position on top of a parson's table, then covered with a protective piece of glass, makes a very interesting coffee table as well as a game table.

The window seat is easily constructed of rectangular cushions with shirred boxings, and is placed on top of a plywood frame. To ensure proper balance and support, the matching canopy should be constructed by an awning contractor.

Bridge Tablecloth

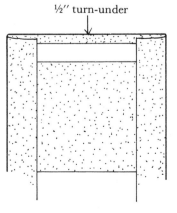

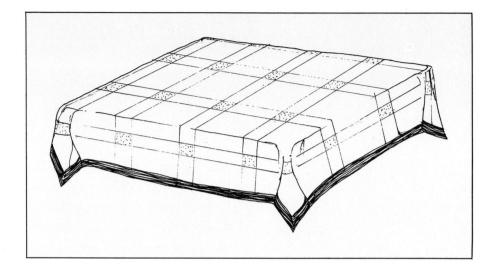

Materials
- 1 yard (91.4cm) lightweight fabric, 44″ (111.8cm) wide
- 1¼ yards (1.1m) contrasting lightweight fabric, 44″ (111.8cm) wide
- tape measure
- tailor's chalk
- fabric shears
- dressmaker's pins
- thread to match

Method

Step 1:

Press fabric.

Measure, mark with tailor's chalk, and cut out a 34″ (86.4cm) square from the 1 yard (91.4cm) piece of fabric.

Measure, mark and cut out a 44″ (111.8cm) square from the contrasting piece of fabric.

Step 2:

Placing right sides together, position the small fabric square in the exact center of the large square. Fold over opposite sides of the large square to meet sides of the small square. Using a ½″ (1.3cm) seam, pin-baste the side edges of both squares together. Stitch in place and press seams open. (See fig. 1.)

Turn right side out and center the small square so that the large square forms a 2″ (5cm) wide border on each side. Press. (See fig. 2.)

Step 3:

Turn under remaining raw edges of large square ½″ (1.3cm). Press. (See fig. 3.)

Fold over remaining opposite sides of the large square to meet sides of small square. Pin-baste in position ½″ (1.3cm) inside raw edges of small square making 2″ (5cm) wide borders. (See fig. 4.)

Miter corners. (See Techniques, Mitered Corners.) Trim excess fabric from underneath and pin-baste in position. (See fig. 5.)

Topstitch around inside edges of margin and along corner diagonals. (See fig. 6.)

Figure 2

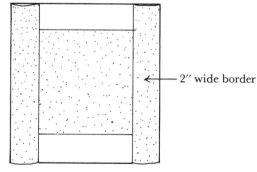

2″ wide border

Figure 1

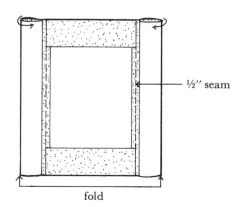

½″ seam

fold

Figure 3

½″ turn-under

Figure 4

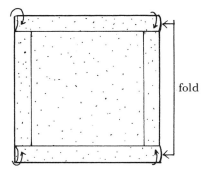

fold

Figure 5

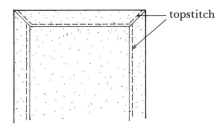

fold

trim

mitered corner

Figure 6

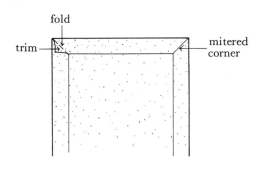

topstitch

Felt Playing Card Coasters

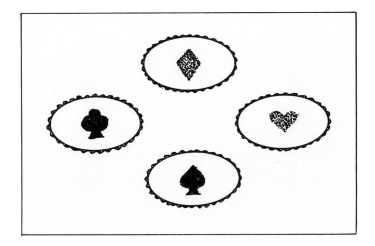

Materials
- three 12″ (30.5cm) felt squares in each of three contrasting colors
- tape measure
- tailor's chalk
- fabric shears
- 1 package medium-size rickrack
- ½ yard (45.7cm) nonwoven fusible bonding web
- lead pencil, #2
- tracing paper, 8½″ x 11″ (21.6cm x 27.9cm)

Method
Step 1:
Measure, mark with tailor's chalk, and cut out eight 3¼″ (8.3cm) diameter circles from one felt square. Place circles on ironing board.

Step 2:
Cut eight lengths of rickrack, each the circumference of the circle. Position rickrack around and beyond perimeters of the circles. (See fig. 1.)

Step 3:
Measure, mark with tailor's chalk, and cut out eight 3¼″ (8.3cm) diameter circles of fusible bonding web. Carefully place web on top of rickrack. Top each with a second felt circle. Press to fuse layers, according to the directions on the package of bonding web.

(Continued)

Step 4:
Transfer playing card symbols, from fig. 2.
onto tracing paper. Cut out symbols and use
as patterns to cut out contrasting color felt
symbols and fusible bonding web.

Place a bonding web shape in the center
of each coaster. Place the corresponding felt
shape on top, and press to fuse symbol,
according to the directions on the package of
bonding web. (See fig. 3.)

Figure 2

Figure 1

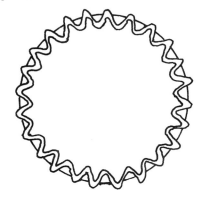

Figure 3

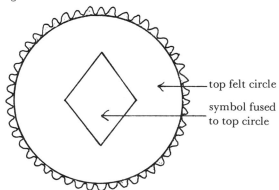

top felt circle

symbol fused
to top circle

Chair Seat Cushions

These popular accents may be elegant or casual depending upon the mood you wish to create. The materials and directions given apply to any size chair seat.

Materials
- light- to medium-weight fabric
- polyurethane foam pad, ½″ (1.3cm) thick
- cable cord
- tape measure
- tailor's chalk
- fabric shears
- dressmaker's pins
- brown wrapping paper
- lead pencil, #2
- 2 yards (1.8m) grosgrain ribbon, ½″ (1.3cm) wide
- thread to match

Method
Step 1:
Measure seat of chair, and cut out a pattern with these measurements from brown wrapping paper.

Using the paper pattern, cut out a piece of foam to fit on the chair seat.

Step 2:
Press fabric.

Using paper pattern, measure, mark with tailor's chalk, and cut two pieces of fabric, allowing for ½″ (1.3cm) seams on all sides.

Step 3:
From the remaining fabric, prepare a continuous bias strip 2½″ (6.4cm) wide and slightly longer than the perimeter of the cover. (See Techniques, Bias Trim.) Cover cable cord with the bias strip as directed to make piping.

Pin-baste piping to right side of one fabric section, ½″ (1.3cm) in from the outer edge with raw edge of piping even with raw edge of fabric. (See fig. 1.) Using a zipper foot attachment, stitch piping in place.

For a smooth finish where ends of the piping overlap, pull cording out of covering and clip it so that the cut ends of both sides meet. Stitch ends in place.

Step 4:
With right sides together, place remaining fabric piece on top of piped fabric piece; pin-baste. Using a zipper foot attachment, stitch in place exactly on top of piping stitching, leaving back side open for turning and stuffing.

Trim seam allowances to ¼″ (6mm), and clip as necessary to release fullness. Turn right side out. Insert foam cushion.

Step 5:
Cut ribbon into four equal lengths. Stitch lengths in place on top and bottom of back seam. Make sure they tie around chair frame.

Slip-stitch back opening closed. (See Techniques, Hand Stitches.)

Figure 1

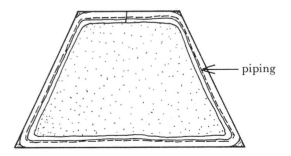

piping

Chair Back Covers

Covers for chair backs dress up ordinary folding chairs and make them more comfortable. The materials and directions given apply to any size folding chair.

Materials
- light- to medium-weight fabric
- cable cord or commercial piping
- tape measure
- brown wrapping paper
- lead pencil, #2
- dressmaker's pins
- fabric shears
- 2 yards (1.8m) grosgrain ribbon, ½″ (1.3cm) wide (optional)
- thread to match

Method
Step 1:
Trace the chair back onto brown wrapping paper, making the outline 1″ (2.5cm) larger on all sides than the chair. (These covers look their best when the finished length reaches the seat of the chair.) To ensure a very snug fit, measure carefully. You may wish to enlarge the pattern a bit.

Following the wrapping paper pattern, cut out front and back sections of the chair cover.

Step 2:
If you choose not to use commercial piping, from the remaining fabric prepare a continuous bias strip 2½″ (6.4cm) wide and slightly

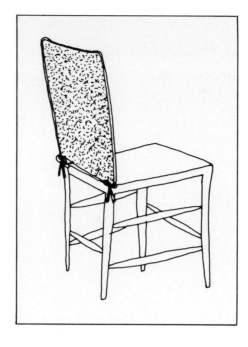

longer than the perimeter of the cover. (See Techniques, Bias Trim.) Cover the cable cord with the bias strip as directed to make piping.

Pin-baste piping to right side of one fabric section, ½″ (1.3cm) in from outside edge with raw edge of piping even with raw edge of fabric. Using a zipper foot attachment, stitch in place, leaving one end unpiped. (See fig. 1.)

Step 3:
With right sides together, place remaining fabric section on top of piped fabric; pin-baste. Try cover on chair, and make any necessary seam adjustments. Using a zipper

foot attachment, stitch in place exactly on top of piping stitching, leaving unpiped end open for turning.

Clip seam allowances to release fullness.

Step 4:
To hem the bottom, turn up raw edges ¼″ (6mm), then ¼″ to ½″ (6mm to 1.3cm) again. Press; then stitch in place. (See fig. 2.)

Step 5: (optional)
Cut grosgrain ribbon into four equal lengths. Pin lengths in place on front and back of

Figure 1

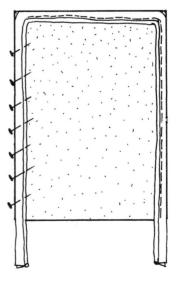

wrong side of cover, positioned so that they will tie around the chair back frame. (See fig. 2.)

Try cover on chair to check positioning of ribbons. Remove cover from chair, and tack ribbons in place.

Press cover.

Note: If you wish to add a decorative touch, cut out a felt design and attach it to the cover with fusible bonding web. Instructions are packaged with the webbing.

Figure 2

Bull's-Eye Floor Pillow

The materials and directions given are for a round pillow, 30″ (76.2cm) in diameter.

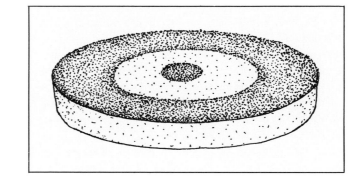

Materials
- one 34″ (86.4cm) square polyurethane foam pad, 4″ (10.2cm) thick
- 3½ yards (3.2m) black corduroy, 44″ (111.8cm) wide
- ¾ yard (68.6cm) bright yellow corduroy, 44″ (111.8cm) wide
- ½ yards (45.7cm) bright red corduroy, 44″ (111.8cm) wide
- 6 yards (5.5m) cable cord, ¼″ (6mm) thick

- serrated knife
- felt tip pen
- yardstick
- tape measure
- tailor's chalk
- fabric shears
- thread to match

Method
Step 1:
Using a felt tip pen, mark a dot in the exact center of the polyurethane square.

Measuring with a yardstick, make a circle of dots 15″ (38cm) from the center, thus outlining a 30″ (76.2cm) diameter circle.

(Continued)

Holding a serrated knife firmly, cut through the foam from the top with a sawing motion. Be sure to cut the foam so that the side edge of the circle is straight, not slanted.

Step 2:
Press fabric.

Measure, mark with tailor's chalk, and cut out a 36″ x 72″ (91.4cm x 182.9cm) rectangle of black corduroy. Cut the rectangle in half to form two 36″ (91.4cm) squares.

Fold each square into quarters and press.

Using a tape measure, measure and mark an arc 17″ (43.2cm) from the folded point of one square. Cut along the arc to form a circle 34″ (86.4cm) in diameter for the pillow top.

Repeat procedure on remaining square of black corduroy for the pillow bottom.

Measure, mark, and cut out a 24″ (61cm) square of yellow corduroy. Fold it into quarters and press. Measure and mark an arc 10″ (25.4cm) from the folded point. Cut along the arc to form a circle 20″ (50.8cm) in diameter for the middle ring of bull's eye.

Measure, mark, and cut out a 12″ (30.5cm) square of red corduroy. Fold it into quarters and press. Measure and mark an arc 5″ (12.7cm) from the folded point. Cut along the arc to form a circle 10″ (25.4cm) in diameter for the center of the bull's eye.

Step 3:
Center the yellow circle on top of one black circle, right sides up. Fold edges of yellow circle under ½″ (1.3cm), and pin-baste in place. Topstitch just inside the folded edge to attach yellow circle to black one. (See fig. 1.)

Repeat procedure with red circle on top of yellow circle. (See fig. 1.)

Step 4:
From remaining black corduroy, carefully measure, mark, and cut out bias strips 4½″ (11.4cm) wide to make a side panel for the pillow. (See Techniques, Bias Trim.) Cut enough strips to make a 3 yard (2.7m) length when stitched together end to end.

Cut additional bias strips 1½″ (3.8cm) wide. Cut enough to make a 6-yard (5.5m) length when stitched together end to end. (See Techniques, Bias Trim.) Fold this bias strip around cable cord, right side out. Using a zipper foot attachment, stitch in place to make piping.

Step 5:
Center bull's eye cover on top of foam circle and pin-baste.

Pin-baste piping with rounded edge facing in toward the center of the bull's eye, so that the stitching line rests exactly on the edge of the foam. (See fig. 2.)

For a smooth finish where ends of the piping overlap, pull cord out of the covering, and clip it so that the cut ends of both sides meet. Stitch ends in place.

Remove pillow top with piping pin-basted in place. Using a zipper foot attachment, stitch exactly on top of the piping stitching line.

Repeat this procedure to attach piping to the bottom edges of the pillow.

Step 6:
With right sides together and using ½″ (1.3cm) seams, pin-baste remaining 4½″ (11.4cm) bias strip to top and bottom sections of pillow. Leave a large opening along the bottom edge for turning and stuffing. The finished cover should measure 3½″ (8.9cm) deep for a snug fit over the foam. Try the cover on the pillow, and make any necessary adjustments.

Figure 1

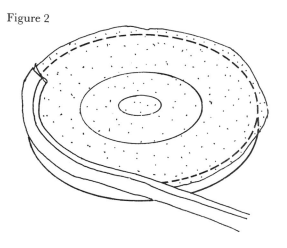

Figure 2

Using a zipper foot attachment, stitch side panel in place.

Trim and clip seam allowances as necessary. Turn pillow cover right side out, and slip over foam circle.

Slip-stitch opening closed.

Ribbon Chess/Checker Cloth

The materials and directions given are for a 30″ (76.2cm) square game cloth designed to fit on a standard-size card table.

Materials
- 4 yards (3.7m) red grosgrain ribbon, 2″ (5cm) wide
- 4 yards (3.7m) black grosgrain ribbon, 2″ (5cm) wide
- 2 yards (1.8m) fusible interfacing, 18″ (45.7cm) wide
- 2 yards (1.8m) black felt, 72″ (182.9cm) wide
- tape measure
- fabric shears
- newspapers
- yardstick
- tailor's chalk
- four 10-yard (9m) spools red silk twist thread for topstitching
- black thread
- size 16 sewing machine needle

Method
Step 1:
Measure and cut each color of ribbon into eight 18″ (45.7cm) strips.

Measure and cut interfacing into two 36″ (91.4cm) lengths.

Step 2:
Spread several layers of newspapers on a large smooth surface suitable for ironing, such as a floor.

Place the two pieces of interfacing, fusible sides up, side by side on top of the newspapers.

Position the black ribbons side by side on top of the fusible interfacing. Weave the red ribbons through the black to create a checkered effect. (See fig. 1.) Make sure that the sides of the ribbons touch each other with no overlaps or spaces.

Carefully press ribbons onto the fusible interfacing. Trim excess interfacing.

Step 3:
Measure, mark, and cut black felt into three 30″ (76.2cm) squares.

In the exact center of one felt square, measure, mark, and cut out a 16″ (40.6cm) square (See fig. 2.) Pin-baste the checkered ribbons inside the cut out square so that the raw edges of ribbon are underneath and the checkered design is bordered with black felt.

Pin-baste the remaining two felt squares underneath the square with the checkered ribbon insert.

Step 4:
Fill the sewing machine bobbin with silk twist thread. Replace the standard size (size 14) sewing machine needle with a size 16 needle.

Using silk twist in the needle, topstitch on the black felt just outside the checkered insert. Topstitch around the checkered insert again, ¼″ (6mm) outside the first row of top-stitching. (See fig. 3.)

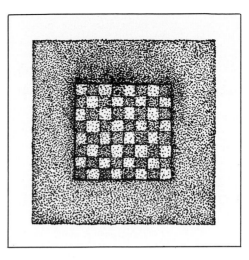

Figure 1

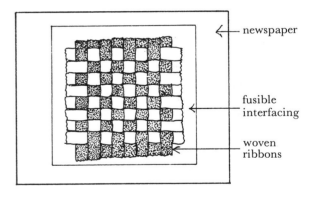

newspaper

fusible interfacing

woven ribbons

Topstitch ½″ (1.3cm) in from the outer edge of the chess/checker cloth. Topstitch around the cloth again ¼″ (6mm) inside the first row of topstitching. (See fig. 4.)

Using black thread and a large zigzag stitch, sew the outer edges of the cloth together. (See fig. 4.)

(Continued)

Figure 2

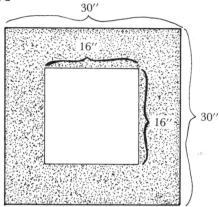

30″

16″

16″

30″

Figure 3

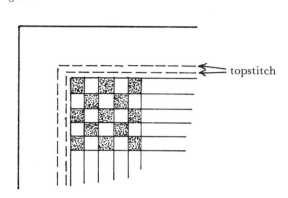

topstitch

Figure 4

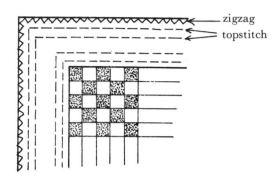

zigzag

topstitch

Window Seat Cushion with Shirred Boxing

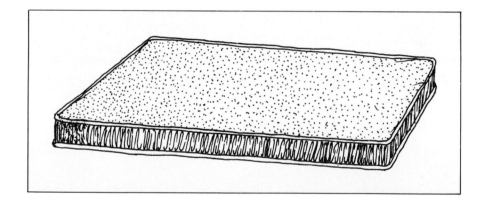

The materials and directions given are for any size cushion.

Materials
- medium-weight fabric
- polyurethane foam pad
- piping in accent color, ¼″ (6mm) thick
- tape measure
- tailor's chalk
- fabric shears
- dressmaker's pins
- thread to match

Method
Step 1:
Press fabric.

Measure, mark with tailor's chalk, and cut out two sections of fabric 1″ (2.5cm) longer and wider than the desired finished measurements of the cushion.

Step 2:
From the remaining fabric, measure, mark, and cut out enough 2″ (5cm) wide strips to equal 2½ times the distance around the cushion.

With right sides of strips together and using ½″ (1.3cm) seams, join ends of strips to make one long strip. Measure and press raw edges under ½″ (1.3cm) on long sides.

Run basting threads along each fold line of the fabric strip and pull threads to gather. (See fig. 1.) Distribute gathers evenly to make fabric strip 1″ (2.5cm) longer than the distance around the foam cushion.

Step 3:
Using a zipper foot attachment and ½″ (1.3cm) seams, pin-baste and stitch piping to each side of the shirred strip, right side up, making sure rounded edge of piping faces in toward center of fabric. (See fig. 2.) Press.

Using ½″ (1.3cm) seams, pin-baste; then stitch piped, shirred boxing strip to one piece of fabric, right sides together, starting and ending in the center of one short side. (See fig. 3.) Stitch boxing strip ends together and press.

Pin-baste; then stitch remaining fabric piece to shirred boxing strip, right sides together, leaving an opening in the center of one short side for turning and stuffing.

Step 4:
Turn cover right side out and press. Insert foam pad and slip-stitch opening closed.

Figure 1

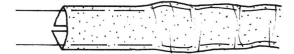

Figure 2

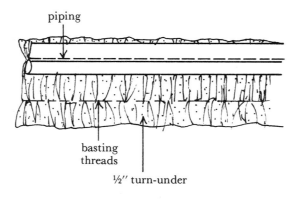

piping

basting threads

½″ turn-under

Figure 3

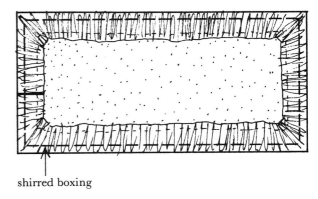

shirred boxing

Sports Room

Sports Room

After a hard day of play, what better place is there to relax than in this cozy, sports-oriented rumpus room with highly polished wood floor and cozy brick fireplace?

The log tote is a very practical accent easily made out of sturdy fabric and heavy braid.

The usual place to begin "story telling" is at the bar. This and the matching chairs can be covered quickly and simply with a practical, synthetic, leather-type fabric from which most spills can easily be wiped. Brass upholstery tacks lend a masculine accent to the furniture.

The oversize fireplace cushion can be easily executed by adapting the directions for the Turkish Corner Floor Pillow found in the Eclectic Living Room. The bright multicolored afghan is really an authentic Irish horse blanket. Even the zebra rug can be made from fake fur and backed with felt!

There are quite a few items in this room which, when they are not in use, serve as decorations for atmosphere. One color theme does not dominate this room; the idea is to people the room with evidence of an active life. The tennis racquet covers, tennis tote, and golf club head covers are all stored in full view; why hide your sports equipment or your talents?

Golf Club Socks

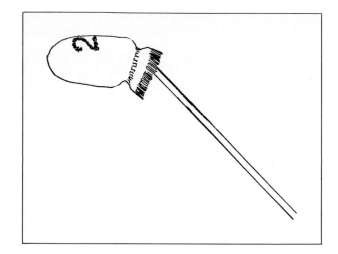

These handy covers not only serve as protection for expensive woods but are also great for cleaning all your clubs.

The materials and directions given are for four covers.

Materials
- 2 fingertip terry cloth towels with fringe
- felt scraps in assorted colors
- tracing paper
- lead pencil, #2
- dressmaker's pins
- fabric shears
- thread to match
- 1 yard narrow elastic (optional)

Method

Step 1:
Enlarge and transfer pattern from fig. 1 onto tracing paper. This will be the pattern for the covers.

Step 2:
Smooth towels. Fold each fingertip towel in half horizontally and cut.

Fold each half in half vertically and cut.

Working with one layer of towel at a time, pin paper pattern in place and cut out shape. Repeat this procedure with each piece of terry until all eight pieces are cut.

Step 3:
With right sides together, use ½″ (1.3cm) seams, and stitch covers together. Trim excess, and turn right side out. (See fig. 2.)

Step 4: (optional)
Stitch elastic around wrong side of cover, 3″ (7.6cm) from bottom fringe edge. (See fig. 2.)

Step 5: (optional)
Embellish each cover with a felt number, hand stitched in place. (See fig. 3.)

Figure 1

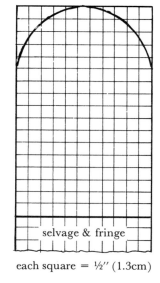

selvage & fringe

each square = ½″ (1.3cm)

Figure 2

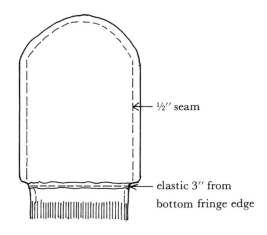

½″ seam

elastic 3″ from bottom fringe edge

Figure 3

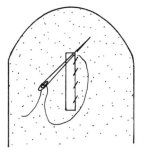

Canvas Log Carrier

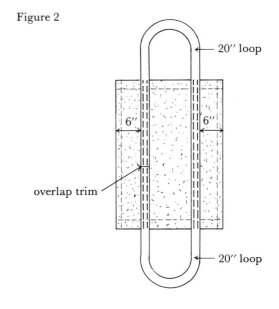

Materials

- 1 yard (91.4cm) heavyweight canvas, 42″ to 45″ (106.7cm to 114.3cm) wide
- tape measure
- tailor's chalk
- fabric shears
- dressmaker's pins
- 3 yards (2.7m) heavy braid, 1¼″ (3.2cm) wide
- heavy-duty thread to match

Method

Step 1:
Press fabric.

Measure, mark with tailor's chalk, and cut out a rectangle of fabric 27″ x 36″ (68.6cm x 91.4cm).

Step 2:
Hem long sides of rectangle by turning raw edges under ⅝″ (1.6cm), then another ¾″ (1.9cm). Press; then topstitch in place. (See fig. 1.)

Hem short sides of rectangle by measuring and turning raw edges under ¾″ (1.9cm), then another 1″ (2.5cm). Press; then topstitch in place. (See fig. 1.)

Step 3:
Pin-baste one end of heavy braid to right side of rectangle, 6″ (15.2cm) in from one long side and midway between the short sides. Continue pinning trim so that it

extends to form a 20″ (50.8cm) loop at each short side and rests 6″ (15.2cm) inside the opposite long edge. (See fig. 2.) Turn under raw edge where braid meets. Topstitch along edges of trim.

Figure 1

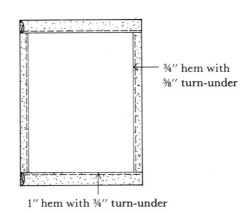

¾″ hem with ⅝″ turn-under

1″ hem with ¾″ turn-under

Figure 2

20″ loop

6″   6″

overlap trim

20″ loop

Tennis Racquet Cover

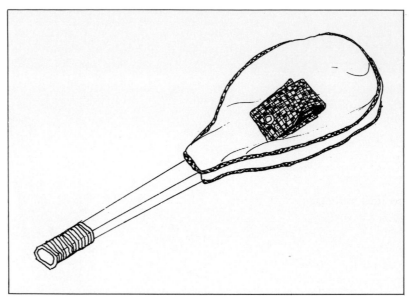

The directions given may apply to any size racquet: tennis, squash, etc.

Materials
- 1 yard (91.4cm) medium- to heavyweight fabric, 48″ (121.9cm) or wider
- ½ yard (45.7cm) contrasting medium- to heavyweight fabric, 48″ (121.9cm) or wider
- 2½ yards (2.3m) cable cord, ¼″ (6mm) thick
- invisible zipper, 22″ (55.9cm) long
- fabric shears
- tailor's chalk
- dressmaker's pins
- tape measure
- thread to match
- 1 shank button, ¾″ (1.9cm) in diameter
- 12″ (30.5cm) grosgrain ribbon, 1½″ (3.8cm) wide

Method
Step 1:
Press fabric.

Place tennis racquet on wrong side of the 1 yard (91.4cm) piece of fabric as shown in fig. 1. Using tailor's chalk, draw an outline 1″ (2.5cm) larger than the racquet frame and throat. Make a second outline, also 1″ larger than the racquet. (See fig. 1.) Cut out shapes.

Step 2:
From the ½ yard (45.7cm) piece of fabric, measure, mark, and cut off a 12″ x 18″ (30.5cm x 45.7cm) rectangle for the outside pocket. (See fig. 2.)

From the remaining fabric, prepare 3 yards (2.7m) of 1¾″ (4.4cm) wide continuous bias. (See Techniques, Bias Trim.) Cover cable cord with the bias strip as directed to make piping.

Step 3:
Beginning at lower throat part of cover and using ½″ (1.3cm) seams, pin piping around outer edge of right side of one racquet shape. Raw edges of piping should be even with the raw edge of fabric. Baste in place. Pull cording out of covering about ½″ (1.3cm) on each side, and clip. Overlap the covering ends at the lower throat part of the cover. (See fig. 3.)

Using a zipper foot attachment, stitch piping to fabric section, sewing directly on top of the piping stitches.

Repeat procedures on the remaining racquet shape.

Figure 1

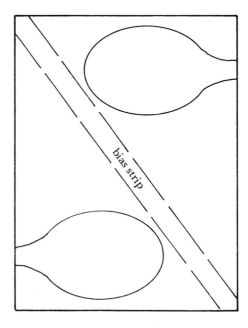

bias strip

Step 4:
Place one cover section, wrong side up, on a flat surface so that the piping is underneath.

Open the invisible zipper. Pin-baste the left side of it face down to the left side of the cover so that the teeth rest on top of the stitching line which attached the piping to the cover. (See fig. 4.) Before stitching, close zipper to double-check placement. Make sure that after it is stitched in place and closed, the teeth are right side up.

Attach zipper to seam allowances of piping and cover using the sewing machine zipper foot attachment. Stitch as close as possible to the zipper's teeth. (See fig. 5.)

Step 5:
From the same fabric as the racquet cover, cut out a strip of bias 2¼″ (5.7cm) wide and 44″ (111.8cm) long. (See fig. 1.)

Following manufacturer's directions and using the invisible zipper foot attachment, stitch remaining half of invisible zipper to right side of bias strip. Be sure to extend top of bias strip 1″ (2.5cm) beyond the top of the zipper to turn the fabric under to finish the cover.

Close zipper. Using the sewing machine zipper foot attachment, stitch remaining part of the bias to the cover, beginning ½″ (1.3cm) above the base of the zipper.

Step 6:
To prepare the outside pocket from the reserved 12″ x 18″ (30.5cm x 45.7cm) rectangle, measure, mark, and cut out an 8″ x 10″ (20.3cm x 25.4cm) rectangle. Turn under one long side ¼″ (6mm). Turn under again ¼″ (6mm), and stitch.

Fold raw edges of short sides in 2″ (5cm). Fold that fabric allowance in half to make 1″ (2.5cm) pleats. (See fig. 6.) Stitch across bottom ¼″ (6mm) up from raw edge, securing pleats.

Pin stitched end onto racquet cover with right sides facing so that the stitching line rests 5″ (12.7cm) above the throat and 2″ (5cm) in from the piping on each side. (See fig. 7.)

Attach pocket to cover by stitching from the edge of one fold to the edge of the other.

Flip pocket upward so that the hemmed edge faces the widest part of the cover. Turn side seams under 1″ (2.5cm) and top-stitch through bottom pleat. (See fig. 8.)

(Continued)

Figure 2

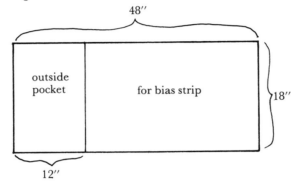

Figure 3

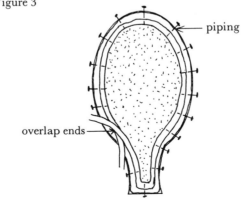

Figure 4

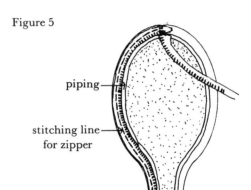

Figure 5

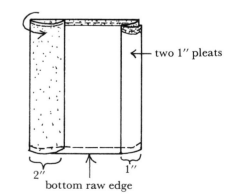

Figure 6

Step 7:

From remaining contrasting fabric, measure, mark, and cut out an 8″ x 10″ (20.3cm x 25.4cm) strip. Fold strip in half lengthwise, wrong side out, and press. Using ¼″ (6mm) seams, stitch long edges together to form a tube. Turn tube right side out, center the seam, and press.

   Turn raw edges of tube to inside ½″ (1.3cm) and topstitch. You now have a "flap."

   Position and pin-baste flap ½″ (1.3cm) down into the pocket, wrong side out. Top-stitch. (See fig. 9.)

   Using a buttonhole machine attachment, make a horizontal buttonhole 1″ (2.5cm) wide, centered, and 1¼″ (3.2cm) from top edge of flap. (See fig. 9.)

   Sew button to pocket 1¼″ (3.2cm) up from bottom edge. (See fig. 10.)

Step 8:

With right sides together, pin-baste front and back sections of racquet cover together. Using a zipper foot attachment, stitch bias strip (which becomes a boxing to the back cover section) to racquet cover.

   Turn under raw edges of bias strip at throat of completed racquet cover. Slip-stitch.

   Finish the inside throat edge by pinning grosgrain ribbon over all raw edges. Tack in place.

Figure 7

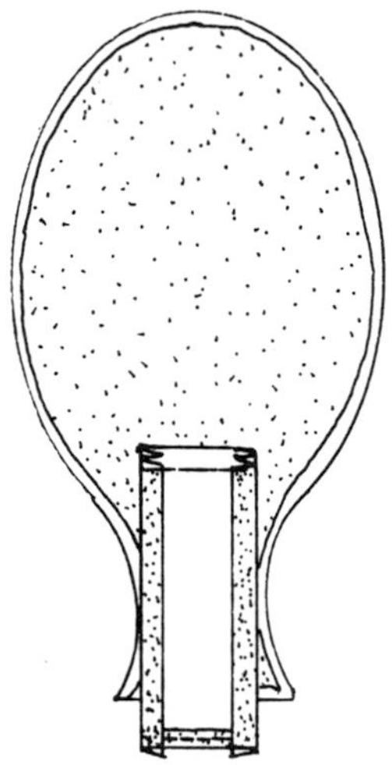

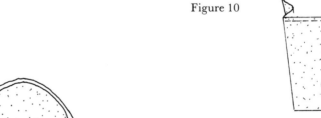

Figure 9

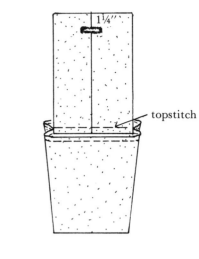

topstitch

Figure 10

Figure 8

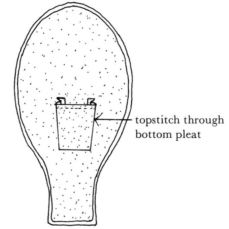

topstitch through bottom pleat

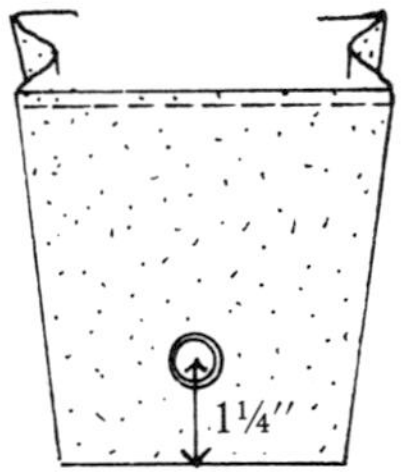

Figure 11

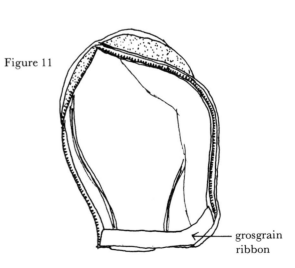

grosgrain ribbon

Tennis Racquet Tote

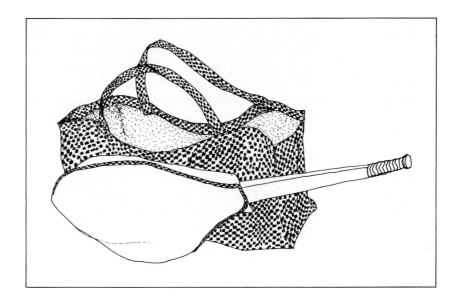

The materials and directions given are for an 18″ x 12″ x 4½″ (45.7cm x 30.5cm x 11.4cm) bag.

Materials
- 2 yards (1.8m) heavyweight fabric, 48″ (121.9cm) or wider
- 1 yard (91.4cm) contrasting heavyweight fabric, 48″ (121.9cm) or wider
- 1½ yards (1.4m) cable cord, ¼″ (6mm) thick
- invisible zipper, 22″ (55.9cm) long
- tape measure
- tailor's chalk
- fabric shears
- dressmaker's pins
- thread to match
- cardboard rectangle, 17½″ x 5″ (44.5cm x 12.7cm)

Method
Step 1:
Press fabric.

From the 2 yard (1.8m) piece of fabric, measure, mark with tailor's chalk, and cut out a rectangle 24″ x 36″ (61cm x 91.4cm). Fold, right side out, to make a rectangle 24″ x 18″ (61cm x 45.7cm). Press.

Step 2:
To prepare handles from excess fabric, measure, mark, and cut out two bias strips, each 4″ x 25″ (10.2cm x 63.5cm). (See Techniques, Bias Trim.) Fold each strip in half lengthwise, wrong side out, and press. Using ½″ (1.3cm) seams, stitch long edges together to form two tubes.

Turn tubes right side out. Position seams along one side. Topstitch tubes ⅛″ (3mm) in from long edges. (See fig. 1.)

Trim corners at an angle ½″ (1.3cm) from the points. Fold raw edges inside each tube. Press; then pin. (See fig. 2.)

Step 3:
From remaining excess fabric, measure, mark, and cut out a bias strip 1½″ x 45″ (3.8cm x 114.3cm). (See Techniques, Bias Trim.) Cover cable cord with bias strip as directed to make piping.

Step 4:
Place tennis racquet on top of the folded rectangle of fabric. Center racquet face 3½″ (8.9cm) from the top and 3½″ (8.9cm) in from the side fold. (See fig. 3.) Trace around the racquet.

(Continued)

Figure 1

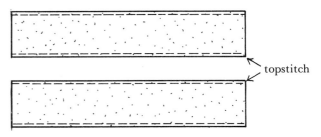

topstitch

Figure 2

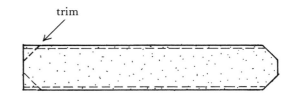

trim

Remove racquet from fabric. Position invisible zipper so that when closed, the left side tape will be attached to the rectangle of fabric and the right side will be attached to the racquet cover. (See fig. 4.)

Open up rectangle. Following manufacturer's directions and using the invisible zipper foot attachment, stitch the left side tape to one layer of the fabric rectangle. Make sure the edge of the zipper tape rests exactly on top of the traced outline of the racquet. Before stitching, check to make sure the teeth are in the correct position so the zipper can be opened and closed correctly.

Step 5:
Place tennis racquet on top of contrasting piece of fabric and draw an outline 1″ (2.5cm) larger than the racquet frame and throat. Cut around outline.

Beginning at lower throat part of cover and using ½″ (1.3cm) seams, pin piping around outer edge of racquet cover, right side up, and with the raw edges of the piping even with the raw edges of the fabric. Pull cable cord out of its covering ½″ (1.3cm) on each side. Clip cord. Overlap the covering ends at the lower throat part of the cover. (See fig. 5.)

Using a zipper foot attachment, stitch piping to fabric section sewing directly on top of piping stitches.

Step 6:
From remaining contrasting piece of fabric, measure, mark, and cut out a bias strip 2¼″ x 45″ (5.7cm x 114.3cm). (See Techniques, Bias Trim.)

Place right sides of racquet cover and bias strip together. With raw edges even, use a zipper foot attachment and stitch bias strip to racquet cover. (See fig. 6.)

Step 7:
Pin-baste racquet cover to single layer of the fabric rectangle, making sure the edge of the bias strip rests exactly on top of the traced outline of the racquet. Carefully position invisible zipper and allow bias strip to extend 1″ (2.5cm) beyond the top of the zipper so that is can be turned under for finishing.

Remove pin-basting. Following manufacturer's directions and using the invisible zipper foot attachment, stitch remaining half of invisible zipper to bias strip. Close zipper.

Step 8:
Using a zipper foot attachment, stitch remaining part of the racquet cover to the fabric so that the raw edge of the seam allowance rests exactly on top of the traced outline of the racquet.

Stitch small pieces of excess piping to the ends of bias strip. Finish the inside throat edge by pinning grosgrain ribbon over all raw edges. Tack in place.

Figure 3

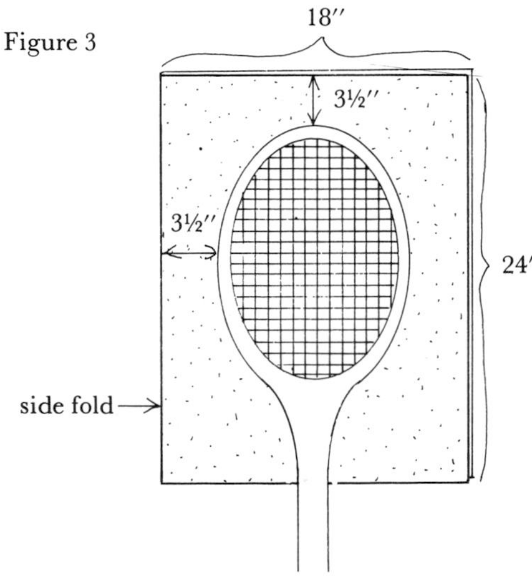

Figure 4

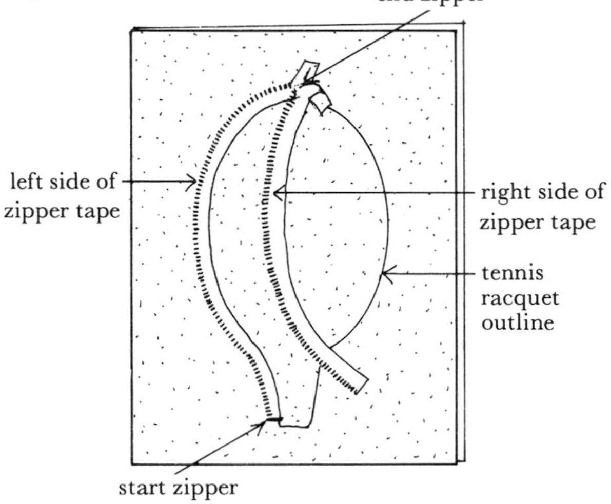

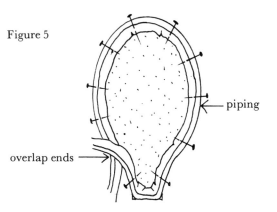

Figure 5

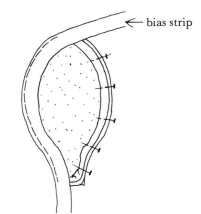

Figure 6

Step 9:
Using ½" (1.3cm) seams, and with right sides together, pin-baste and stitch sides of the tote together.

   Pinch bottom inside corners so that the side seam rests exactly on the bottom fold. Stitch across the triangle formed 2¼" (5.7cm) down from the point. (See fig. 7.) Press seams open; then turn tote right side out.

Turn top edge of tote under 1" (2.5cm) three times to make a triple hem. Topstitch ⅛" (3mm) down from top fold and up from bottom fold.

   Pinch four top corners of the tote. Topstitch ⅛" (3mm) in from the fold, beginning at top edge and ending at base of hem. (See fig. 8.)

Step 10:
Pin-baste handles on inside of tote, 3" (7.6cm) in from each end. (See fig. 9.) Topstitch to the tote.

Step 11:
Measure, mark, and cut out a piece of contrasting fabric large enough to wrap around the cardboard rectangle. Topstitch through cardboard to hold fabric in place.

   Place covered cardboard section in the bottom of the tote.

Figure 7

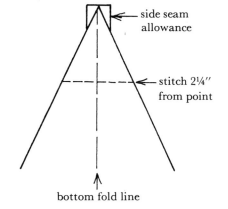

side seam allowance

stitch 2¼" from point

bottom fold line

Figure 8

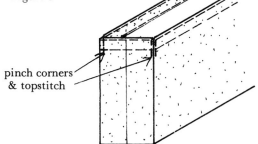

pinch corners & topstitch

Figure 9

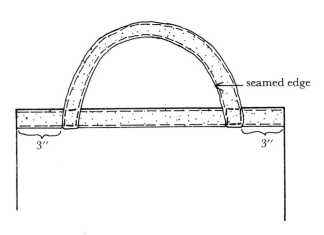

seamed edge

3"   3"

Mr. & Mrs. Bedroom

Mr. & Mrs. Bedroom

A cool and serene atmosphere of several shades of blue makes the master bedroom a refuge for frazzled nerves.

The focal point of this Mr. & Mrs. Bedroom is the elegant canopy bed, an invitation to many comfortable hours. The bed frame itself is really not complicated to build as long as you have guidance from a knowledgeable lumberyard salesperson or cabinetmaker. The canopy is simply a series of curtains, two different lengths, shirred onto curtain rods and hung from a frame.

The walls are easily covered with fabric pasted into place. The print shown here softens the solid blue atmosphere of this sophisticated room. The night spread, dust ruffle, and pioneer knot comforter are all components designed to encourage pleasant dreams. A heavier bedspread may replace the light spread during cooler months of the year.

Directions for the floor-length tablecloth are found in the Williamsburg Living Room, and directions for a reversible cloth are found in the Eclectic Living Room.

Directions for the slip-seat bench cover at the foot of the bed can be adapted from the ones found in the Williamsburg Dining Room.

An assortment of lush greenery adds to the restful atmosphere.

Night Spread

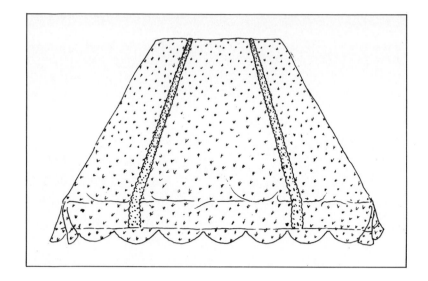

A very elegant and practical item, a night spread protects the blanket and may be used instead of a spread to give a lighter, more delicate look to the bed.

Materials
- lightweight washable fabric
- double-edged eyelet, lace, or ribbon trim, 5″ (12.7cm) wide, 2 times the length of the night spread
- tape measure
- tailor's chalk
- fabric shears
- dressmaker's pins
- thread to match

Method

Step 1:
Estimate the amount of fabric required. The night spread should be 4″ (10.2cm) wider than a flat sheet (2″ [5cm] below the top of the dust ruffle) and 12″ (30.5cm) longer than the mattress.

Step 2:
Press fabric.

Measure, mark with tailor's chalk, and cut out a center and two side panels. The center panel should be one-half the width of your flat sheet and 12″ to 14″ (30.5cm to 35.6cm) longer than the length of the mattress.

Each side panel should be one-quarter the width of your flat sheet plus 2″ (5cm)

and 12″ to 14″ (30.5cm to 35.6cm) longer than the length of the mattress.

Figure 1

Step 3:
Lay the panels out, right side up, on a smooth, flat working surface.

Measure and cut eyelet, lace, or ribbon trim to the length of the panels.

Using ½″ (1.3cm) seams, pin-baste trim on top of raw edges along each long side of the center panel and the adjoining long side of each side panel. (See fig. 1.)

Topstitch in place, trim fabric seam allowances, and press.

Step 4:
Finish night spread by making a 1″ (2.5cm) double hem around the entire spread. Turn raw edges under 1″ (2.5cm) and press. Turn under 1″ (2.5cm) again and press. Stitch hem in place, mitering corners. (See Techniques, Mitered Corners.)

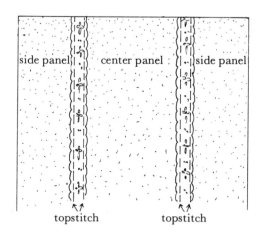

side panel | center panel | side panel

topstitch   topstitch

Instead of a double hem, you may wish to make a scalloped border with a hand-rolled hem. (See Techniques, Hand-Rolled Hem.)

Dust Ruffle

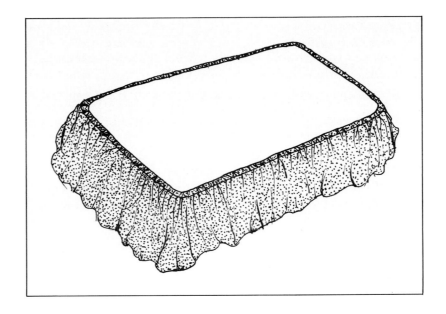

A dust ruffle is an attractive decorative accent that is relatively easy to make. For best results, use a lightweight fabric; it will ruffle nicely and give a fresh, feminine effect.

Measure the innerspring mattress carefully to insure a perfect fit. The materials and directions given are for a standard twin-size bed, approximately 38″ x 72″ (96.5cm x 182.9cm).

Materials
- 8 yards (7.3m) lightweight fabric, 48″ (121.9cm) or wider
- 12 yards (11m) sturdy cotton string
- tape measure
- tailor's chalk
- fabric shears
- thread to match
- safety pin

Method

Step 1:
Measure your innerspring mattress to calculate the amount of fabric needed for the dust ruffle. (See fig. 1.)

Length: distance from head to foot x 2

Width: distance from side to side x 2

Total distance around bed: length + width (as figured above)

Total length of ruffle: total distance around bed x 2.5

Total depth of ruffle: distance from top of innerspring mattress to floor + 3½″ (8.9cm)

Step 2:
Press fabric.

Measure, mark with tailor's chalk, and cut out a section of fabric for the "underlay" (that part of the dust ruffle which rests between the mattress and the innerspring). The underlay should be 1″ (2.5cm) smaller on all sides than the surface area of the innerspring mattress.

Measure, mark, and cut out strips of fabric for the ruffle. Each strip should extend the full width of the fabric and be as wide as the ruffle depth calculated in Step 1.

Figure 2 illustrates a typical layout for a standard twin-size dust ruffle.

Assuming the innerspring mattress measurements to be as follows:

144″ (3.7m): length

76″ (1.9m): width

220″ (5.6m): total distance around bed

550″ (14m): total length of ruffle

18″ (45.7cm): total depth of ruffle

Figure 1

you will need 8 yards (7.3m) fabric, 48″ (121.9cm) wide, cut into twelve 18″ x 48″ (45.7cm x 121.9cm) strips for the ruffle.

(Continued)

Note: If you use wider fabric, you will need less yardage because each ruffle strip will be longer. It is important to measure carefully and calculate the exact amount of fabric required.

Step 3:
Place ruffle strips right sides together and stitch, end to end, using ½" (1.3cm) seams to form one long strip. Press seams open.

For the standard twin-size bed, the twelve 48" (121.9cm) long strips yield one strip 565" (14.4m) long (slightly over the necessary 550" [14m]).

Fold under top raw edge 1" (2.5cm) and press. Stitch ¼" (6mm) above the raw edge to form a casing. (See fig. 3.)

Turn under the bottom raw edge of the ruffle strip ¼" (6mm); then turn up a 1¼" (3.2cm) deep hem. (See fig. 3.) Machine-stitch, slip-stitch, or machine blindstitch the hem.

Tie one end of the cotton string to a safety pin and pull the string through the ruffle casing. (See fig. 4.) Draw up gathers until the ruffle section is the exact length of all four sides of the innerspring mattress (total distance around bed as calculated in Step 1).

Note: You can also gather this ruffle by using gathering stitches on your sewing machine or a ruffler attachment. For large areas, such as a dust ruffle, many people find the casing/drawstring method more satisfactory. Select the technique which seems to work best for you.

Step 4:
Pin-baste the gathered ruffle to the underlay, right sides together, so that the stitching line which formed the ruffle casing rests ½" (1.3cm) inside the outer edge of the underlay.

With the ruffle side up, stitch the two pieces together just to the left of the casing stitch. In this way, the casing line will be enclosed in the seam when the dust ruffle is completed and placed on the bed.

A zipper foot attachment may be used in order to stitch close to the casing line.

Step 5:
After the ruffle has been attached to the underlay, complete the final side seam by sewing the short ends of the ruffle together.

Press thoroughly and turn right side out.

Place dust ruffle over innerspring mattress.

Figure 3

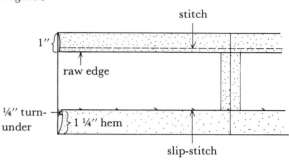

Figure 2

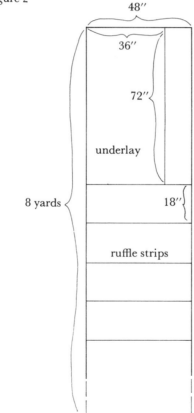

Figure 4

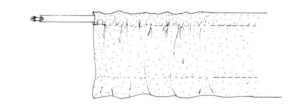

Fabric Covered Walls—Paste

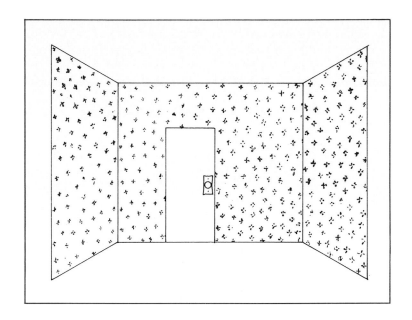

Before beginning this project, refer to Techniques, Walls.

Fabric pasted to walls tends to reveal any imperfections in the walls. To prepare the wall for pasting, repair any cracks and smooth out all bumps or lumps. Clean the wall thoroughly.

Unless your fabric is very dark, make sure the walls you are covering are white or off-white. Colored walls tend to make the fabric appear tinted.

Materials
- fabric
- steel yardstick
- steel ruler
- fabric shears
- fabric-to-wall paste
- paintbrush, 3″ (7.6cm) wide
- wallpaper brush
- single-edge razor blades

Method
Step 1:
To calculate the exact amount of fabric needed, measure the height of the wall and add 4″ (10.2cm), and measure the width of each wall area to be covered. If the fabric you've selected has a repeat, add one extra repeat in length to your calculations.

Step 2:
Press fabric and cut off selvages.

Cut fabric panels 4″ (10.2cm) longer than the height of the area to be covered. If more than one width of fabric is needed, match design and/or repeats very carefully. (See fig. 1.)

Step 3:
If fabric-to-wall paste is not premixed, prepare it according to manufacturer's directions. If desired, a light wash of diluted paste may be applied to the wall area before you begin. This will help the fabric adhere to the wall more readily. Allow wash to dry thoroughly before beginning to apply the fabric.

Establish vertical fabric placement with a plumb line. (See Techniques, Walls.)

Step 4:
Working from the ceiling down, brush fabric-to-wall paste onto wall, covering an area slightly wider than the fabric panel. Allowing 2″ (5cm) extra fabric at the top and bottom of the wall area, align the fabric and smooth out all wrinkles and air bubbles with your hands or a dry wallpaper brush.

(Continued)

Figure 1

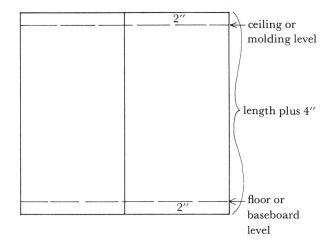

Avoid stretching fabric. Repeat this procedure with each fabric panel until the entire wall area is covered. Vertical edges of the fabric may either be overlapped ⅛″ (3mm) or simply butted together.

Step 5:
Wipe excess paste off fabric with a damp sponge. Allow walls to dry. Trim excess fabric from top and bottom edges using a single-edge razor blade and a steel yardstick or ruler as a guide. (See fig. 2.)

Decorative molding may be used to conceal raw edges of the fabric. Or you may wish to use undiluted white household glue to attach braid, self-welting, or ribbon around the perimeter of the covered wall area. This adds a more tailored, finished effect to the room.

Figure 2

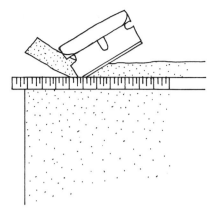

Pioneer Knot Comforter

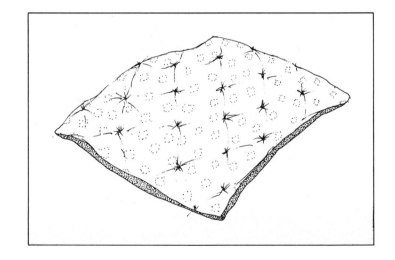

Comforters are usually the same length as the bed's mattress with a 12″ (30.5cm) drop on each side of the mattress's width.

This comforter is designed as a "throw" for a chaise lounge or a twin bed. Directions given apply to any size comforter.

Materials
- lightweight fabric
- polyester batting
- wool knitting yarn in an accent color
- sharp needle with a large eye
- tape measure
- tailor's chalk
- fabric shears
- thread to match

Method
Step 1:
Press fabric.

Measure, mark with tailor's chalk, and cut out two sections of fabric the width and length of the finished comforter plus 1″ (2.5cm) seam allowance on all sides.

Measure, mark, and cut out two sections of batting the width and length of the fabric sections.

Step 2:
Place right sides of top and bottom fabric sections together and place two layers of batting against one wrong side.

Using 1″ (2.5cm) seams, pin-baste, then stitch around comforter leaving an opening in the center of one side for turning. (See fig. 1.)

Trim batting and seam allowances to ½″ (1.3cm).

Turn right side out, press, and slip-stitch opening closed.

Step 3:
Using tailor's chalk, mark the top side of the comforter every 3″ to 4″ (7.6cm to 10.2cm) for placement of the "pioneer knots."

Thread the needle with a double strand of knitting yarn, approximately 18″ (45.7cm) long.

Working on the top side of the comforter, hold end of yarn and push the needle down through the three layers at the marked spot. Bring the needle back up to the top side again. Trim yarn to approximately 2″ (5cm). (See fig. 2.)

Tie the two strands on the left to the two strands on the right. Then separate the strands and tie again, this time with the alternate strands paired.

Tuft the entire comforter in this manner. Trim all of the pioneer knots to about ½″ (1.3cm).

When the comforter is washed, the pioneer knots will fluff up into small pom-poms.

Figure 1

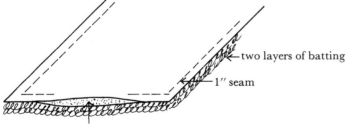

two layers of batting

1″ seam

opening

Figure 2

Ms Bedroom

Ms Bedroom

A blend of crisp greens and elegant white, this feminine and efficient bedroom is perfect for any lady, Ms, Miss, or Mrs. However, here we have the career-oriented Ms in mind, and organization is the key when trying to get to the office on time.

The shirred panel screen behind a plain box spring and mattress creates a very soft headboard, and the fabric can be easily removed for cleaning. Each fabric panel is gathered two and one-half to three times the width of each panel. The finished screen can stand free behind the bed or be secured to the wall.

The crisp, white, ruffled bedspread, pillow shams, neck roll pillow, and boudoir pillow all offer a softness to the room, which is extended to the floor-length table skirt. A quick fabric switch on the bedspread, shirred panel screen, and table skirt can alter the entire mood of the room to suit the seasons. Directions for the ruffled pillow shams (as well as tailored shams) are found in the Little Girl's Bedroom.

A place for everything and everything in its place, this closet is so well organized with coordinated garment bags, shoe caddy, and handbag caddy that it's no wonder the louvered doors are left open. Covered hat boxes and assorted storage boxes rest on the shelf.

The smooth lampshade could be covered with an accent fabric by following the directions in the Country French Dining Room.

Ruffled Bedspread

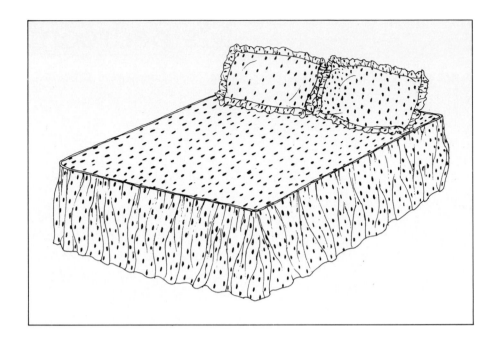

The materials and directions given are for a mattress approximately 60″ x 80″ (152.4cm x 203.2cm).

Materials
- 13 ½ yards (12.3m) lightweight fabric, 44″ (111.8cm) or wider
- 6 ½ yards (5.9m) cable cord, ¼″ (6mm) thick
- 8 yards (7.3m) sturdy cotton string
- tape measure
- tailor's chalk
- dressmaker's pins
- fabric shears
- large safety pin
- thread to match

Method
Step 1:
Press fabric

Measure, mark with tailor's chalk, and cut out a 42″ x 84″ (106.7cm x 213.4cm) rectangle for the center of the spread.

Measure, mark and cut out two 10 ½″ x 84″ (26.7cm x 213.4cm) fabric strips for each side of the center piece.

With right sides together and using ½″ (1.3cm) seams, pin-baste, then stitch strips to each side of the center panel. Press seams open.

Step 2:
Prepare a 1½″ (3.8cm) wide continuous bias strip, 6½ yards (5.9m) long. (See Techniques, Bias Trim.) Cover cable cord with the bias strip as directed to make piping.

Step 3:
From remaining fabric, measure, mark, and cut out 12 fabric strips, each the full width of the fabric and 24″ (61cm) long. Stitch strips right sides together, end to end, using ½″ (1.3cm) seams to make one strip approximately 517″ (13m) long and 24″ (61cm) wide. Press all seams open.

Turn bottom raw edge of ruffle strip to wrong side to form a 1¼″ (3.2cm) hem with a ¼″ (6mm) turn-under. Pin-baste; then stitch in place. (See fig. 1.)

Turn down top edge 1¼″ (3.2cm) to wrong side. Stitch a casing line ½″ (1.3cm) below the fold. (See fig. 1.)

Tie one end of the sturdy cotton string to the safety pin, and draw it through the casing. Gather the ruffle to approximately 223″ (5.7m). Distribute gathers evenly, and pin-baste through the string to hold gathers in position.

Figure 1

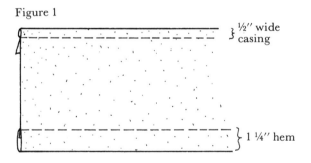

½″ wide casing

1 ¼″ hem

Figure 2

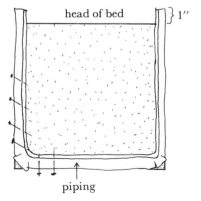

head of bed

1″

piping

Step 4:

Place the top section of the spread on the bed, right side up. Center and smooth the spread carefully so that it rests exactly as you want the finished spread to rest.

Pin-baste piping to the spread, starting at the head of the bed. The raw edges of the piping should extend 1″ (2.5cm) beyond the hemmed edge of the spread and be pinned so that the rounded side faces toward the center of the bed and the stitching line on the piping rests exactly on the edge of the bed. (See fig. 2.)

Step 5:

Fold under the raw edges of the piping and the bedspread hem. Pin-baste the ruffle sec-tion underneath the piping so that the gathered edge extends ½″ (1.3cm) inside the rounded side of the piping. (See fig. 3.)

Turn under raw edges of the ruffle at the head of the spread to form a 1″ (2.5cm) hem with a ½″ (1.3cm) turn-under on each side. Slip the raw edges of the piping inside this hem. Stitch in place to secure.

Attach ruffle section to the top of the spread by topstitching on top of the stitching line attaching the bias strip to the cable cord.

Trim excess string from the ruffle and other seam allowances or excess fabric as necessary.

Press spread and ruffle.

Figure 3

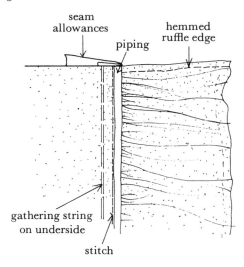

seam allowances

piping

hemmed ruffle edge

gathering string on underside

stitch

Boudoir Pillow with Ruffled Cover

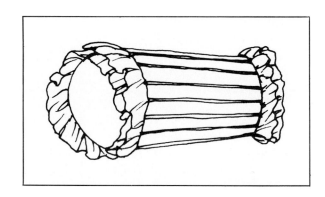

The materials and directions given are for an 18″ x 13″ (45.7cm x 33cm) pillow and a 22 ½″ x 13″ (57.2cm x 33cm) ruffled cover.

Materials for Pillow
- 1 yard (91.4cm) lightweight fabric, 45″ (114.3cm) wide
- tape measure
- tailor's chalk
- dressmaker's pins
- fabric shears
- thread to match
- polyester fiber fill

Materials for Cover
- 2½ yards (2.3m) lightweight fabric, 42″ to 45″ (106.7cm x 114.3cm) wide
- 1½ yards (1.4m) double-edge ruffle trim, 2″ (5cm) wide
- 1½ yards (1.4m) narrow ribbon-threaded eyelet trim, ¼″ (6mm) wide
- 6 yards (5.5m) cable cord, ¼″ (6mm) thick

Method for Pillow
Step 1:

Press fabric.

Measure, mark with tailor's chalk, and cut out a 19″ x 27″ (48.3cm x 68.6cm) rectangle.

(Continued)

Fold the rectangle, wrong side out, to measure 19″ x 13½″ (48.3cm x 34.3cm). Pin-baste and stitch a ½″ (1.3cm) seam down one side, across the bottom, and half-way up the other side.

Turn rectangle right side out and press.

Step 2:
Stuff pillow with polyester fiber fill, packing corners firmly. Turn in raw edges and slip-stitch opening closed.

Method for Cover
Step 3:
Press fabric.

Measure, mark with tailor's chalk, and cut out a 27″ (68.6cm) square of fabric.

Fold the square in half, right side out. Make a French seam along the side opposite the fold by stitching ⅛″ (3mm) in from the raw edge. Trim as close as possible to the stitching line, and turn fabric so that right sides are together. Stitch to enclose first seam. (See Techniques, Seams.)

Turn raw edges at both ends onto the wrong side of the fabric to form 2″ (5cm) hems with ½″ (1.3 cm) seams. (See fig. 1.) Pin-baste; then stitch in place.

Step 4:
From remaining fabric, cut bias strips 5½″ (14cm) wide. Join strips together, end to end, with French seams to make two 52″ (132cm) bias strips.

Edgestitch along one long side of each bias strip. Trim as close as possible to stitching line, and make a very narrow rolled hem. (See Techniques, Hand-Rolled Hem.)

Form a casing on the remaining long side of each bias strip by turning under raw edge ½″ (1.3cm) and stitching in place. (See fig. 2.)

Attach cable cord to a safety pin, and thread it through the casings. Gather fabric evenly to make a ruffle.

Cut additional bias strips, each 3¾″ (9.5cm) wide. Join strips together, end to end, with French seams to make an additional two 52″ (132cm) bias strips.

Repeat procedure in Step 4.

Step 5:
When all four ruffle sections are complete, pin-baste ruffles 2″ (5cm) in from side openings of pillow cover, with the narrow ruffle on top of the large ruffle. (See fig. 3.) Stitch in place.

As an optional finishing touch, pin-baste, then stitch the 2″ (5cm) wide double-edge eyelet trim at the base of the ruffles, and attach ribbon to center of eyelet.

Slip pillow inside cover.

Figure 2

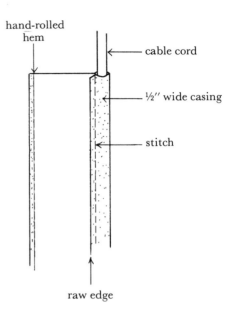

hand-rolled hem

cable cord

½″ wide casing

stitch

raw edge

Figure 1

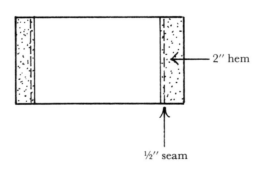

2″ hem

½″ seam

Figure 3

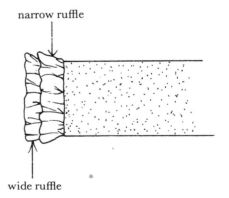

narrow ruffle

wide ruffle

Fabric Covered Round Hat Box

The materials and directions given are for one round hat box 11″ (27.9cm) in diameter.

Materials
- 1 yard (91.4cm) lightweight fabric, 44″ (111.8cm) wide
- tape measure
- tailor's chalk
- fabric shears
- white household glue
- small disposable container
- paintbrush, 1″ (2.5cm) wide
- 1 yard (91.4cm) ribbon or braid, 1″ (2.5cm) wide
- ¾ yard (68.6cm) cable cord or braid, ¼″ (6mm) thick

Method
Step 1:
Press fabric.

Measure, mark with tailor's chalk, and cut out sections of fabric for the top, bottom, and sides of the round hat box: Two 14″ (35.6cm) squares; one 2″ x 36″ (5cm x 91.4cm) strip; one 8″ x 36″ (20.3cm x 91.4cm) strip.

Fold and press one of the 14″ (35.6cm) squares into quarters. Measure and mark an arc 6½″ (16.3cm) from the folded point. Cut along the arc to make a 13″ (33cm) diameter circle. Repeat procedure with remaining square.

Step 2:
Pour glue into disposable container and dilute with water until it spreads evenly with a paintbrush—approximately two parts glue to one part water.

Brush diluted glue onto bottom of hat box. Carefully center and smooth one fabric circle into position on bottom of box. Notch the overlap and glue these flaps to the side of the box. (See fig. 1.)

Repeat procedure to cover top of hat box lid.

Step 3:
Brush diluted glue around side of hat box lid. Wrap and smooth the 2″ (5cm) wide strip around side of lid, making sure raw edge is just below the curve. Butt seam edges together. (See fig. 2.) Turn remaining raw edge to underside of top and glue securely in place.

Repeat above procedure using the 8″ (20.3cm) wide strip to cover the side of the box, placing one raw edge just above bottom curve of box. (See fig. 3.)

(Continued)

Figure 1

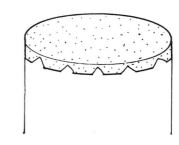

Figure 2

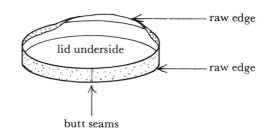

raw edge

lid underside

raw edge

butt seams

Step 4:
Dilute glue to create a wash. Brush over fabric covered box and lid. Smooth fabric to remove any air bubbles or wrinkles.

Step 5:
Using undiluted glue, attach ribbon or braid trim around side of lid, covering the raw edge.

Place top and bottom of hat box separately on table, and allow each to dry thoroughly.

Step 6:
Clip open covered holes in sides of hat box. Knot one end of the cable cord or braid. Pull other end through single hole to outside of box. (See fig. 4.)

Carry cord up and over the open hat box top, and push in through top hole on opposite side. Next, thread cord out one of the bottom two holes and into the last hole. Knot end of cord. (See fig. 5.)

Figure 3

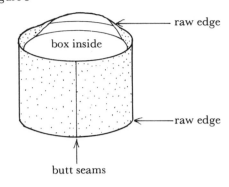

box inside — raw edge

— raw edge

butt seams

Figure 4

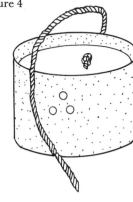

Figure 5

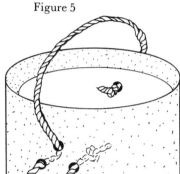

Neck Roll Pillow with Ruffled Cover

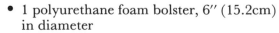

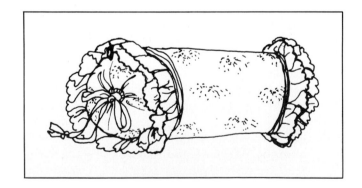

The materials and directions given are for a 12 ½″ x 6″ (31.8cm x 15.2cm) pillow and cover.

Materials for Pillow
- 1 yard (91.4cm) lightweight fabric, 45″ (114.3cm) wide
- 1 polyurethane foam bolster, 6″ (15.2cm) in diameter
- tape measure
- tailor's chalk
- dressmaker's pins
- fabric shears
- thread to match

Materials for Cover

- 1 yard (91.4cm) lightweight fabric, 42″ to 45″ (106.7cm to 114.3cm) wide
- 1½ yards (1.4m) double-edge ruffle trim, 2″ (5cm) wide
- 5 yards (4.6m) cable cord, ⅛″ (3mm) thick
- 1½ yards (1.4m) narrow ribbon, ¼″ (6mm) wide (optional)

Method for Pillow

Step 1:
Using a serrated knife, cut a 12½″ (31.8cm) long section from the polyurethane foam bolster.

Step 2:
Press fabric.

Measure, mark with tailor's chalk, and cut out a 13″ x 20″ (33cm x 50.8cm) rectangle. Fold rectangle in half horizontally, wrong side out, and stitch a ¼″ (6mm) seam along the horizontal raw edges to form a tube. Press seam open.

Turn tube right side out, and slip over foam bolster.

Step 3:
Measure, mark, and cut out two 7″ (17.8cm) diameter circles from remaining fabric.

Place circles over ends of bolster, and tuck raw edges inside fabric tube. Fold raw edges of fabric tube inside, and slip-stitch both circles and tube together to complete the pillow. (See fig. 1.)

Method for Cover

Step 4:
Press fabric.

Measure, mark with tailor's chalk, and cut out a 20″ (50.8cm) square.

Fold square in half, right side out. Make a French seam along the side opposite the fold by stitching ⅛″ (3mm) in from the raw edges. Trim as close as possible to stitching line, and turn fabric so that right sides are together. Stitch to enclose first seam. (See Techniques, Seams.)

Step 5:
Fold in raw edges of both sides of tube to form two ½″ (1.3cm) wide casings. (See fig. 2.) Pin-baste; then stitch casings, leaving a 1″ (2.5cm) opening for the cable cord.

Cut cable cord into two equal lengths, attach to a safety pin, and thread through casings.

Step 6:
From remaining fabric, cut bias strips, each 5¼″ (13.3cm) wide. Join strips together, end to end, with French seams to make two lengths, each 40″ (101.6cm) long. This will be your ruffle trim.

Edgestitch along one long side of each bias strip. Trim as close as possible to the stitching line and make a very narrow hand-rolled hem. (See Techniques, Hand-Rolled Hem.)

Form a casing on remaining long side of each bias strip by turning under raw edge ½″ (1.3cm) twice and stitching in place. (See fig. 3.)

Step 7:
Attach cording to a safety pin, and thread it through casings. Gather fabric to make a ruffle.

Pin-baste ruffles 5″ (12.7cm) in from each end of pillow cover and topstitch in place. (See fig. 4.)

Pin-baste and stitch 2″ (5cm) wide ruffle trim on top of stitching line of first ruffle. Stitch ribbon to center of trim, if desired.

Pull cover over pillow, tighten draw strings at each end, tie in place, and tuck cable cord ends inside.

Figure 1

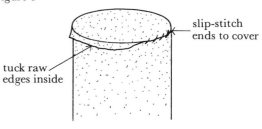

tuck raw edges inside

slip-stitch ends to cover

Figure 2

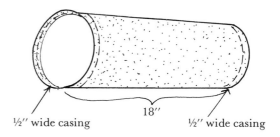

½″ wide casing   18″   ½″ wide casing

Figure 3

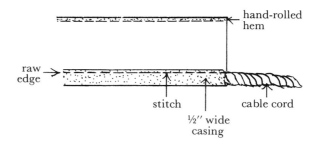

hand-rolled hem

raw edge

stitch   ½″ wide casing   cable cord

Figure 4

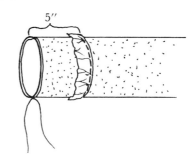

5″

Garment Bag

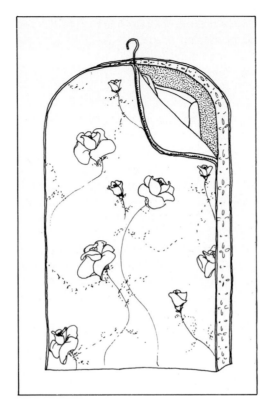

Materials
- 3 yards (2.7m) medium-weight fabric, 52″ (132cm) wide
- 8 yards (7.3m) cable cord, ¼″ (6mm) thick
- 2 separating zippers, each 25″ (63.5cm) long
- 4 yards (3.7m) flat eyelet trim, 2″ (5cm) wide
- tape measure
- tailor's chalk
- fabric shears
- thread to match

Method

Step 1:
Press fabric.

Measure, mark with tailor's chalk, and cut out two rectangles of fabric, each 25″ x 50″ (63.5cm x 127cm).

Cut the remaining piece of fabric in half crosswise to make two more rectangles, each 27″ x 58″ (68.6cm x 147.3cm). (See fig. 1.)

From one 27″ (68.6cm) wide section, prepare 8 yards (7.3m) of 2″ (5cm) wide continuous bias. (See Techniques, Bias Trim.) Cover cable cord with the bias strip as directed to make piping.

From the remaining 27″ (68.6cm) wide section, prepare 4 yards, (3.7m) of 3″ (7.6cm) wide continuous bias. (See Techniques, Bias Trim.)

Step 2:
Place the two 25″ x 50″ (63.5cm x 127cm) rectangles together, right sides out. Measure a 5″ (12.7cm) diagonal from the top corner points toward the center of the fabric. (See fig. 2.) Measure 10″ (25.4cm) from top corner points along sides. Mark a curved line following these marks. Trim along chalked lines.

Step 3:
Using ½″ (1.3cm) seams, pin-baste piping around right side of outer edge of one garment bag fabric section. Raw edges of piping should be even with raw edges of fabric.

Figure 1

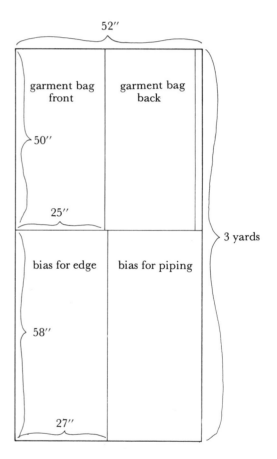

Baste in place. Pull cable cord out of covering about ½″ (1.3cm) on each end and clip cord. Overlap ends of the cording cover at the lower edge of the garment bag. (See fig. 3.)

Using a zipper foot attachment, stitch piping to fabric section sewing directly on top of the piping stitches.

Repeat procedure on remaining garment bag fabric section.

Step 4:
Open both separating zippers completely and pin-baste one half of each to the top of one garment bag section so that the teeth are covered by piping and, when closed, the zippers will meet at the top center of the garment bag. (See fig. 4.)

Using a zipper foot attachment, sew zippers in place by stitching through seam allowance of piping. Zip remaining zipper halves in place and overcast the bottom of each to prevent separating.

Step 5:
Center eyelet trim on right side of 3″ (7.6cm) wide continuous bias strip. Topstitch in place ½″ (1.3cm) in from raw edges.

Pin-baste eyelet trim to garment bag section without the zippers. With eyelet right side up, place raw edge of the strip under the piped edge so that it extends ½″ (1.3cm) beyond the stitching line used to attach the piping to the garment bag section.

Using a zipper foot attachment, stitch eyelet trim in place along the piped edge.

Step 6:
With wrong sides together, place the garment bag section with zippers on top of the garment bag section with eyelet trim.

Complete zipper application by turning raw edge of eyelet strip under ½″ (1.3cm) to form a lapped zipper cover. Using a zipper

foot attachment, topstitch through the eyelet to secure the lap in place. (See fig. 5.) Pin-baste, then stitch each zipper half to the eyelet strip.

Step 7:
Open the zippers and continue pin-basting the rest of the eyelet strip around the garment bag by placing the raw edge of the strip under the piping as before.

Using a zipper foot attachment, and working from the top of the garment bag down, attach the eyelet trim to the front of the garment bag by stitching through the bag and strip at the base of the piping.

If necessary, hand-stitch the inch or so below the zipper to secure.

Trim and notch seam allowances as necessary.

Figure 4

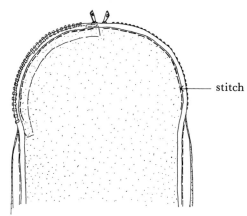

stitch

Figure 2

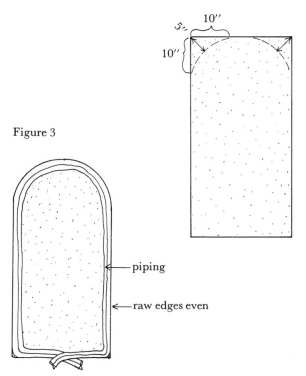

Figure 3

piping

raw edges even

Figure 5

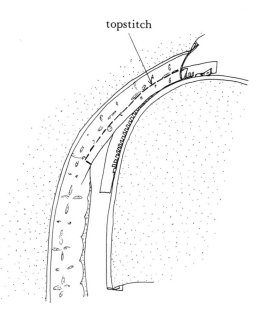

topstitch

Shoe Caddy

Materials
- 1½ yards (1.4m) medium-weight reversible fabric, 54″ (137.2cm) wide
- tape measure
- tailor's chalk
- fabric shears
- dressmaker's pins
- 5 yards (4.6m) flat eyelet trim, 2″ (5cm) wide
- thread to match
- round wooden curtain rod, 18″ (45.7cm) long and 1¼″ (3.2cm) thick
- wooden curtain rod brackets

Method
Step 1:
Press fabric.

Measure, mark with tailor's chalk, and cut out an 18″ x 52″ (45.7cm x 132cm) rectangle. Turn strip so that the 52″ (132cm) side becomes the length.

Fold top raw edge down 3½″ (8.9cm) onto the right side of the fabric; press. This will form a rod casing with its hem allowance on the front side of the finished shoe caddy.

Measure and cut off an 18″ (45.7cm) long piece of eyelet trim. Place trim ½″ (1.3cm) up from the raw edge. Working through a single layer of fabric, pin-baste, then stitch in place along top and bottom of trim.

Step 2:
From remaining fabric, measure, mark, and cut out three rectangles, each 10″ x 29″ (25.4cm x 73.7cm). Fold raw edges of one long side onto wrong side ¼″ (6mm) and press. Fold down again ¼″ (6mm) and press. (See fig. 1.) Stitch in place forming finished edges.

Keeping hems on top, press each rectangle to form four shoe-size pockets. Begin 1½″ (3.8cm) in from each side and make each pocket 4″ (10.2cm) wide with ½″ (1.3cm) folds on each side. (See fig. 2.) Press and pin-baste in place.

When all three rectangles have been pin-basted, stitch along unfinished bottom edges of pockets to hold folds in place. (See fig. 3.)

Step 3:
Position and pin-baste the first shoe pocket section to the right side of the back fabric 7½″ (19cm) below the top fold. Pin-baste second pocket section 21″ (53.3cm) below the top fold. Pin-baste the third pocket section 35½″ (90.2cm) below the top fold. (See fig. 4.)

Stitch sides of each pocket section to the back fabric.

Turn bottom raw edge up 2″ (5cm) and press.

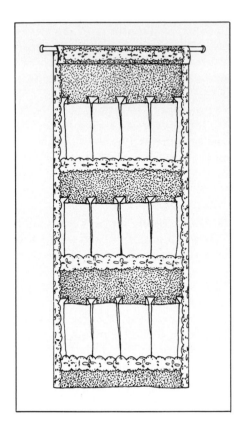

Figure 1

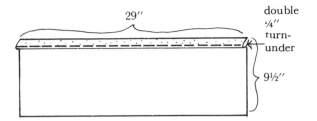

29″

double ¼″ turn-under

9½″

Step 4:
Measure and cut three 18″ (45.7cm) lengths of eyelet trim. Position it across the bottom of each pocket section so that it covers raw edges of pockets and the top edge of the trim rests 1″ (2.5cm) above the bottom edge of each pocket section. Pin-baste, then stitch in place along top and bottom of trim. (See fig. 5.) Bottom row of eyelet should cover 2″ (5cm) hem. This secures the pockets in place while adding a decorative finish.

Stitch the middle of each pocket beginning at the top hem and ending at the top of the bottom trim. (See fig. 6.)

Step 5:
Cut remaining length of eyelet trim in half. Fold it around the raw side edges of the shoe caddy, to bind the edges making sure both sides are even. Fold under raw edges of trim at top and bottom. Topstitch trim ¾″ (1.9cm) in from the outer edge.

Turn under top raw edge ½″ (1.3cm). Stitch across and on top of eyelet stitching to form rod casing. (See fig. 7.)

Step 6:
Attach wall brackets according to manufacturer's instructions. Slip shoe caddy onto rod and place in brackets.

Figure 3

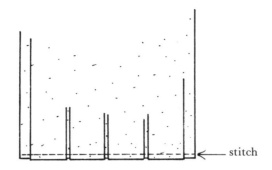

← stitch

Figure 4

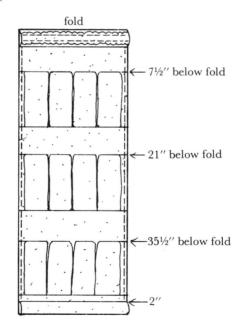

fold

← 7½″ below fold

← 21″ below fold

← 35½″ below fold

← 2″

Figure 2

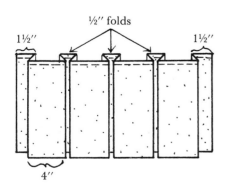

½″ folds

1½″   1½″

4″

Figure 5

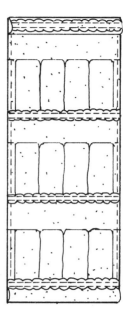

Figure 6

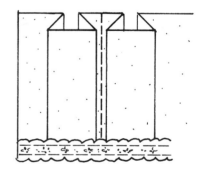

Figure 7

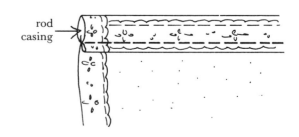

rod casing →

Handbag Caddy

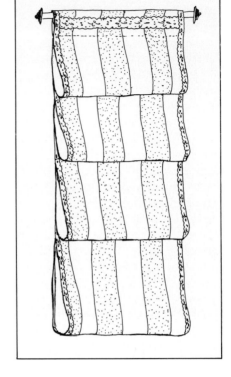

Materials

- 3 yards (2.7m) medium-weight reversible fabric, 54" (137.2cm) wide
- tape measure
- tailor's chalk
- fabric shears
- dressmaker's pins
- 6½ yards (5.9m) flat eyelet trim, 2" (5cm) wide
- thread to match
- round wooden curtain rod, 18" (45.7cm) long and 1¼" (3.2cm) thick
- wooden curtain rod brackets

Method

Step 1:
Press fabric.

Measure, mark with tailor's chalk, and cut a strip of fabric 16" (40.6cm) wide and 3 yards (2.7m) long.

Measure and cut eyelet trim into two 3-yard (2.7m) long pieces. Reserve extra ½ yard (45.7cm).

Step 2:
Fold trim around long raw edges of fabric, making sure both sides are even. Topstitch in place ¾" (1.9cm) in from the outer edge. (See fig. 1.)

Stitching through a single layer of fabric, attach remaining ½ yard (45.7cm) of eyelet trim across width of fabric between the two lengthwise strips of trim, 3½" (8.9cm) down from the top raw edge on the right side of the fabric. (See fig. 2.)

To form a casing for the curtain rod, turn down top raw edge 3" (7.6cm) onto wrong side of fabric and press. (See fig. 3.)

Step 3:
Double the length of fabric back on itself, right side out, to make a compartment 8" (20.3cm) deep. The top of the compartment should rest ¼" (6mm) above the raw edge which was pressed down on the wrong side in Step 2. Stitch across the width of the fabric securing the compartment and the top rod casing in place. (See fig. 4.)

Follow the same procedure to form another 8" (20.3cm) compartment. The top of this second compartment should be 7½" (19cm) below the stitching line of the first

Figure 1

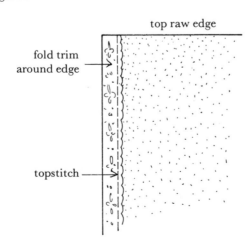

Figure 2

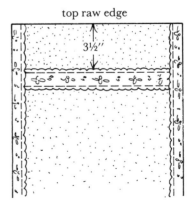

compartment. Stitch across the width of the fabric to secure in place, taking care not to stitch through the bottom of the first compartment. (See fig. 4.)

Repeat the above procedure to form a 10″ (25.4cm) compartment. The top of this third compartment should be 7″ (17.8cm) below the stitching line of the previous compartment. (See fig. 4.)

Finish by folding the last part of fabric under to form a 12″ (30.5cm) compartment. The top of this fourth compartment should be 9″ (22.9cm) below the stitching line of the previous compartment, and the bottom raw edge should be turned under ½″ (1.3cm). Stitch across the width of fabric to secure in place. (See fig. 4.)

Step 4:
Attach wall brackets according to manufacturer's instructions. Slip handbag caddy onto rod and place in brackets.

Figure 3

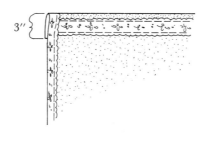

Figure 4

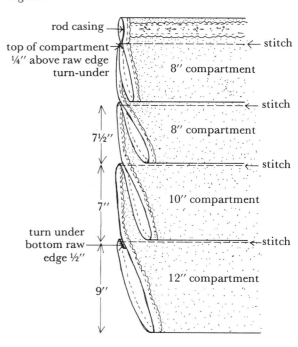

rod casing
top of compartment ¼″ above raw edge turn-under
stitch
8″ compartment
stitch
7½″
8″ compartment
stitch
7″
10″ compartment
turn under bottom raw edge ½″
stitch
9″
12″ compartment

Shirred Folding Screen

As unusual headboards or handy room dividers, screens of all types add to the versatility of your home.

With the help of your local lumberyard, construct four open framework panels of any size out of 1″ x 2″ (2.5cm x 5cm) strips of wood held together with Skotch wood joiners and then joined together with bifold hinges. Paint or stain the panels.

Prepare casement curtains according to the directions given in the Country French Living Room. Thread the curtains onto pressure curtain rods; then insert the rods inside each open framework panel.

Changing the effect is as simple as changing the curtain fabric.

Mr. Bedroom

Mr. Bedroom

This masculine bedroom is obviously designed with the romantic in mind. The monochromatic gray-blue tones of the room suggest relaxation and exude a cool, serene atmosphere.

The half canopy over the bed, which is a simple box spring and mattress, sets the dramatic tone of the room. The panel is relatively uncomplicated to make and is supported above the bed by the use of café curtain rods.

The bedspread, matching bolsters, and rectangular pillows are all extremely tailored. The darker colored club chair adds dimension to the room.

The one large window in the room is topped with a cornice which is covered in the same fabric as the bedspread. The three curtain panels are each two and one-half times the width of the curtain rod from its outer edge to its center. When the tiebacks are removed, an opulent effect of lush fullness is achieved. The fabric-covered window shade with dowel pull heightens the tailored effect. The lampshade may be covered, following directions in the Country French Dining Room.

To lighten the entire room, a pale blue/white, plush, wall-to-wall carpet is added. And to warm the room and give it life, plants are added.

Tailored Bedspread and Canopy

🧵 🧵 🧵 🧵

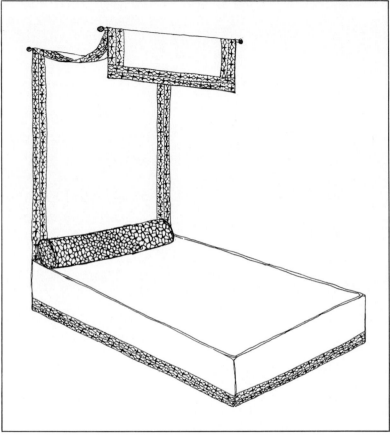

The materials and directions given are for a full-size spread, approximately 54″ x 75″ (137.2cm x 190.5cm), and a canopy.

Materials
- 18 yards (16.5m) medium-weight fabric, solid or nondirectional print, 44″ (111.8cm) or wider
- 5 yards (4.6m) contrasting medium-weight fabric, solid or nondirectional print, 44″ (111.8cm) or wider
- 7 yards (6.4m) cable cord, ¼″ (6mm) thick
- 2 narrow round curtain rods, each 57″ (144.8cm) long
- tape measure
- yardstick
- tailor's chalk
- fabric shears
- staple gun and staples

Method for Bedspread
Step 1:
Press fabric.

Measure, mark with tailor's chalk, and cut out a 42″ x 95″ (106.7cm x 241.3cm) rectangle from the 18 yard (16.5m) piece of fabric for the center of the spread.

Measure, mark, and cut out two 7½″ x 95″ (19cm x 241.3cm) fabric strips for each side of the center piece.

With right sides together and using ½″ (1.3cm) seams, pin-baste, then stitch strips to each side of the center panel. Press seams open.

Step 2:
From fabric remaining after lengthwise strips have been cut, or from the ½ yard (45.7m) of contrasting fabric, prepare a continuous bias strip, 1½″ (3.8cm) wide and approximately 7 yards (6.4m) long. (See Techniques, Bias Trim.) Cover cable cord with the bias strip as directed to make piping.

Step 3:
Measure, mark, and cut out seven fabric strips, each the full width of the fabric and 24″ (61cm) wide. Using ½″ (1.3cm) seams,

pin-baste, then stitch the strips together end to end, making one long strip, approximately 305″ (774.7cm) long and 24″ (61cm) wide. This is the side panel or "drop." Press all seams open.

Step 4:
Place the top of the spread on the bed, right side up. Center and smooth the spread carefully so that it rests exactly as you want the finished spread to rest.

Pin-baste piping to the spread, starting at the head of the bed. The raw edges of the piping should extend 1″ (2.5cm) beyond the top edges of the spread and be pinned so that the rounded side faces toward the center of the bed and the stitching line on the piping rests exactly on the edge of the bed. (See fig. 1.) Using a zipper foot attachment, stitch piping in place.

Step 5:
With right sides together and using ½″ (1.3cm) seams, pin-baste drop to top section.

At each corner at the foot of the bed, double the fabric back to make a pleat extending 8″ (20.3cm) in each direction. (See fig. 2.)

Continue pin-basting the drop to the spread. Using a zipper foot attachment, stitch in place.

Step 6:
Place spread on bed. Using a yardstick, carefully measure and mark off the bottom of the spread; it should rest about 1″ (2.5cm) above the floor or carpet.

If you are planning to accent the bottom edge with contrasting trim, cut along the marked line to remove excess fabric.

Measure, mark, and cut out fabric lengths 10″ (25.4cm) wide. Stitch strips together end to end to make one long strip approximately 275″ (7m). Press seams open.

Turn raw edges under ½″ (1.3cm) and press. Fold trim around the bottom raw edge of the spread, pin-baste, and topstitch in place. (See fig. 3.)

If you plan to hem the bottom edge of the spread without trimming it in a contrasting fabric, allow 2½″ (6.4cm) to form a 2¼″ (5.7cm) hem with a ¼″ (6mm) hem allowance. Stitch hem.

Turn under raw edge of spread at the head of the bed. Fold fabric to form a 1½″ (3.8cm) hem with a ¼″ (6mm) turn-under. Stitch in place and press.

Method for Canopy

Step 7:
Measure, mark, and cut out a strip of fabric the full width of the fabric and 170″ (4.3m) long.

Measure, mark, and cut out two additional strips, each 7¼″ (18.4cm) wide by 170″ (4.3m) long.

Using ½″ (1.3cm) seams, stitch narrow strips to wider strip to make a panel 57″ (144.8cm) wide. Press seams open.

Step 8:
Prepare a 57″ x 12″ (144.8cm x 30.5cm) fabric strip. Using a French seam, stitch strip to the end of the canopy that will be hanging above the foot of the bed. (See Techniques, Seams.)

Step 9:
To prepare trim, measure, mark, and cut 10″ (25.4cm) wide lengthwise strips from contrasting fabric. Stitch strips end to end to make one long strip, approximately 11 yards (10m) long.

Press long strip to make a lengthwise fold in the center. Turn under the raw edges ½″ (1.3cm) and press. Pin-baste trim around four sides of the canopy. Topstitch trim in place.

Step 10:
Mount the two curtain rods on the ceiling using the bolts or screws recommended by your local hardware store and suited to the construction of your ceiling.

Mount rod directly over the head of the bed, about 1″ (2.5cm) from the angle where the wall meets the ceiling.

Mount the other rod on the ceiling, spaced according to the amount of drop you desire.

With the seam allowances facing the wall, thread the canopy up behind the bed, across the ceiling and over the second rod.

Secure the bottom edge of the canopy behind the bed with staples.

Figure 1

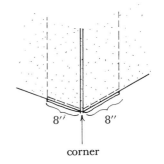

Figure 2

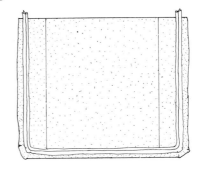

8″   8″

corner

Figure 3

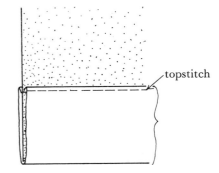

topstitch

Round Bolster

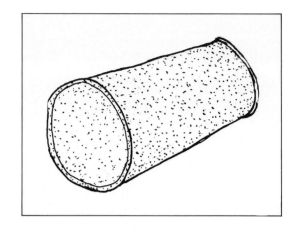

A polyurethane foam bolster can be made to any size you desire by simply cutting it with a serrated knife.

The materials and directions given are for a 36″ x 8″ (91.4cm x 20.3cm) bolster.

Materials
- 1 polyurethane foam bolster, 36″ x 8″ (91.4cm x 20.3cm)
- tape measure
- tailor's chalk
- 1¾ yards (1.6cm) medium- to heavyweight fabric, 42″ to 45″ (106.7cm to 114.3cm) wide
- fabric shears
- one 20″ to 22″ (50.8cm x 55.9cm) zipper to match
- 2 yards (1.8m) cable cord, ¼″ (6mm) thick
- thread to match

Method
Step 1:
Press fabric.

Measure the circumference and the distance around the length of the bolster. Then measure, mark, and cut out a rectangle of fabric 1″ (2.5cm) more than the circumference and 2″ (5cm) more than the length around the bolster. (See fig. 1.)

From the remaining fabric, measure, mark with tailor's chalk, and cut out two 12″ (30.5cm) squares. Fold each square into quarters and press. Measure and mark an arc 4½″ (11.4cm) from the folded points.

(See fig. 2.) Cut along the arcs to make two 9″ (22.9cm) circles.

Step 2:
Fold the rectangle of fabric wrong side out with long sides together. Measure, mark, and pin-baste ½″ (1.3cm) seams extending 8″ (20.3cm) in from each end. (See fig. 3.) Press seams open.

Turn tube right side out. Pin-baste zipper in position in center opening, and stitch in place according to manufacturer's directions. (See fig. 4.)

Step 3:
From remaining fabric, prepare 2 yards (1.8m) continuous bias strip 1¾″ (4.4cm) wide. (See Techniques, Bias Trim.) Cover cable cord with bias as directed to make piping.

Keeping fabric right side out, slip tube over foam bolster. Close zipper. Pin-baste piping around bolster edges so that the raw edges of the piping are even with raw edges of the fabric tube. (See fig. 5.)

Figure 1

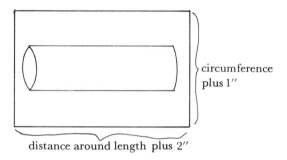

circumference plus 1″

distance around length plus 2″

Figure 2

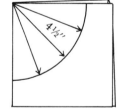

4½″

Figure 3

½″ seam extending 8″ in from end

Carefully remove fabric tube from bolster, and stitch piping in place using zipper foot attachment. Trim and notch seam allowances to remove excess fabric.

Step 4:
Turn fabric tube wrong side out.

Position fabric circles, wrong side out, on each end of the tube. Pin-baste in place so that the ½″ (1.3cm) seam allowances of the circles extend just a bit beyond the stitching line attaching the piping to the tube. (See fig. 6.)

Using a zipper foot attachment, stitch circles to ends of tube by sewing directly on top of stitching line which attaches piping to tube.

Notch seam allowances around circles to make cover fit smoothly.

Turn cover right side out, press, and insert bolster.

Figure 4

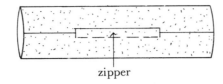

zipper

Figure 6

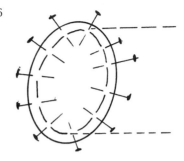

Figure 5

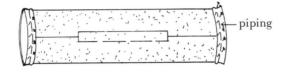

piping

Fabric Covered Window Shade with Dowel Pull

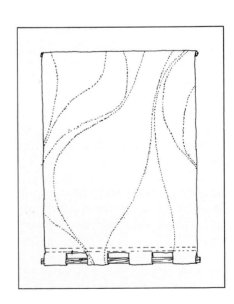

For best results, be sure the shade to be covered is in good condition.

Materials
- 1 window shade, 35″ wide by 66″ long (88.9cm x 167.6cm)
- 4 yards (3.7m) nonwoven fusible bonding web, 18″ (45.7cm) wide
- 2 yards (1.8m) lightweight fabric, 42″ to 45″ (106.7cm to 114.3cm) wide

- tape measure
- tailor's chalk
- fabric shears
- dressmaker's pins
- thread to match
- masking tape
- staple gun and staples
- 1 wooden dowel, 35″ (88.9cm) long and 1″ (2.5cm) thick

(Continued)

Method

Step 1:

Press fabric.

Measure, mark with tailor's chalk, and cut out a section of fabric 1″ (2.5cm) larger on all sides than the window shade.

Remove roller from window shade, and cut off bottom slat casing ⅛″ (3mm) above the stitching line. (See fig. 1.)

Place an old sheet on top of a table protected by a cutting board. Lay shade on top of sheet, right side up.

Step 2:

Cut fusible bonding web into two strips, each 1″ (2.5cm) longer than shade. Place strips on top of shade, making sure they extend beyond shade sides ¼″ (6mm), beyond top and bottom ½″ (1.3cm), and overlap each other ½″ (1.3cm) in the center. (See fig. 2.)

Carefully center and place fabric, right side up, on top of fusible bonding web.

Put iron on synthetic setting. Fuse fabric to shade by holding iron in the same spot for five seconds; then move iron slowly to next spot and hold for five seconds. (Do not allow iron to touch fusible bonding web; it will stick to the iron and be difficult to remove.) Repeat procedure until entire shade is fused. At this point move shade to ironing board, which is protected with an old sheet.

(If your window shade is vinyl, it will become quite limp.) Allow to dry thoroughly, and repeat above procedure two more times.

Step 3:

Trim excess fabric and bonding web from edges after shade has dried for the third time.

Using a very small zigzag stitch (15) on your sewing machine, stitch around the perimeter of the window shade to keep raw edges from fraying. If your machine does not have a zigzag stitch, brush trimmed raw edges with clear nail polish.

Step 4:

Turn bottom edge of window shade onto wrong side 7″ (17.8cm) and press.

Open up bottom fold. Measure, mark with tailor's chalk, and cut out 5″ x 6″ (12.7cm x 15.2cm) rectangles, each 5″ (12.7cm) apart. (See fig. 3.) Size of these openings may vary according to size of window, size of dowel, and personal preference.

Turn bottom edges of cut sections under and up to fold line. Pin-baste; then stitch in place directly above cut out areas and again 1″ (2.5cm) above that. (See fig. 4.)

Step 5:

Make sure tension spring is on right side of roller as you hold it facing the window so that the shade will roll front to back. (See fig. 5.)

Attach top of window shade to roller with masking tape. Place shade up at window in roller sockets to make sure it rolls up and down evenly. Staple shade to roller, tighten roller spring, and hang in window.

Slide dowel through loops at bottom of shade.

Figure 2

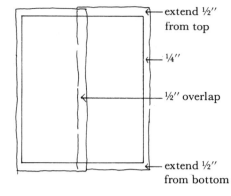

←extend ½″ from top

←¼″

←½″ overlap

←extend ½″ from bottom

Figure 3

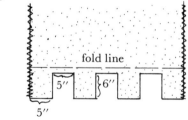

fold line

5″   6″

5″

Figure 4

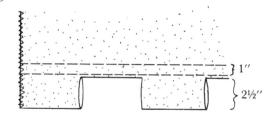

1″

2½″

Figure 1

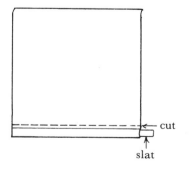

cut

slat

Figure 5

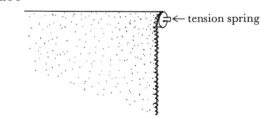

←tension spring

Rectangular Pillow with Boxing

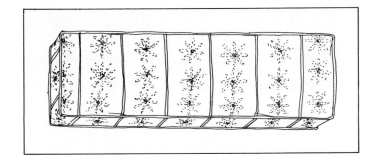

The materials and directions given are for a 36″ x 11″ x 1″ (91.4cm x 27.9cm x 2.5cm) rectangular pillow.

Materials
- polyurethane foam pad, 36″ x 11″ x 1″ (91.4cm x 27.9cm x 2.5cm)
- 1 yard (91.4cm) light- to medium-weight fabric, 44″ to 52″ (111.8cm to 132cm) wide
- 6 yards (5.5m) commercial piping in an accent color, ¼″ (6mm) thick
- tape measure
- tailor's chalk
- fabric shears
- dressmaker's pins
- thread to match

Method

Step 1:
Press fabric.

Measure, mark with tailor's chalk, and cut out two 36½″ x 11½″ (92.7cm x 29.2cm) rectangles of fabric. (See fig. 1.)

From remaining fabric, measure, mark, and cut out three strips, each the full width of the fabric and 1½″ (3.8cm) wide. (See fig. 1.)

Using ½″ (1.3cm) seams and with right sides together, join strips end to end to make one strip 100″ (2.5m) long.

Step 2:
Using a zipper foot attachment and ¼″ (6mm) seams, pin-baste, then stitch commercial piping to each side of the long strip, right side out, making sure rounded edge of piping faces in toward the center of the fabric. (See fig. 2.) Press.

Step 3:
Using ¼″ (6mm) seams and with right sides together, pin-baste, then stitch piped strip to one cover section, starting and ending in the center of one short side. (See fig. 3.) Stitch boxing strip ends together and press.

With right sides together, pin-baste, then stitch remaining cover section to piped strip, leaving an opening in the center of one short side for turning and stuffing. (See fig. 4.)

Turn cover right side out and press. Insert foam pad and slip-stitch opening closed.

Figure 2

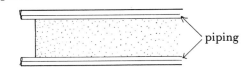

piping

Figure 3

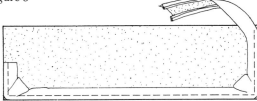

Figure 1

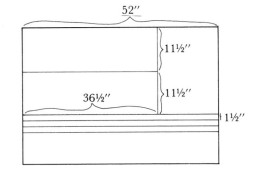

52″

11½″

36½″

11½″

1½″

Figure 4

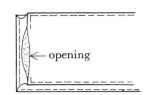

opening

Teenager's Bedroom

Teenager's Bedroom

Designed for today's active teenager, a cheerful and durable bedroom. The studio couch and matching bolsters are covered in a sturdy cotton corduroy. The café window curtains are made of the same fabric, but only the bottom half of the window is covered in order to bring more color into the room without blocking the light. The soothing pale walls soften the brightness of the yellows and reds while the thick rug blends and also helps to soften the brighter colors.

Large cubes constructed of 1'' (2.5cm) thick plywood are painted in bright colors and used as tables, extra seating, or step stools to reach the higher shelves of the bookcase.

The backrest with arms is a comfortable addition to any bedroom and a must for reading in bed. Relatively indestructable, the backrest makes studying into the wee hours much more enjoyable.

Pillows are a favorite with any teenager, and the array shown here are patterned after traffic symbols, school emblems, and bright geometrics. A good item to include in this room to help organize unnecessary clutter would be a covered album holder. The directions for the practical holder are located in the Music Room.

Studio Couch Cover

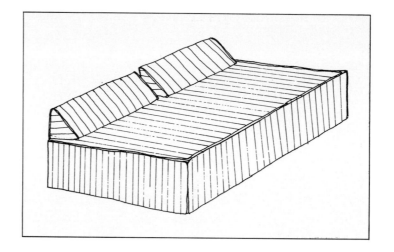

The materials and directions given are for a cover approximately 39" x 75" (99cm x 190.5cm).

Materials
- 7½ yards (6.9m) medium-weight fabric, 44" (111.8cm) or wider
- 7 yards (6.4m) cable cord, ¼" (6mm) thick
- tape measure
- dressmaker's pins
- tailor's chalk
- fabric shears
- yardstick
- thread to match

Method

Step 1:
Press fabric.

Measure, mark with tailor's chalk, and cut off a section of fabric the full width of the fabric and 78" (198cm) long for the top cover.

Prepare a 1½" (3.8cm) wide continuous bias strip, 7 yards (6.4m) long. (See Techniques, Bias Trim.) Cover cable cord with the bias strip as directed to make piping.

Step 2:
Place fabric section for top of couch cover on the bed, right side up. Center, and smooth it to rest exactly as you want the finished spread to rest.

Pin-baste the piping to the spread, starting at the head of the bed. Pin piping so that the rounded side faces toward the center of the bed and the stitching line on the piping rests exactly on the edge of the bed. (See fig. 1.)

Continue pin-basting piping around all four sides of the studio couch top. Using a zipper foot attachment, stitch in place. For a smooth finish where ends of the piping overlap, pull cord out of covering and clip cord so that the cut ends of both sides meet. Stitch ends in place. Replace cover on couch.

Step 3:
Measure, mark, and cut out seven fabric strips, each the full width of the fabric and 24" (61cm) wide. Stitch strips together end to end, right sides together, using ½" (1.3cm) seams, to make one long strip approximately 8½ yards (7.8m) long and 24" (61cm) wide. Press all seams open.

Remove cover from the couch. With right sides together, and using ½" (1.3cm) seams, pin-baste drop to couch cover top.

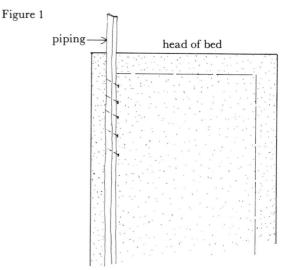

Figure 1

piping→   head of bed

Figure 2

corner

8"   8"

Step 4:
At each corner, double the fabric back to make a deep pleat extending 8″ (20.3cm) in each direction. (See fig. 2.)

Continue pin-basting the drop to the top of the cover. Using a zipper foot attachment, stitch drop to cover.

Step 5:
Replace cover on couch. Using a yardstick, carefully measure and mark off the bottom of the cover; the finished hem should rest about 1″ (2.5cm) above the floor or carpet. Mark the bottom of the hem with dress-maker's pins or tailor's chalk. (See fig. 3.)

Remove cover from couch, and press bottom edge up to form a 1½″ (3.8cm) hem with a ½″ (1.3cm) turn-under. Machine- or hand-stitch to finish.

Figure 3

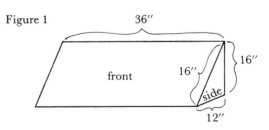

mark hem

Wedge-Shaped Bolster

🧵 🧵 🧵

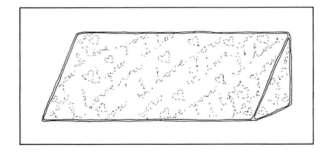

The materials and directions given are for a bolster approximately 36″ (91.4cm) wide, 16″ (40.6cm) high, and 12″ (30.5cm) deep at the base.

Materials
- 1 polyurethane foam bolster, 36″ x 16″ x 12″ (91.4cm x 40.6cm x 30.5cm)
- 2½ yards (2.3m) medium- to heavyweight fabric, 44″ (111.8cm) or wider
- 6 yards (5.5m) cable cord, ¼″ (6mm) thick
- tape measure
- tailor's chalk
- fabric shears
- upholstery zipper (optional)
- dressmaker's pins
- thread to match

Method
Step 1:
Press all fabric.

Measure, mark with tailor's chalk, and cut out all five fabric sections, each approximately 2″ (5cm) larger than the bolster dimensions. (See figs. 1 & 2.)

If you want to be able to remove the cover for cleaning, cut the bottom section 2″ to 3″ (5cm to 7.6cm) wider than the bolster dimensions in order to attach a zipper. Insert upholstery zipper according to manufacturer's instructions with a lapped or centered application in the middle of the bottom panel of the bolster cover.

Figure 1

36″

16″

front   16″

side

12″

Step 2:
Prepare 6 yards (5.5m) of continuous bias, 1½″ (3.8cm) wide. (See Techniques, Bias Trim.) Cover cable cord with the bias strip as directed to make piping.

(Continued)

Position one of the 38″ x 18″ (96.5cm x 45.7cm) rectangles on the bolster front. Pin-baste piping across top edge of the fabric with rounded edge facing toward the bolster front. Piping should extend 1″ (2.5cm) beyond the cut edge of the fabric on either side. (See fig. 3.)

Following the same procedure, pin-baste a row of piping along the bottom edge of the bolster front fabric. (See fig. 3.)

Remove fabric from bolster and using a zipper foot attachment, stitch piping in place.

Step 3:
With right sides facing and using ½″ (1.3cm) seams, pin-baste the second large rectangle to rectangle with piping attached. Using a zipper foot attachment, stitch along the piping at the top edge.

Turn cover right side out and place on bolster. Firmly smooth into position.

Following the procedure outlined in Step 2, pin-baste a row of piping along the bottom of the back section. Remove fabric from bolster and stitch in place.

Step 4:
Replace cover on bolster. Position bottom section, turn under raw edges and pin-baste in place. When cover is pinned to fit snugly, remove it from bolster and replace pins to the inside. Using a zipper foot attachment, stitch along bottom rows of the piping to attach bolster cover bottom.

Step 5:
Slip cover onto bolster. Pin-baste piping around side edges of bolster ends so that the rounded part of cord faces toward center of side panel.

Remove cover from bolster and using a zipper foot attachment, stitch piping in place.

Replace cover on bolster. Position side panels and trim to triangular shape. Turn under raw edges, and pin-baste in position following the same techniques as you used to attach the bottom section to the cover in Step 4.

When cover is pinned to fit snugly, remove from bolster by opening zipper or pins in the bottom. Replace pins to the inside. Using a zipper foot attachment, stitch along the base of the piping to attach the side sections.

Figure 2

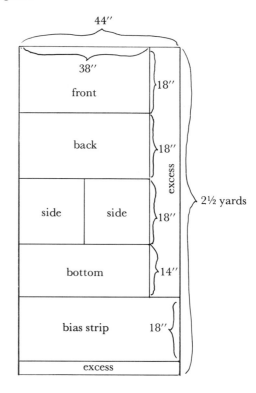

Figure 3

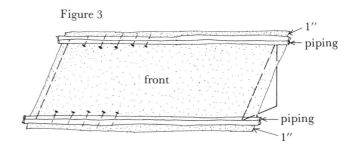

Backrest Pillow with Arms

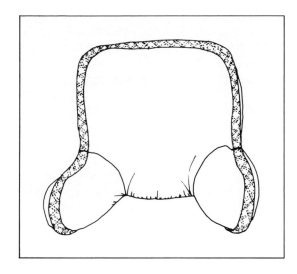

Materials
- 2 yards (1.8m) medium- to heavyweight fabric, 48" (121.9cm) or wider
- one 16-ounce (448g) package polyester fiber fill
- three 16-ounce (448g) packages polyester fiber fill
- graph paper
- yardstick
- tape measure
- fabric shears
- dressmaker's pins
- thread to match

Method
Step 1:
Transfer the outline of the shaped pillow sections, including the front, back, and sides, to square ruled paper. (See fig. 1.)

Step 2:
Press fabric and place it on top of a large, flat working surface.

Fold up one corner of the fabric so that the cut end rests exactly on the selvage. Press along this diagonal fold to locate the true bias. (See Techniques, Bias Trim.)

Use the true bias fold as a guide to cut two strips of bias, each 5" (12.7cm) wide. Attach these strips, end to end, to make a strip of bias approximately 2½ yards (2.3m) long and 5" (12.7cm) wide. This will be used for the large welting around the back of the pillow.

(Continued)

Figure 1

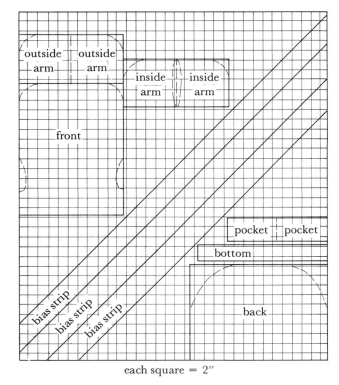

each square = 2"

Cut along the same diagonal edge to prepare another bias strip 4½″ (11.4cm) wide and 1 yard (91.4cm) long. This strip will be used for the welting along the armrests.

Step 3:
Position pattern pieces for the front, back, sides and pockets on the remaining fabric, following fig. 1. Cut out the pieces.

Step 4:
From a double layer of polyester batting, cut strips 6″ (15.2cm) wide and the exact length of the two bias strips prepared in Step 2.

Roll the 6″ (15.2cm) batting strips lengthwise to form two smooth tight tubes of polyester. Using a zipper foot attachment, cover each tube with the bias strips to make welting. (See fig. 2.)

Pin-baste the thicker welting made from the 5″ (12.7cm) wide bias strip around the raw edges of the pillow back. Make sure raw edges of the welting face in the same direction as fabric section's raw edges. (See fig. 3.)

Using ½″ (1.3cm) seams and a zipper foot attachment, stitch welting in place. Where welting meets, pull batting out of its covering about ½″ (1.3cm) on each end, and clip. Overlap the covering ends at the lower corner of the pillow. (See fig. 3.)

Step 5:
To hem the outside arm pockets, turn under ½″ (1.3cm) then turn under a ½″ (1.3cm) hem. Stitch in place.

Stitch pockets in place, right sides up, ¼″ (6mm) in from the side and bottom edges of the outer armrest sections. (See fig. 4.)

Step 6:
Pin-baste the narrower welting made from the 4½″ (11.4cm) bias strip around the curved edge of the outer arm section. (See fig. 5.) Raw edge of welting should face the same direction as raw edges of fabric. Stitch

in place using a zipper foot attachment and ½″ (1.3cm) seams. Repeat Step 6 to attach welting to the second armrest.

Step 7:
Pin-baste the inside section of the armrest to the outside section which has the welting attached. The sections should be right sides together with the welting resting in between them.

Using a zipper foot attachment, stitch along the base of the welting to attach the two armrest sections. Repeat this procedure to complete the second armrest. Turn both armrests right side out.

Step 8:
With right sides facing, pin the armrests to the inside front of the pillow on each side. The curved seams at the base of the armrests fit exactly into the curved seams on the inside back pillow section. (See fig. 6.) Stitch.

With right sides together, stitch ½″ (1.3cm) seams directly underneath the outer pockets to finish the bottom of the armrests and form the base of the cushion.

Step 9:
With right sides together, pin-baste; then stitch the narrow bottom strip along the wider bottom edge of the cushion. Stitch directly on top of the stitching line which attached the thick welting to the pillow back.

Figure 3

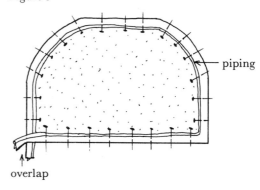
—piping
↑
overlap

Figure 4

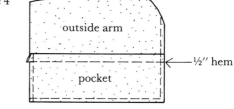
outside arm
←½″ hem
pocket

Figure 5

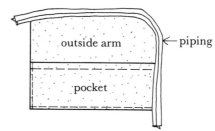
outside arm
←piping
pocket

Figure 2

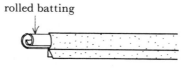
rolled batting

Step 10:

Place the pillow front, with the completed arm sections on top of the pillow back so that the right sides are together.

Pin-baste along the welting. Where welting overlaps, clip excess polyester batting, and fold the ends of the welting so that they meet for a finished effect with a minimum of bulk.

Starting at one lower corner, stitch the front and back pieces together, stitching around the outer edge to the opposite lower corner.

Trim seam allowances as necessary, and turn cover right side out.

Step 11:

Stuff polyester fiber fill into the pillow, being careful to fill the armrests and back areas evenly and firmly. (If filling compresses when used over a long period of time, open pillow and add more fiber fill.)

Pin-baste the bottom edge of the pillow, and slip-stitch the opening closed. Be careful to spread the ease of this bottom strip across the entire width of the pillow. This will create a shirred, full effect.

Figure 6

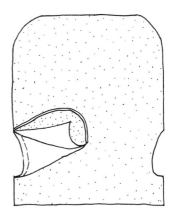

Little Girl's Bedroom

Little Girl's Bedroom

A very feminine room is in store for your special little Miss. Tones of pink accented with pastel colors and white work together to create the perfect haven for sugar and spice dreams.

The covered padded headboard is easy to construct using a 1'' (2.5cm) thick plywood base. In any bedroom, it adds a decorator touch to an otherwise ordinary box spring and mattress.

The pillow shams, ruffled or tailored, are a soft cushion for listening to bedtime stories. For special dreams, the Tooth Fairy Pillowcase in the foreground is sure to be a favorite. The instructions are easily altered to make a masculine Tooth Fairy Pillowcase for your young lad.

The charming patchwork quilt may be an heirloom or one you design yourself. For an easy, yet luxurious substitute, adapt the directions for the pioneer knot comforter in the Mr. & Mrs. Bedroom, or choose the bunk quilt style in the Little Boy's Bedroom using bright feminine colors. Directions for the dust ruffle may also be found in the Mr. & Mrs. Bedroom.

The ruffled dressing table skirt adds a bit of fluff to the room and transforms a worn, unused table into a child's delight. With pieces remaining from the skirt, tack a ruffled frame around the mirror. Make a rectangular bench cushion by adapting directions from the Mr. Bedroom, and add a ruffle there too!

Padded Headboard

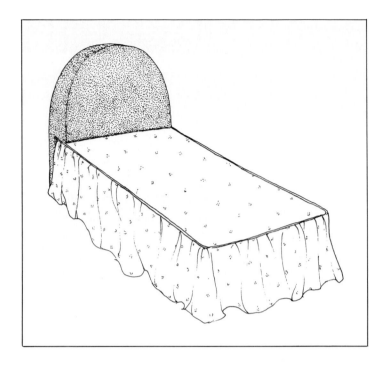

Simple or elaborate, a headboard adds dramatic interest to any bed. When using sheeting, you have wide widths to work with. The materials and directions given are for a double bed-size headboard.

Materials
- 1 double-size flat sheet
- newspaper
- scotch tape
- lead pencil, #2
- fabric shears
- ½" (1.3cm) thick plywood
- 3" (7.6cm) thick polyurethane foam
- rubber cement
- paintbrush, 3" (7.6cm) wide
- polyester batting, double bed size
- staple gun and staples
- drill
- 4 molly plugs and bolts

Method

Step 1:
Cover wall area where headboard is to be placed with sheets of newspaper taped together. Outline the shape you wish headboard to be on the newspaper. The headboard should be 1" (2.5cm) wider than the mattress; begin drawing at floor level and draw up to a height of 49" (124.5cm). Carefully remove the newspaper from the wall and cut out the pattern.

Take the pattern to your local lumberyard to have the shape traced and cut out of ½" (1.3cm) thick plywood.

Step 2:
Cut polyurethane foam into the shape of the plywood from mattress level up. (See fig. 1.) Trim around top very carefully.

Liberally coat one side of the plywood with rubber cement, and attach polyurethane foam. If you have to piece the foam, join section edges together with rubber cement.

Step 3:
Cover polyurethane foam and plywood part of headboard with one layer of batting, wrapping it around all edges of the headboard to give a rounded effect. (See fig. 2.) Staple to back of plywood.

Wrap again with a second layer of batting. (See fig. 2.)

Step 4:
Open all hems of sheet and press. Fold and cut sheet in half horizontally.

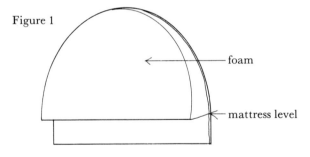

Figure 1

foam

mattress level

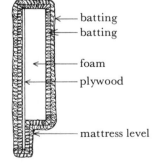

Figure 2

batting
batting
foam
plywood

mattress level

Place headboard, foam side up, on top of one half of the sheet. Allowing a 5″ (12.7cm) margin of fabric all around the headboard, cut fabric to the shape of the headboard. (See fig. 3.)

Center the sheet, right side up, on top of the batting covered foam. Carefully and firmly wrap it around to the back of the headboard and staple in place 1″ (2.5cm) in from the edge.

Step 5:
Using remaining half of sheet, cut it to the shape of the plywood. Turn raw edges under ¼″ (6mm) and press. Staple sheet, right side up, to back of plywood headboard, covering batting and raw edges of wrapped sheet. (See fig. 4.)

Step 6:
Set headboard on the floor flush against the wall. On each side, 3″ (7.6cm) up from the

floor and 1″ (2.5cm) below the foam, drill through the headboard with a ¼″ (6mm) drill, marking the wall in the same spots.

Remove headboard, and drill marked wall spots with a ⅜″ (9mm) drill. Insert molly plug. Replace headboard and attach bolt through it into the molly plug; thus securing headboard to the wall. (See fig. 5.)

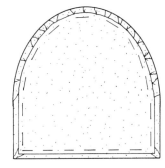

Figure 4

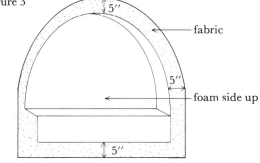

Figure 3

5″ ← fabric

5″

5″ ← foam side up

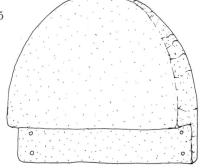

Figure 5

Tooth Fairy Pillowcase

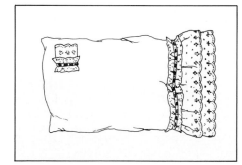

A special surprise for a special occasion, the Tooth Fairy Pillowcase has a pocket small enough to hold a lost tooth and large enough for the Tooth Fairy to drop in a coin or two. The case is designed to fit over an 18″ x 13″ (45.7cm x 33cm) boudoir pillow. (See Ms Bedroom.)

To alter the design to suit a little boy, simply replace the ruffles with regimental striped ribbon or piping.

(Continued)

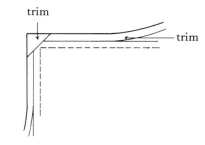

Figure 1

trim

trim

Materials

- ½ yard (45.7cm) light- to medium-weight washable fabric, any width
- tape measure
- tailor's chalk
- dressmaker's pins
- fabric shears
- 2 yards (1.8m) eyelet trim, 5″ (12.7cm) wide
- 1 yard (.9m) narrow, ribbon-threaded, double-edge eyelet trim, 2″ (5cm) wide

Method

Step 1:
Press fabric.

Measure, mark with tailor's chalk, and cut out two sections of fabric, each 19″ x 15″ (48.3cm x 38cm).

Step 2:
Place right sides of fabric together. Using a ½″ (1.3cm) seam allowance, pin-baste, then stitch around three sides leaving one 15″ (38.1cm) side open.

Trim seam allowances and excess fabric from corners. (See fig. 1.) Turn right side out and press.

Step 3:
Cut the 5″ (12.7cm) wide eyelet trim into two equal lengths. Place right sides of trim and fabric together. Using a ½″ (1.3cm) seam, pin-baste one length around the open end of the pillowcase. Cut off any excess trim. Stitch trim in place. (See fig. 2.)

Step 4:
Join ends of trim together with small whipping stitches, turning raw edges to the inside as you do so. (See Techniques, Hand Stitches.) Turn the eyelet so that the ruffle extends away from the pillowcase. (See fig. 3.)

Step 5:
Fasten the second row of eyelet 1½″ (3.8cm) below the bottom of the first row of trim, and repeat procedure in Steps 3 and 4. (See fig. 3.)

Step 6:
Attach the ribbon-threaded, double-edge eyelet trim to the pillowcase directly on top of the bottom edge of the second row of eyelet. (See fig. 4.) Pin-baste; then stitch in place. Turn ends under.

Step 7:
Make a 3½″ x 5″ (8.9cm x 12.7cm) pocket out of remaining scraps of 5″ (12.7cm) wide trim. (See fig. 5.) Turn raw side edges under, and stitch in place.

Attach a remaining scrap of ribbon-threaded eyelet to the bottom of the larger eyelet, and stitch in place. (See fig. 6.) Turn raw edges under, and pin in place.

Step 8:
Pin pocket in position in the upper left-hand corner of the pillowcase, 2″ (5cm) in from the side edge and 1½″ (3.8cm) in from the top edge. Topstitch around sides and bottom edges.

Figure 2

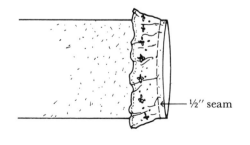
½″ seam

Figure 3

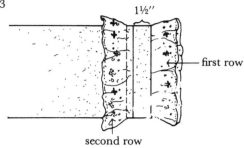
1½″ — first row — second row

Figure 4

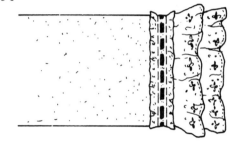

Figure 5

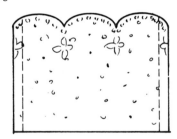

Figure 6

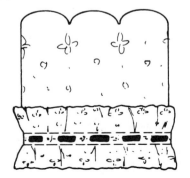

Tailored Pillow Sham

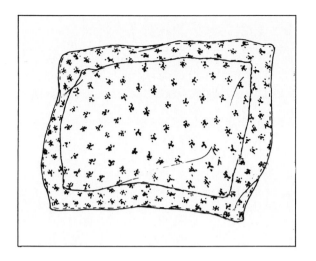

An unruffled pillow cover is particularly attractive when grouped with ruffled pillow shams. Try this one for a nice contrast.

Materials
- 1 yard (91.4cm) light- to medium-weight fabric, 42″ to 45″ (106.7cm to 114.3cm) wide
- tape measure
- tailor's chalk
- fabric shears
- thread to match

Method
Step 1:
Press fabric.

Carefully measure the pillow you plan to cover. Measure, mark with tailor's chalk, and cut out a section of fabric 2 times the length of the pillow plus 20″ (50.8cm), and the width of the pillow plus 7″ (17.8cm).

Step 2:
Hem the short sides of the fabric section by measuring and turning raw edges under ½″ (1.3cm), then under 1½″ (3.8cm). Press; then stitch in place.

Fold fabric wrong side out so that side hems are centered with edges overlapping to form a tube 6″ (15.2cm) longer than the length of your pillow. (See fig. 1.)

Step 3:
Measure, mark, and stitch ½″ (1.3cm) seams along each open end of the tube. Trim excess at each corner. (See fig. 2.)

Turn tube right side out and press. Edge-stitch around the entire perimeter of the pillow sham. Form a border by measuring, marking, and stitching 3″ (7.6cm) in from the outside edge. (See fig. 3.)

Insert pillow.

Figure 2

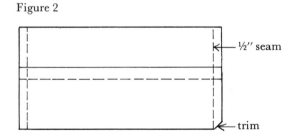

½″ seam

trim

Figure 1

center & overlap side hems

Figure 3

edgestitching

border stitching 3″ from edge

Ruffled Dressing Table Skirt

This is also a very pretty way to dress up an old bathroom sink. The materials and directions given are for a table approximately 40″ x 18″ x 28″ (101.6cm x 45.7cm x 71cm).

Materials
- 7½ yards (6.9m) lightweight fabric with all-over design, 44″ to 52″ (111.8cm to 132cm) wide
- 28 yards (25.6m) cable cord, ¼″ (6mm) thick
- tape measure
- tailor's chalk
- fabric shears
- dressmaker's pins
- small safety pin
- 1 yard (91.4cm) lightweight fabric in matching or contrasting color, 44″ x 52″ (111.8cm x 132 cm) wide
- thread to match
- 1⅙ yards (106.7cm) snap tape
- staple gun and staples

Method
Step 1:
Press fabric.

From the 1-yard (91.4cm) piece of fabric, prepare 20 yards (18.3m) of continuous bias 1¼″ (3.2cm) wide. (See Techniques, Bias Trim.) Cover 20 yards (18.3m) of cable cord with the bias strip as directed to make piping.

From the 7½-yard (6.9m) piece of fabric, measure and cut off a piece 228″ (5.8m) long. Measure this piece, mark with tailor's chalk, and divide it into three lengthwise strips, each 12″ (30.5cm) wide by 228″ (5.8m) long.

Step 2:
Measure and turn one long raw edge of each strip under ½″ (1.3cm) and press.

Using a zipper foot attachment, stitch piping to each fabric strip, topstitching as close as possible to the fold. (See fig. 1.)

Turn down top raw edge of one strip 2¼″ (5.7cm) and press. Make a ½″ (1.3cm) wide casing by stitching 1″ (2.5cm) below the fold and ½″ (1.3cm) below that. (See fig. 2.)

Step 3:
To form casings on remaining two strips, fold top raw edges down 1½″ (3.8cm) and press. Make a ½″ (1.3cm) wide casing by stitching ½″ (1.3cm) below the fold and ½″ (1.3cm) below that. (See fig. 3.)

Step 4:
Measure and cut remaining cable cord into three equal lengths. Attach safety pin to one end of each cord and pull them through casings. Gather each ruffle evenly to 78″ (198cm), allowing for a 1″ (2.5cm) turn-under on the sides. (See fig. 4.) Secure cording at each side by stitching in place.

Figure 1

Figure 2

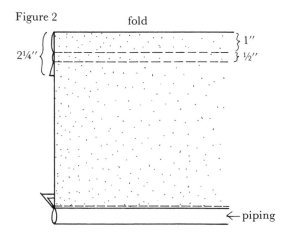

When each ruffle is completed, it should be as wide as the distance around the side, front, and opposite side of your dressing table.

Step 5:
To prepare a backing for the ruffles, measure the length of the dressing table from the top to the floor and add 4″ (10.2cm). Measure the distance around the side, front, and opposite side of the dressing table and add 2″ (5cm). Measure, mark, and cut out a piece of fabric according to those dimensions.

Fold top raw edge of backing onto wrong side 1″ (2.5cm) and press. Fold in each side edge 1″ (2.5cm), press, and stitch in place. Fold under bottom raw edge 2″ (5cm), press, and stitch in place. (See fig. 5.)

Step 6:
Position male side of snap tape on wrong side of backing along top fold. Pin-baste in place. Using a zipper foot attachment, stitch snap tape to backing. (See fig. 6.)

Staple female side of snap tape around side, front, and opposite side of the dressing table top, making sure the snaps align with the snaps on the backing.

Step 7:
Lay backing out on a flat surface, right side up, and place ruffle with 1″ (2.5cm) wide heading at top of backing. Make sure the casing rests on top of the snap tape and that the heading extends 1″ (2.5cm) beyond the fold edge of the backing. (See fig. 7.) Pin-baste in place.

Using a zipper foot attachment, stitch ruffle to backing directly above casing.

In the same manner, attach the bottom ruffle so that its bottom edge is even with the bottom hem edge of the backing.

Attach remaining middle ruffle to backing so that it is in between and in proportion to the other ruffles.

Snap completed ruffle skirt onto dressing table.

Figure 3

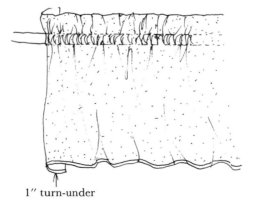

fold

1½″

½″
½″

Figure 4

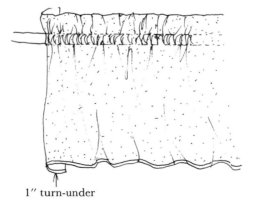

1″ turn-under

Figure 5

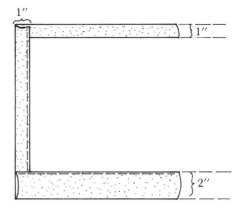

1″

1″

2″

Figure 6

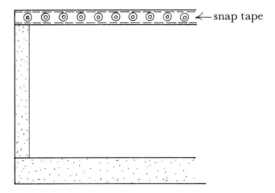

← snap tape

Figure 7

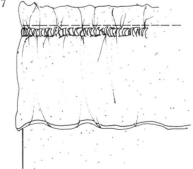

Ruffled Pillow Sham

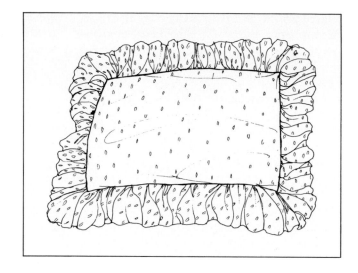

The materials and directions given are for a sham to fit a 20″ x 30″ (50.8cm x 76.2cm) pillow.

Materials
- 1½ yards (1.4m) lightweight fabric for the cover, 44″ (111.8cm) wide
- 1½ yards (1.4m) lightweight fabric for the ruffle, 44″ (111.8cm) wide
- tape measure
- tailor's chalk
- fabric shears
- thread to match
- 5 yards (4.6m) cable cord, ¼″ (6mm) thick
- small safety pin

Method
Step 1:
Press fabric.

Measure, mark with tailor's chalk, and cut out a 20″ x 30″ (50.8cm) x 76.2cm) rectangle from the cover fabric.

Step 2:
From the ruffle fabric, prepare 8 yards (7.3m) of continuous bias, 8″ (20.3cm) wide. (See Techniques, Bias Trim.)

Fold the bias in half lengthwise, right side out, and make a ½″ wide (1.3cm) casing 2½″ (6.4cm) in from the fold. (See fig. 1.)

Attach cable cord to safety pin and thread it through the casing. (See fig. 2.) Gather fabric to make a ruffle long enough to fit around the perimeter of the front of the pillow sham.

Step 3:
Beginning in the middle of one side, distribute ruffle fullness evenly and pin-baste the ruffle around the pillow sham top, with the widest part of the ruffle facing towards the center. (See fig. 3.) Continue pin-basting until both ends of the ruffle meet. Remove cording from casing. Overlap ends of ruffle to form a narrow flat-felled seam. (See Techniques, Seams.)

Attach ruffle to pillow sham top with a wide zig-zag stitch, sewing between the stitching lines that formed the ruffle casing. (See fig. 3.)

Step 4:
From remaining cover fabric, measure, mark, and cut out two 22″ x 20″ (55.9cm x 50.8cm) rectangles for the back of the pillow sham.

Place the two pieces of fabric on a flat surface, overlapping each at the center, forming a 31″ x 20″ (78.7cm x 50.8cm) rectangle.

Figure 1

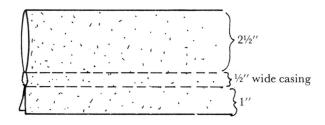

2½″
½″ wide casing
1″

Figure 2

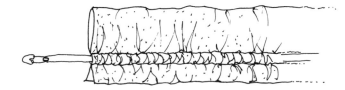

To make double 2" (5cm) hems on the overlapping ends, turn raw edges under 2" (5cm) and press. Turn under 2" (5cm) again and press. Stitch in place and press. (See fig. 4.)

Pin-baste the overlap in place. (See fig. 5.)

Step 5:
With right sides together, position sham back on top of the front, with ruffle section in between.

Using ½" (1.3cm) seams, stitch around entire pillow sham to attach back to front.

Trim and notch ruffle section to within ¼" (6mm) of the stitching line. Trim corners of the pillow sham front and back to remove excess fabric. (See fig. 6.)

Turn right side out and press. Slip a standard-size bed pillow inside.

Figure 3

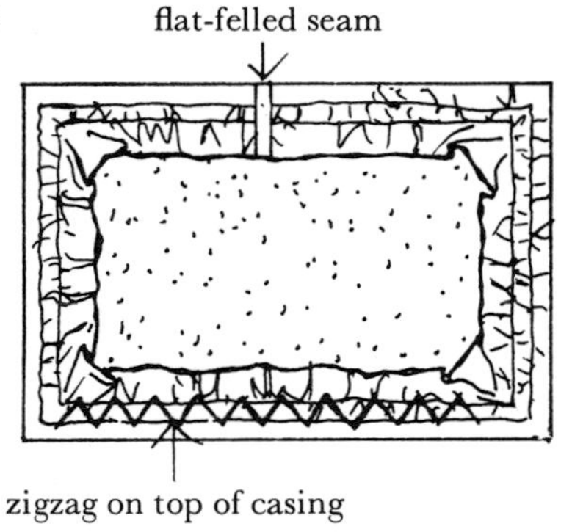

flat-felled seam

zigzag on top of casing

Figure 5

Figure 4

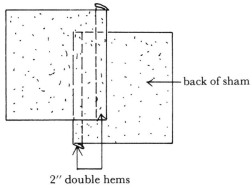

2" double hems

back of sham

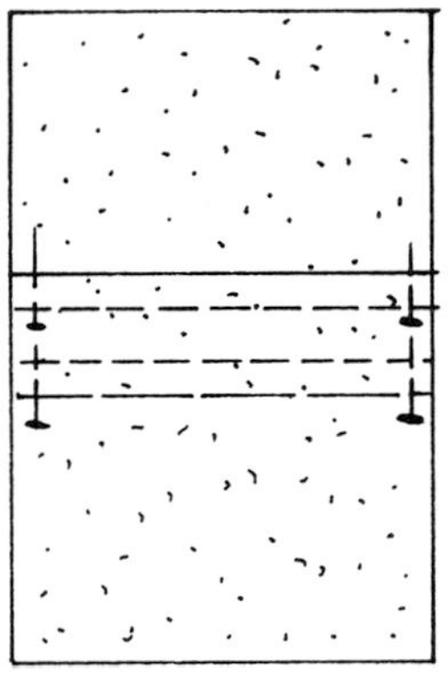

Figure 6

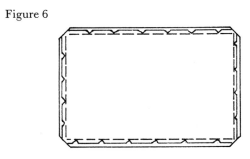

Little Boy's Bedroom

Little Boy's Bedroom

Campaign furniture was developed in the late 18th century and was used by British officers to store their gear while traveling in the colonies. The styling is simple with brass-bound corners and handles on either side. This type of furniture is ideally suited for your own little officer and can be purchased, unfinished, then stained to the desired color.

The floor here is covered with very durable indoor-outdoor carpeting in a dark color—perfect for planning strategic field maneuvers.

The bunk beds make sharing a bedroom or having a friend stay overnight relatively easy, especially when the bed unit folds out to reveal a desk and several drawers.

The 6-foot tall guardsman is really a clothes rack—plywood covered with felt, snappy brass buttons, and brass hooks. Your tiny general will learn to salute as he hangs up his clothes.

The covered mirror frame adds a military dash above the dresser and coordinates with the striped, channel-quilted bunk quilt. To cover the mirror frame, simply increase the dimensions and materials and follow the basic directions given in the Photography Studio for open-backed picture frames.

Finally, the drum hassock is just a handy little seat to have around. Cute to look at and fun to use, its base is a giant sausage tin from the meat market.

Bunk Quilt

This is an easy way to brighten up any bedroom. The directions given will apply to any size quilt.

Materials
- lightweight washable fabric in two or more contrasting colors
- polyester batting
- tape measure
- tailor's chalk
- fabric shears
- dressmaker's pins
- thread to match
- thread to contrast for quilting

Method
Step 1:
Press fabric.

Measure, mark with tailor's chalk, and cut out strips of fabric 8″ (20.3cm) wide and 12″ (30.5cm) longer than the length of the mattress. Cut enough strips for the top of the quilt so that the finished width is equal to the width of mattress plus 10″ to 12″ (25.4cm to 30.5cm) for a drop on each side. Join long sides of the strips together using ½″ (1.3cm) seams.

Repeat this procedure to cut and stitch strips for the underside of the quilt.

Step 2:
Measure, mark, and cut out one layer of polyester batting to equal the dimensions of the top and bottom fabric sections.

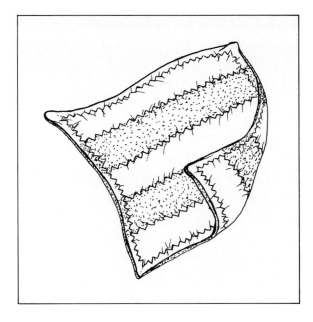

Place right sides of top and bottom quilt sections together, and place batting against one wrong side. (See fig. 1.)

Using ½″ (1.3cm) seams, pin-baste, then stitch around the quilt leaving an opening in the center of one end for turning. (See fig. 2.)

Trim batting as close as possible to stitching line; then trim seam allowances.

Turn quilt right side out, press, and slip-stitch opening closed.

Step 3:
To quilt, use contrasting thread and a large zigzag stitch. Topstitch ¼″ (6mm) in from the outer edges around entire quilt. (See fig. 3.)

Pin-baste each vertical seam, making sure the under seam is perfectly aligned with the top one. Topstitch in place along seam lines using a large zigzag stitch. (See fig. 3.)

Figure 1

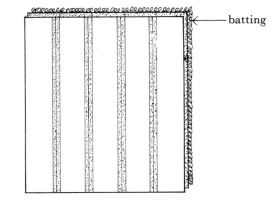

batting

Figure 2

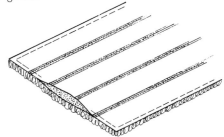

Figure 3

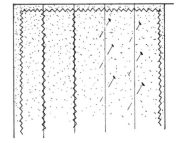

Drum Hassock

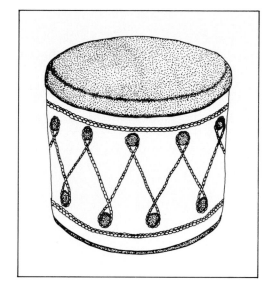

The amount of fabric listed under Materials to be used in the hassock are just enough. If you wish to make a larger hassock, increase the quantity of fabric accordingly.

Materials
- 1 round container with a top and bottom, wood, metal, or plastic, approximately 15″ (38cm) high and 15″ (38cm) in diameter
- polyester batting
- ½ yard (45.7cm) medium blue heavy-weight fabric, 44″ (111.8cm) wide
- ½ yard (45.7cm) red corduroy, 44″ (111.8cm) wide
- 2 ½ yards gold military braid trim, ½″ to ¾″ (1.3cm to 1.9cm) wide
- 16 shank-type, military design brass buttons, ¾″ (1.9cm) in diameter
- 5 yards (4.6m) red, round braid trim ⅛″ (3mm) in diameter
- tape measure
- tailor's chalk
- fabric shears
- cellophane tape
- thread to match

Method
Step 1:
Clean and dry round container thoroughly.

Measure, mark, and cut out a double layer of polyester batting approximately 22″ x 44″ (55.9cm x 111.8cm) to extend over the top and around the sides of the container. (See fig. 1.) The bottom should not be padded since it must sit on the floor.

Using double thread and large overcast stitches, sew the batting up the side of the container. (See fig. 1.) Make folds in the batting extending above the container's top to create a soft seat. Overcast the folds into position. (See fig. 2.)

Step 2:
Measure, mark, and cut out a section of blue fabric which is 1″ (2.5cm) larger than the height of the padded container and 1″ (2.5cm) larger than the distance around it, approximately 17″ x 48″ (43.2cm x 121.9cm).

Position and pin-baste the military braid onto the right side of the blue fabric 1¾″ (4.4cm) in from each long side. Using a zipper foot attachment, topstitch braid in place. (See fig. 3.)

Step 3:
About ½″ (1.3cm) below the top row of braid, attach a row of brass buttons 5½″ to 6″ (14cm to 15.2cm) apart depending upon the exact size of your container. (See fig. 3.)

Figure 1

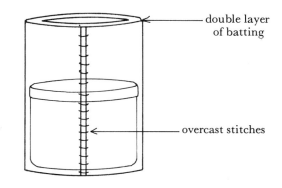

double layer of batting

overcast stitches

Figure 2

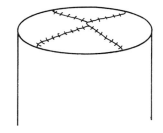

Sew the buttons in place with a ⅛″ (3mm) thread shank so that the red braid trim can be laced around them easily.

When the top row of buttons is complete, sew on a second row ½″ (1.3cm) above the lower row of braid. Position these buttons midway between the top row of buttons. (See fig. 3.)

(Continued)

Step 4:
Measure and divide the red corduroy in half lengthwise forming two sections, each 22″ x 18″ (55.9cm x 45.7cm). These will be used for the top and bottom of the hassock.

Fold each rectangle into quarters and press.

On one folded piece of fabric use a tape measure to mark off an arc 8″ (20.3cm) from the folded point. (See fig. 4.) Cut along the arc to form a 16″ (40.6cm) circle for the top of hassock.

On the second piece of folded fabric, measure and mark off an arc to form a 14″ (35.6cm) circle for the bottom of the hassock.

Step 5:
Turn blue fabric tube inside out.

Placing right sides together, pin-baste the 16″ (40.6cm) circle to the top end of the tube.

The circle will have quite a bit of fullness which is necessary to give the padded seat effect on the finished hassock. Ease the circle onto the tube with a series of small gathers, but with no pleats or puckers. To do this, hold the cylinder so that you can roll the blue fabric over your index finger; then roll the red fabric over the blue as you pin. This distributes the fullness evenly. It may be necessary to place pins about every inch along this seam to avoid puckering.

Use ½″ (1.3cm) seams on the circle, and make sure that the final seam line is ¾″ (1.9cm) from the braid on the blue fabric. Stitch seam in place.

Turn cover right side out and slip onto padded container.

Center remaining circle over bottom of container. Turn under raw edges and pin-baste in place ¾″ (1.9cm) from braid. (See fig. 5.) This will give a snug-fitting cover.

Slip-stitch bottom cover in place. (See Techniques, Hand Stitches.)

Step 6:
Cut one end of the red braid evenly; then wrap with tape. Lace braid around buttons. (See fig. 6.)

When lacing is complete, trim ends to meet each other exactly, and wrap with tape. Wind thread, the color of the braid, around the taped ends. (See fig. 7.)

Using double thread, tack braid in place underneath each button to reduce stress on buttons.

Figure 6

Figure 3

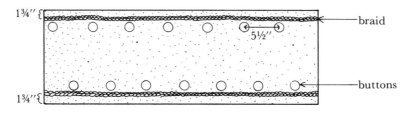

1¾″ {

braid

5½″

buttons

1¾″ {

Figure 4

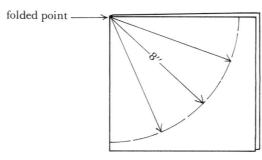

folded point

8″

Figure 5

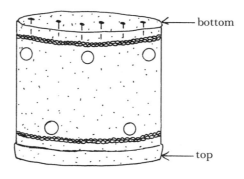

bottom

top

Figure 7

taped ends

thread

Guardsman Clothes Rack

🧵 🧵 🧵 🧵

This handy organizer may be made as large or as small as you wish. It is a bright and happy accent to either a bedroom or a rumpus room.

Materials
- 1 sheet of plywood, 6' x 2' (180cm x 60cm), ½" (1.3cm) thick
- yardstick or steel measure
- lead pencil, #2
- saber saw with fine blade
- sandpaper, medium grade
- dowel, ½" (1.3cm) in diameter
- ½ yard (45.7cm) bright red felt, 72" (182.9cm) wide
- ½ yard (45.7cm) black felt, 72" (182.9cm) wide
- ½ yard (45.7cm) royal blue felt, 72" (182.9cm) wide
- ¼ yard (22.9cm) white felt, 72" (182.9cm) wide
- paint—red, white, blue, and black
- 2 paintbrushes, each 2" (5cm) wide
- 2 yards (1.8m) gold braid trim, ½" (1.3cm) wide
- 9 to 11 shank-type, military design brass buttons, 1¾" (4.4cm) in diameter
- 6 brass hooks, approximately 1" (2.5cm) high and 1" (2.5cm) deep
- 1 brass belt buckle, 2" (5cm) square
- 7 screws, 1¼" (3.2cm) long, suitable for mounting figure (exact type depends upon wall construction)
- small electric drill
- staple gun and staples
- 12 wire paper clips, 1" (2.5cm) long
- tape measure
- fabric shears
- white household glue
- small disposable container

Method

Step 1:

Using a yardstick or steel measure, draw two lines to indicate the lengthwise and crosswise centers of the sheet of plywood. Following these guidelines, continue drawing lines 2" (5cm) apart over the entire sheet to make a grid for transferring the guardsman design.

Transfer the design from fig. 1 to the plywood.

Using the saber saw, cut out the plywood design.

Sand all edges and the surface of the guardsman's face.

Step 2:

Cut three ¼" (6mm) thick disks from the ½" (1.3cm) dowel for the eyes and nose of the guardsman.

Paint the eyes blue with a small black dot in the center for the iris. Paint the nose bright red. Allow disks to dry thoroughly.

Following the guardsman diagram, sketch and cut out a mustache and eyebrows from the remnants of the plywood sheeting. Paint these pieces black and allow to dry thoroughly.

(Continued)

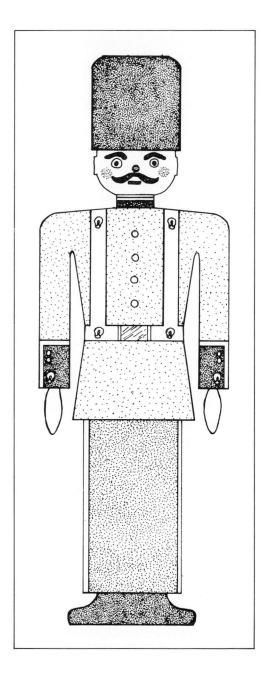

Mix red and white paint together to create a light flesh tone. Paint the face area of the guardsman with this color, and allow to dry thoroughly.

Using undiluted glue, glue the eyebrows, eyes, nose and mustache in place. (See fig. 2.)

Add a bit of red to the flesh-toned paint to create a slightly darker pink tone. Paint circles to indicate cheeks, and paint a red dot or line under the mustache to indicate a mouth. (See fig. 2.)

Step 3:
Pour glue into disposable container and dilute with water until it spreads evenly with a paintbrush—approximately one part water to four parts glue.

Sketch and cut out the differently colored felts to the exact shapes of the hat, shirt, collar, cuffs, trousers, straps, and belt as illustrated in fig. 1. Allow a 1″ (2.5cm) margin around the outside edges of each felt shape that meets the edge of the plywood shape. These margins will be glued or stapled to the wrong side of the plywood outline.

Be very careful when cutting the felt so that no parts on the front side overlap, causing the surface to look lumpy.

Brush diluted glue onto the areas to be covered and attach the felt pieces. Glue or staple outside margins to the back of the plywood. Allow felt shapes to dry thoroughly.

Step 4:
Screw brass hooks onto the shoulders, cuffs, and belt of the guardsman. (See fig. 3.)

Step 5:
Using a pencil, mark the location of the buttons down the center jacket front and on the cuffs as illustrated in fig. 1. Using a small

Figure 1

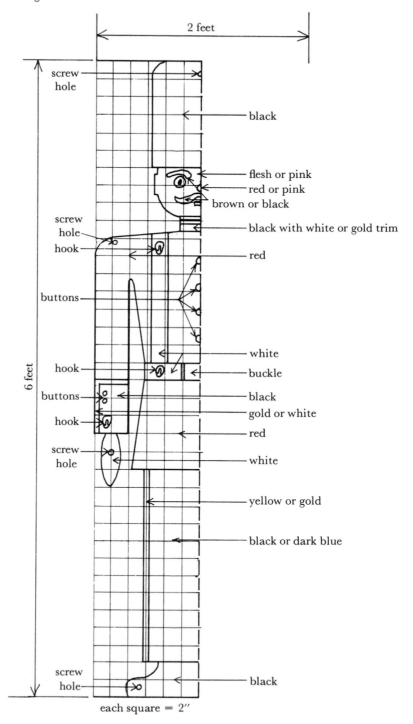

each square = 2″

electric drill, make ⅛″ (3mm) diameter holes through the plywood at each button location.

Unbend the paper clips. Pass a single wire through each buttonhole in the plywood from the wrong side to the front. Slip the wire through the button shank and back through the plywood to the wrong side. (See fig. 4.) Twist wire and flatten ends against the back to secure button in place. Repeat this procedure to attach all buttons.

Following the same procedure as for the buttons, drill holes for mounting and attaching the belt buckle.

Step 6:
Using undiluted glue, attach gold braid to the collar, cuffs, and trouser edges as illustrated in fig. 1. Allow trim to dry thoroughly.

Step 7:
Drill holes for the mounting screws at the top of the hat, shoulders, cuffs, and shoes. Mount figure on wall.

Paint the heads of the screws the same color as the fabric on which they are placed.

Figure 4

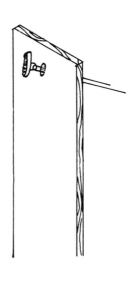

Figure 3

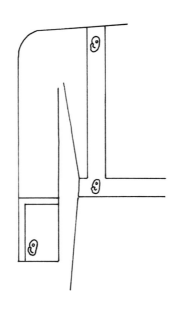

Figure 2

Mrs. Bathroom

Mrs. Bathroom

A private Shangri-la is created here with an abundance of greenery which flourishes in the warm humid atmosphere created by hours of hot, relaxing baths. Pale yellow walls and varying tones of stronger yellow on the fabric covered walls highlight the natural sunlight from the window to make this a refreshing and feminine room on even the gloomiest of days.

Here the fabric covered walls are stapled in place. Pasting fabric to walls in a room destined for excessive moisture creates a problem: most fabric-to-wall paste is water soluble so the fabric would forever be drooping.

The shirred shower curtains and tiebacks carry out the feminine statement and are relatively easy to make. The same method of making the curtain can be applied to making very pretty window curtains in any room.

Mundane bath accessories such as the tissue box and wastebasket are instantly transformed into pretty accents by covering them with scraps of fabric left over from the wall. The toilet lid cover is made from a solid color bath towel to match the ones currently in use in the room. To pull the entire room together, the floor is covered with plush wall-to-wall washable carpeting. To heighten the luxurious richness, try placing matching or contrasting protective throw rugs on top of the carpeting.

Shirred, Floor-Length Shower Curtains with Tiebacks

Each curtain panel is made of fabric 2½ times the length of a standard size bathtub, usually 56″ (1.4m), and extends from the ceiling to the floor, usually 8′ (2.4m) minus 1½″ (3.8cm). Panels may be narrower if desired.

The materials and directions given are for two 140″ x 94½″ (3.6m x 2.4m) curtain panels. This shower curtain creates a very feminine atmosphere and also works very well as a window curtain.

Materials for Curtains
- 14½ yards (13.3m) light- to medium-weight fabric, 60″ (152.4cm) wide
- tape measure
- tailor's chalk
- fabric shears
- 18 yards (16.5m) shirring tape, four strings wide
- dressmaker's pins
- thread to match
- curtain rod as long as shower curtain rod
- drapery hooks

Materials for Tiebacks
- ½ yard (45.7cm) light- to medium-weight fabric, 42″ to 45″ (106.7cm to 114.3cm) wide
- tape measure
- tailor's chalk
- fabric shears
- dressmaker's pins

- 2 large cup hooks
- 2 upholstery rings
- thread to match

Method for Curtains
Step 1:
Press fabric.

Measure, mark with tailor's chalk, and cut curtain fabric into five equal lengths, each 103½″ (2.6m) long. Cut one length in half lengthwise.

To make one panel, place right sides of two full widths and one half width together and join long sides with flat-felled seams. (See Techniques, Seams.) (See fig. 1.) Repeat procedure for remaining panel. Turn top edge of each panel down 1″ (2.5cm) onto wrong side and press. Turn down another 2″ (5cm) and press.

Step 2:
Cut shirring tape into four equal lengths each 4″ (10.2cm) narrower than the width of each panel. Place 2 lengths of shirring tape on wrong side of each panel, 2″ (5cm) in from each side and with ridges of drawstrings facing up and top edge of tape resting ⅛″ (3mm) inside pressed hem edge. Stitch in place ⅛″ (3mm) above and below each drawstring. (See fig. 2.)

Overlap the second length of shirring tape on top of the first length and stitch in place ⅛″ (3mm) above and below each drawstring.

Figure 1

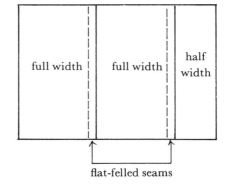

Pull drawstrings from both sides of each panel, and gather fabric evenly, making sure each curtain is 40″ (101.6cm) wide. Secure drawstring ends with several rows of stitching.

Step 3:
To make double hems along both side edges of each shirred panel, turn raw edges under 1″ (2.5cm) and press. Turn under 1″ (2.5cm) again and press. Stitch in place and press. (See fig. 3.)

To make the bottom hem, measure, mark, and turn up 6″ (15.2cm) to form a 5″ (12.7cm) hem with a 1″ (2.5cm) turn-under. Press, stitch in place, and press again.

Step 4:
Attach curtain rod 1½″ (3.8cm) below the ceiling, and hang shower curtains with drapery hooks.

Method for Tiebacks
Step 5:
Press fabric.

Measure, mark with tailor's chalk, and cut out two 9″ x 25″ (22.9cm x 63.5cm) rectangles. The overall width of the tiebacks may be smaller or larger, depending upon the effect you desire.

Step 6:
Fold rectangles in half lengthwise, wrong sides out. Using ½″ (1.3cm) seams, stitch long sides together. Turn tubes right side out and press.

Turn in raw edges at both ends of each tube, and topstitch in place.

Fold each end into a point, and tack in place on underside. (See fig. 4.) Wrap points around upholstery rings, and tack in place on underside. (See fig. 5.)

Step 7:
Attach cup hooks 30″ to 35″ (76.2cm to 88.9cm) up from the floor to hold tiebacks in position.

Figure 4

Figure 2

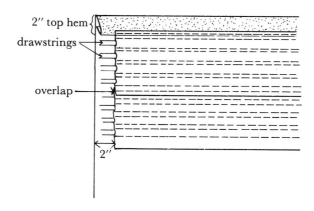

2″ top hem

drawstrings

overlap

2″

Figure 5

Figure 3

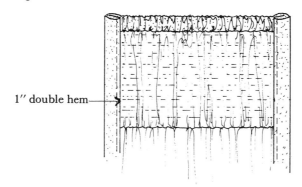

1″ double hem

Tissue Box Cover

This attractive bathroom accent may be constructed in any size you desire; simply select various size tissue boxes as the pattern.

Materials
- ½ yard (45.7cm) light- to medium-weight fabric, 36″ (91.4cm) wide
- 1 sheet foam-core board, 30″ x 40″ (76.2cm x 101.6cm)
- straight-edged ruler
- lead pencil, #2
- matte knife
- white household glue
- paintbrush, 2″ (5cm) wide
- small disposable container
- sandpaper
- fabric shears
- white masking tape
- 2 yards (1.8m) ribbon, braid, or rickrack trim, ¼″ (6mm) wide

Method
Step 1:
Using a pencil, draw sections of tissue box onto foam-core board in the following dimensions:

Top: 10¾″ x 5½″ (27.3cm x 14cm)
Each side: 10½″ x 2½″ (26.7cm x 6.4cm)
Each end: 5″ x 2½″ (12.7cm x 6.4cm)

Draw a ½″ (1.3cm) wide opening in the center of the top section 1″ (2.5cm) in from each end and 2½″ (6.4cm) in from each side.

Guiding the matte knife along the straight edge of the ruler, cut out shapes from foam-core board.

Cut out opening in top of box.

Step 2:
Glue foam-core board ends and side sections together. (See fig. 1.)

Glue top section in place letting it rest on top of sides and end sections.

Allow to dry thoroughly; then sand any rough edges. This completed shell will cover a regular-size tissue box.

Step 3:
Press fabric.

Measure, mark with tailor's chalk, and cut out a 15″ x 20″ (38cm x 50.8cm) rectangle of fabric.

Pour glue into disposable container and dilute with water until it spreads evenly with a paintbrush—approximately two parts glue to one part water.

Beginning with the top, brush diluted glue onto outside of foam-core shell. Center fabric right side up, and smooth into place.

Miter corners on short ends to create smooth edges. Trim excess fabric from underneath before allowing fabric to dry. (See fig. 2.)

Glue excess fabric to the inside of the shell.

Figure 1

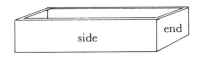

Figure 2

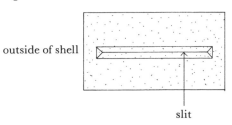

trim excess underneath to here

Figure 3

outside of shell

slit

Step 4:
Carefully slit fabric down center of the top opening, making a V-shape slash at each end. (See fig. 3.)

Push fabric into the opening, and glue in position on the underside. (See fig. 4.) Place white masking tape over raw edges.

Step 5:
When covered shell has dried thoroughly, trim as desired using undiluted glue to hold ribbon, braid, or rickrack securely in place.

Figure 4

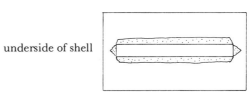

underside of shell

Toilet Lid Cover

Materials
- 1 bath towel
- fabric shears
- dressmaker's pins
- thread to match
- 2 yards (1.8m) cable cord, ¼″ (6mm) thick
- safety pin

Method
Step 1:
Press towel.

Place towel on top of toilet seat lid, and cut out a cover shape 2½″ (6.4cm) larger all the way around than the lid. (See fig. 1.) Zigzag stitch around the entire perimeter of the towel shape to keep edges from fraying.

Step 2:
Fold straight edge of toweling under ¾″ (1.9cm) to wrong side. Pin-baste, then stitch in place.

Fold curved edge of toweling under ¾″ (1.9cm) to wrong side to make a casing. Pin-baste; then stitch in place leaving ends open. (See fig. 2.)

Attach a large safety pin to the cable cord and gently pull it through the casing, shaping the cover as you do so. Pull cord ends even.

Put cover on toilet seat lid, and pull cord ends to make cover fit snugly. Tie ends together in a bow.

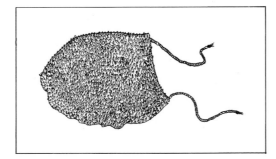

Figure 1

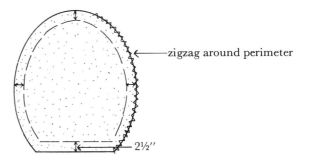

zigzag around perimeter

2½″

Figure 2

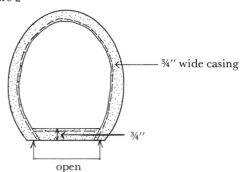

¾″ wide casing

¾″

open

Fabric Covered Walls—Staple

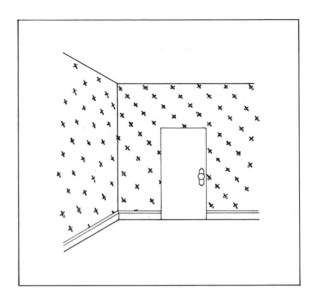

Before beginning this project, refer to Techniques, Walls.

Materials
- fabric
- wood stripping, ½″ (1.3cm) wide x ⅛″ (3mm) thick—enough for the perimeters of each wall to be covered, plus perimeters of doors and windows
- hammer
- headless nails
- push pins
- staple gun and staples
- fabric shears

Method

Step 1:
Nail wood stripping around entire perimeter of wall area to be covered, parallel to and flush with ceiling and baseboard or floor. If the wall area has doors or windows, nail stripping around them as well. (See fig. 1.)

Step 2:
Calculate exact amount of fabric needed by measuring height plus 4″ (10.2cm) and width plus 4″ (10.2cm) of each area to be covered. Do not subtract for door or window areas. If the fabric you select has a repeating pattern, add one extra repeat in length to your calculations.

Step 3:
Plumb line the wall to establish vertical fabric placement. (See Techniques, Walls.)

Step 4:
Press fabric and cut off selvages.

Cut fabric into lengths 4″ (10.2cm) longer than the height of the area to be covered. If more than one width of fabric is needed, match design, pin-baste, and machine-stitch fabric lengths together, allowing ½″ (1.3cm) seams. Press seams open.

Allow 2″ (5cm) extra fabric at top and bottom of each wall area to be covered for correct pattern alignment. Beginning in a corner, tack fabric to wood stripping with push pins inserted into wood stripping at 6″ (15.2cm) intervals. Push-pin fabric into corners as well. (Two people working together can comfortably handle four lengths of fabric sewn together.)

Step 5:
Align fabric. Return to starting point, and staple fabric in position, turning raw edges under and placing staples approximately 1″ (2.5cm) apart in wood stripping along ceiling and down the sides. (See fig. 2.) Gently pull and smooth out wrinkles as you staple. Lastly, staple fabric in place at baseboard or floor area.

Staples may be concealed by applying shoe polish or colored felt-tip markers along the backs of the staples before dropping them into the staple gun.

Figure 1

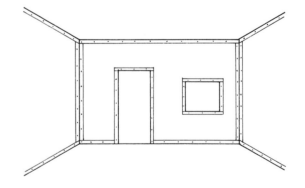

Around windows and doors, follow above procedure and cut out openings allowing for a 2″ (5cm) excess around the perimeters. Turn raw edges under, and staple in place. *Do not* cut out for doors or windows before stapling fabric to the walls; the margin for error is too great.

For a more finished effect, glue braid, ribbon, or self-welting on top of staples with undiluted white household glue.

Figure 2

Covered Drum Wastebasket

If the fabric you select is light in color, make sure the wastebasket is white or off-white or the fabric will appear tinted. Simply spray-paint the drum inside and out, and allow to dry thoroughly.

Materials
- drum wastebasket, 10½″ (26.7cm) high, 9½″ (24cm) in diameter
- ½ yard (45.7cm) medium- to heavyweight fabric, 44″ (111.8cm) wide
- tape measure
- tailor's chalk
- fabric shears
- small disposable container
- white household glue
- paintbrush, 3″ (7.6cm) wide
- ribbon, braid, or rickrack (optional)

Method
Step 1:
Press fabric.

Measure, mark with tailor's chalk, and cut out a section of fabric the exact height and circumference of the wastebasket.

Step 2:
Pour glue into disposable container and dilute with water until it spreads evenly with a paintbrush—approximately two parts glue to one part water.

Beginning at the seam, brush diluted glue onto outside of wastebasket from top to bottom in 8″ (20.3cm) sections. Carefully smooth fabric onto drum. Allow to dry thoroughly.

When covered wastebasket has dried thoroughly, trim as desired using undiluted glue to attach ribbon, braid, or rickrack.

Mr. Bathroom

Mr. Bathroom

A bathroom just for him—no frills and quite masculine—depicts elegance along with practicality. The room is large enough to encompass a space for exercising and an area for relaxing after an invigorating shower or bath.

Soft tones of brown and gold lighten the deep chocolate brown of the tiles surrounding the bath area and highlight the Spanish-type floor tiles with the touches of ecru and soft caramel-yellow patterning. The caramel color walls continue to create a softly spacious effect, while the white furniture and shutters add a brightening accent to the room.

The shower curtain adds a bright note to this neutral area. Reaching from floor to ceiling, it is very tailored with loops at the top rather than the traditional plastic rings. A protective plastic liner is easily buttoned into place on the tub side of the curtain.

The magazine rack next to the tub is a handy way to organize your favorite reading material.

The louvered shutters attached to the outer side edges of the window deceive the eye by making the window appear wider. Shutters across the top of the window are shaped and nailed into place to create a lengthened window effect. Both enlarging techniques are good tricks to keep in mind for any small room.

Since this room offers the luxury of space, a chaise lounge with terry covered foam cushions completes the neutral color theme, as does the terry covered foam exercise mat. When not in use, the mat can be rolled up and easily stored. To make a thick exercise mat for your man, adapt the instructions for the floor mats in the Oriental Porch.

The clothesline covered planter completes the casually masculine effect while hiding an ugly pot. Instructions for the planter appear in the Wicker Porch.

Floor-Length Shower Curtain with Loops

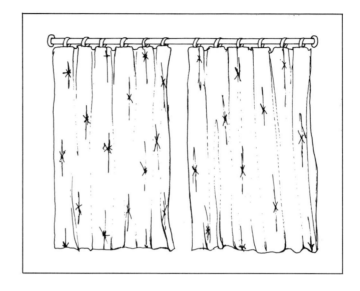

The materials and directions given are for a curtain the width of a standard-size shower curtain, 72″ (182.9cm), and the length from the bottom of the shower curtain rod to the floor, 80″ (203.2cm).

Materials
- 5½ yards (5m) light- to medium-weight fabric, 42″ to 45″ (106.7cm to 114.3cm) wide
- tape measure
- tailor's chalk
- fabric shears
- dressmaker's pins
- 2 yards (1.8m) buckram, 4″ (10.2cm) wide
- thread to match
- buttonhole twist to match
- 12 buttons to match, ⅞″ (2.1cm) in diameter
- shower curtain liner

Method
Step 1:
Press fabric.

Measure, mark with tailor's chalk, and cut fabric into two 89″ (226cm) lengths.

With right sides facing, join two long sides together with a flat-felled seam. (See Techniques, Seams.) Trim excess fabric from each side of the panel to make it 76″ (193cm) wide by 89″ (226cm) long, with the flat-felled seam running top to bottom in the exact center. (See fig. 1.)

To make double hems along both side edges, turn edges under 1″ (2.5cm) and press. Turn under 1″ (2.5cm) again and press. Stitch in place and press.

Step 2:
From remaining fabric, measure, mark, and cut out three strips, each 4½″ (11.4cm) wide and the full width of the fabric long.

Fold strips in half lengthwise, wrong sides out. Using ¼″ (6mm) seams, stitch long sides together to make three tubes.

Turn tubes so that seams are off center. Press seams open while pressing tubes flat.

For first loop, stitch across tube 8½″ (21.6cm) from end of tube. Cut ¼″ (6mm) beyond the stitching line. (See fig. 2.) Repeat procedure to make a total of 12 loops, four loops from each of the three tubes.

Turn all loops right side out and press.

Figure 1

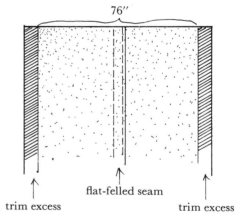

76″

flat-felled seam

trim excess   trim excess

Step 3:
At closed end, make a 1″ (2.5cm) long buttonhole in the center of each loop ½″ (1.3cm) from the end. (See fig. 3.) (See Techniques, Hand-Bound Buttonholes.)

Step 4:
To make a heading for the shower curtain, measure, mark, and cut out a 2″ x 72″ (5cm x 182.9cm) strip of buckram. Pin buckram to wrong side of curtain ½″ (1.3cm) below raw edge at top. (See fig. 4.)

Pin loops to heading on right side of shower curtain matching buttonholes to the holes in the shower curtain liner. If no liner is used, space the buttonhole centers on the two end loops 1½″ (3.8cm) in from the side edges. Position the remaining loops evenly across the width of the curtain with their buttonhole centers 6¼″ (15.9cm) apart. (See fig. 5.) Pin, then stitch in place along top, using ½″ (1.3cm) seams.

Turn attached loops under along stitching line. Fold buckram section down and fold loops back up. Stitch across buckram ¼″ (6mm) up from bottom fold line. Move up ½″ (1.3cm) and stitch across. Move up another ½″ (1.3cm) and stitch across. Move up another ½″ (1.3cm) and stitch across. (See fig. 6.)

Step 5:
To hem the curtain, measure, mark, and turn up the bottom edge 6″ (15.2cm) to form a 5″ (12.7cm) hem with a 1″ (2.5cm) turn-under. Pin-baste, then stitch in place and press.

Hang shower curtain, adjusting loops to proper length; mark button placement with pins. Sew on buttons and hang shower curtain with liner buttoned to it.

Figure 2

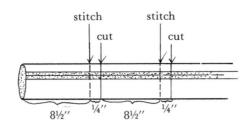

Figure 3

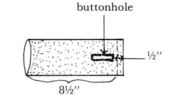

Figure 4

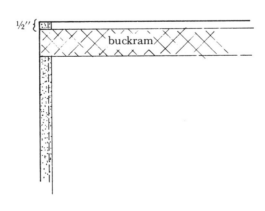

Figure 5

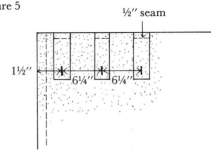

Figure 6

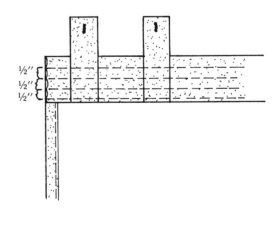

Stenciled Magazine Rack

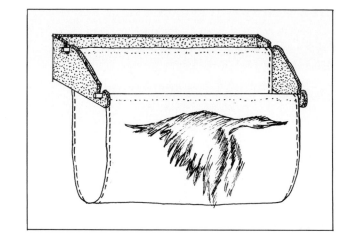

Test the paint on the fabric you have selected. Most oil or latex paints can be used on heavyweight fabrics without the paint running or smudging. Select a paint that will not spread through the fibers. If the paint you use on the wooden rack is not suitable for your fabric, purchase "fabric paint" at a crafts shop.

Materials for Wooden Rack
- 1 board plywood, pine, or similar wood, 27½″ x 3¾″ x ½″ (69.9cm x 9.5cm x 1.3cm)
- jigsaw
- drill with ¼″ (6mm) bit
- white household glue
- 8 headless nails, ¾″ to 1″ (1.9cm to 2.5cm) long
- 2 wooden dowels, each 16″ (40.6cm) long by ¾″ (1.9cm) thick
- 1 sheet medium-grade sandpaper, 8½″ x 11″ (21.6cm x 27.9cm)
- paint
- paintbrush, 1″ (2.5cm) wide
- 2 wood or masonry screws, depending on wall construction, each 1½″ x ¼″ (3.8cm x 6mm)
- screwdriver

Materials for Canvas Holder
- ½ yard (45.7cm) heavyweight fabric, 44″ (111.8cm) wide
- tape measure
- tailor's chalk
- fabric shears

- heavy-duty thread, same color as paint
- stencil
- tracing paper
- lead pencil, #2
- 1 sheet medium-weight cardboard, 8½″ x 11″ (21.6cm x 27.9cm)
- matte knife
- toothbrush or similar small, firm bristle brush
- wooden cutting board covered with brown wrapping paper
- thumbtacks
- fabric paint

Method for Wooden Rack
Step 1:
Using a jigsaw, cut two 6¼″ (15.9cm) sections from the sides of the wooden board. (See fig. 1.)

Following fig. 2, use the jigsaw to shape the two side sections with notches for the dowels.

On remaining middle section of wood, drill two ¼″ (6mm) holes for wood or masonry screws, 2″ (5cm) in from the sides and 1″ (2.5cm) down from the top. (See fig. 3.)

Step 2:
Spread white household glue along the 3¾″ (9.5cm) sides of the middle section of wood.

Position a notched side section to rest exactly on one glued end of the middle piece of wood. Nail in place with four, evenly spaced, headless nails. (See fig. 4.) Repeat procedure for opposite side.

Figure 1

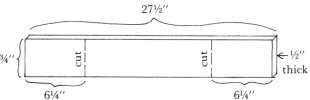

Figure 2

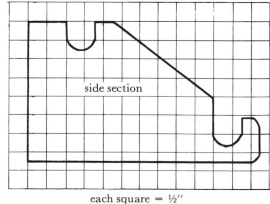

side section

each square = ½″

Step 3:
Sand all wood surfaces—notches, drilled holes, joined edges, and dowels until smooth.

Paint the rack and dowels and allow to dry thoroughly.

Attach rack to wall using wood or masonry screws.

Method for Canvas Holder

Step 4:
Press fabric.

Measure, mark with tailor's chalk, and cut out a 15″ x 44″ (38cm x 111.8cm) rectangle of fabric.

With right sides together and using ½″ (1.3cm) seams, stitch short edges together to form a tube. Press seam open. Turn top and bottom raw edges of tube down ½″ (1.3cm) and stitch in place ¼″ (6mm) in from the fold lines. Turn tube right side out. Position tube so that the seam is 2″ (5cm) in from one side fold.

Step 5:
To make dowel casings, topstitch directly on top of edge stitching lines, beginning 2″ (5cm) in from edge fold and stitching to the center of the tube. (See fig. 5.)

Remove tube from sewing machine, and turn seam away from you. Topstitch again directly on top of edge stitching lines, beginning 2″ (5cm) in from the opposite edge fold and stitching to the center of the tube. (See fig. 6.) Stitching in this manner keeps the tube from stretching out of shape.

Step 6:
Following fig. 7, transfer the duck stencil design onto tracing paper. Cut out design.

Transfer the design to cardboard by drawing around the traced outline. Carefully cut around the outline of the stencil with a matte knife.

Position cardboard stencil so that the top of the design is 2½″ (6.4cm) below the tube

fold which is near the seam. (See fig. 8.) Make sure seam is on the underside of the tube. Secure stencil in place on wooden cutting board with thumbtacks.

Step 7:
Lightly dip toothbrush into paint, being very careful not to put too much paint on it at one time. For best results, coat only ⅛″ (3mm) of the bristles with paint.

Paint the entire outlined area, brushing from the outer edges of the stencil toward the center of the design.

Allow fabric to dry thoroughly.

Slide dowels through casings at each end of fabric tube, and place dowels in rack notches.

Figure 3
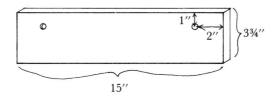

Figure 4
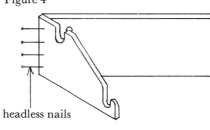
headless nails

Figure 5
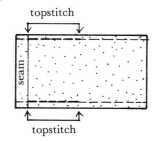
topstitch
seam
topstitch

Figure 6
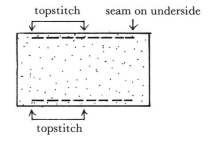
topstitch   seam on underside
topstitch

Figure 7
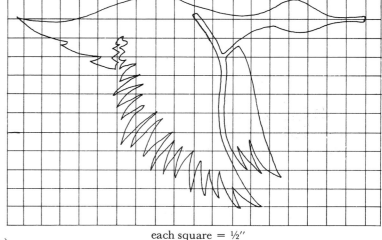
each square = ½″

Figure 8
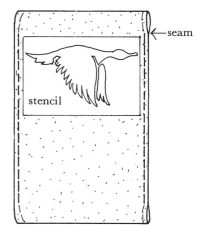
seam
stencil

Little Girl's Bathroom

Little Girl's Bathroom

This is a bathroom to grow in—at present it has a very feminine and captivating charm for your "little lady." As the years progress, it will be a simple matter to transform the room into one of more womanly sophistication.

The walls are all painted in a shade of pale pink to soften and extend the deeper pink of the tiles around the tub area. White used around the baseboard and for the wooden sink cabinet creates an expansive feeling which is extended to the off-white, wall-to-wall, washable plush carpeting.

Right now, the felt bunny grow chart adds a youthful touch to the room. It can easily be replaced later with a full-length mirror. The bunny motif is extended onto the towels to add a light-hearted enchantment reminiscent of a certain well-known white rabbit. The looking glass above the sink is an old mirror with a fabric covered frame which also adds a softening dimension to the wall area.

The washable, ruffle trimmed shower curtains and matching valance extend the luxurious feeling clear to the ceiling.

The terry covered plywood cube is ideal for any age and many uses. When young, your little lady may use it as an aide for reaching the sink. When she is older, it can be turned into a handy tub-side table or bench.

Ruffled Shower Curtain and Valance

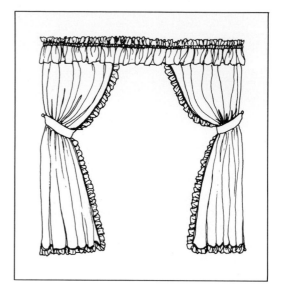

The materials and directions given are for two shower curtain panels, each approximately 60″ x 85″ (152.4cm x 215.9cm), and for one valance, 150″ x 13″ (381cm x 33cm). Directions for the tiebacks appear in the Mrs. Bathroom.

Materials
- 2 king-size flat sheets or 18¼ yards (16.7m) light- to medium-weight fabric, 36″ (91.4cm) wide
- 6 yards (5.5m) sturdy cotton string
- 1 safety pin
- 13 yards (11.9m) trim, ¼″ (6mm) wide
- 1 expansion curtain rod
- tape measure
- tailor's chalk
- fabric shears
- thread to match

Method for Valance
Step 1:
Remove hems from sheets and press.

Measure, mark with tailor's chalk, and cut off a strip 20″ (50.8cm) wide across the top of each sheet. Using ½″ (1.3cm) seams, stitch strips together end to end to make one long strip. Trim to 150″ (381cm). Press seams open.

Step 2:
Turn under the short end raw edges to make 1″ (2 5cm) hems with a ¼″ (6mm) turn-under. Stitch in place.

Fold under top raw edge 3½″ (8.9cm). Stitch 1″ (2.5cm) below top fold. Turn under ½″ (1.3cm) along the raw edge, and stitch in place to form a casing. (See fig. 1.)

Across the bottom of the valance strip, measure and make a 3″ (7.6cm) hem with a ½″ (1.3cm) turn-under. Pin-baste, then stitch in place. (See fig. 1.)

Stitch trim in place across width of top and bottom stitching lines on valance.

Method for Ruffled Curtain
Step 3:
From each of the remaining sheets, cut a rectangle 60″ x 90″ (152.4cm x 228.6cm) and four strips, each 10″ x 90″ (25.4cm x 228.6cm). (See fig. 2.)

Press top of each panel under 3½″ (8.9cm) with a ¼″ (6mm) turn-under. Do not stitch the hem now.

Turn under bottom and side raw edges to form a 1″ (2.5cm) hem with a ¼″ (6mm) turn-under around the panel. Stitch the outside hem which will not have a ruffle attached. The remaining sides will be stitched as the ruffle is attached.

Step 4:
To make the ruffle for the curtain panels, stitch the four narrow fabric strips together end to end to make one strip 357″ (9m) long. Repeat with remaining four strips. Press seams open.

Using ½″ (1.3cm) seams and with right sides together, stitch along the length of the strips to make two tubes. Turn tubes right side out.

Press tubes so that the lengthwise seam is just underneath one edge of the ruffle. Topstitch along this edge to secure the seam line.

Step 5:
Stitch two lines, 1″ (2.5cm) and 1½″ (3.8cm) inside the topstitched edge to form a ½″ (1.3cm) wide casing. Tie one end of the cotton string to a safety pin and pull through the casing. Gather fabric until the ruffles are the exact length of one side and the bottom of the curtain panel, approximately 142½″ (3.6m).

Step 6:
Pin-baste ruffles to the right side of each curtain panel so that the casing rests ¾″ (1.9cm) inside the outer edge. Start pinning at the top edge of the top hem. Remember that

you didn't stitch the top hems before so that now you can open them flat for ease in attaching the ruffles.

Using large stitches, hand-baste the ruffles to the inside edges and bottoms of the curtain panels.

Step 7:
Pin-baste the ¼″ (6mm) wide trim directly on top of the casing. (See fig. 3.) Turn under raw edges of ruffle and hem by machine.

Machine-stitch from the top through the trim, ruffle casings, and curtain panels to attach ruffles and hem the sides and bottoms.

Stitch top hems beginning at the outside edge and stitching toward the inside ruffled edges. Finish top hems by hand under the ruffles.

Step 8:
Move the shower curtain rod so that it is approximately 8″ (20.3cm) below the ceiling.

Place extension rod approximately 2″ (5cm) below the ceiling.

Make sure the rod placements are correct according to the length of the valance and the finished panels. Thread valance onto shower curtain rod and panels onto extension rod.

Figure 1

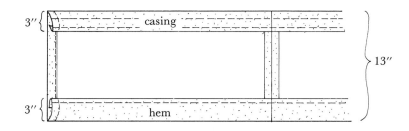

Figure 2

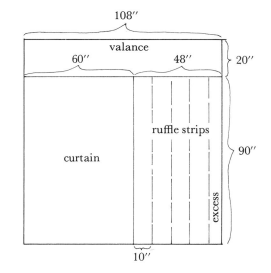

Figure 3

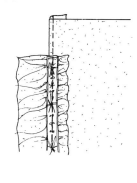

Bunny Bath Towel

Alice in Wonderland spent a lot of time chasing the White Rabbit; your young Miss will too when she sees that he is as close as her bath towel.

Materials
- 1 large piece of tracing paper
- lead pencil, #2
- fabric shears
- 1 bath towel
- 1 hand towel in a contrasting color
- ½ yard (45.7cm) fusible bonding web
- thread in a contrasting color
- polyester fiber fill

Method
Step 1:
Transfer the bunny design in fig. 1 onto a large piece of tracing paper.

Cut out tracing. Pin it in place on top of right side of hand towel, and cut out bunny design.

Cut out fusible bonding web in the shape of the bunny design.

Step 2:
Place fusible bonding web under the terry bunny. Center both on the right side of the bath towel 2½" (6.4cm) up from the bottom edge. Press to fuse design to towel, following manufacturer's directions.

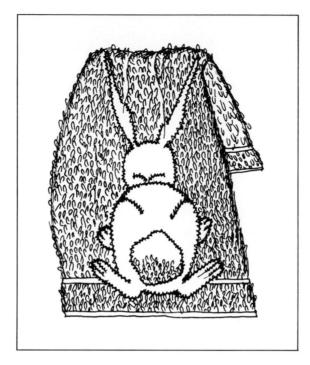

Step 3:
Use scrap hand-towel pieces for testing, and set your sewing machine at a narrow zigzag stitch. Use as many stitches per inch as possible.

Appliqué the bunny to the towel using the narrowest zigzag stitch and a contrasting thread color. For best results, stitch once around the bunny including the design lines which indicate neck, shoulders, and toes. After this, broaden the zigzag stitch very slightly and repeat stitching over the outline and design lines.

Figure 1

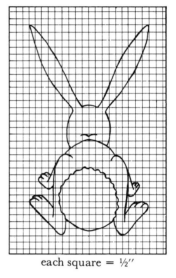

each square = ½"

Step 4:
Sketch a pattern for the bunny's tail on tracing paper. (See fig. 1.) Cut out tracing. Pin it in place on right side of remaining piece of hand towel and cut out tail.

Place a small wad of polyester fiber fill under tail section. Pin-baste tail in position. Attach to bunny using the same zigzag top stitching technique as in Step 3.

Bunny Grow Chart

Materials

- tracing paper
- lead pencil, #2
- scissors
- tape measure
- ¾ yard (68.6cm) white terry cloth, 44" (111.8cm) wide
- ½ yard (45.7cm) contrasting terry cloth, 44" (111.8cm) wide
- ¾ yard (68.6cm) felt, 60" (152.4cm) wide
- 2 yards (1.8m) fusible bonding web
- 1 spool thread, gray or brown
- 1 spool thread to match contrasting terry cloth
- 7" (17.8cm) square of fabric suitable for a bow tie
- embroidery floss or tapestry wool
- embroidery needle
- 24" (61cm) wooden dowel, ¾" (1.9cm) thick
- 2 wooden curtain rod brackets

Method

Step 1:
Transfer the letters needed for your child's name from the alphabet chart appearing in the Country French Living Room, and the bunny outline from fig. 1 onto large pieces of tracing paper.

Cut out tracings. Pin letters in place on right side of contrasting terry cloth; cut out letters.

Pin bunny shape in place on right side of white terry cloth; cut out bunny. Pin shapes for tummy and the inside ears on the contrasting terry cloth; cut out shapes.

Cut out fusible bonding web in the shapes of the bunny design and the letters.

Step 2:
Measure, mark with tailor's chalk, and cut out a 23" x 48" (58.4cm x 121.9cm) rectangle of felt. Turn the felt so that the 48" (121.9cm) side becomes the length.

Place fusible bonding web under terry bunny. Position the terry bunny 13" (33cm) up from the bottom raw edge of the felt rectangle. The lower hand of the bunny should rest 1½" (3.8cm) from the side raw edge. Press to fuse design in place, following manufacturer's directions. Do not fuse bunny's right hand to the felt.

Step 3:
Use scrap terry towel pieces for testing, and set sewing machine at a narrow zigzag stitch. Use as many stitches per inch as possible.

Appliqué the bunny shape to the felt using the narrow zigzag stitch and gray or brown thread. Do not stitch around the bunny's right hand. For best results, stitch once around the bunny including the design lines which indicate the left-hand fingers. Then broaden the zigzag stitch very slightly and repeat stitching over the outline and design lines.

(Continued)

Step 4:
Place fusible bonding web under terry letters. Position the letters 5½″ (14cm) above the bottom raw edge and centered under the bunny; *do not* start letters at the left hand margin. Press to fuse letters in place, following manufacturer's directions.

Appliqué the letters and all contrasting bunny parts to the felt, using the same zigzag stitches as in Step 3.

Step 5:
Measure, mark, and cut out a 6″ (15.2cm) square of fabric for the bow tie. Fold it in half, wrong side out. Using ¼″ (6mm) seams, stitch around the fabric, leaving a small opening in the center of one side for turning. Turn right side out, press, and slip-stitch opening closed.

Gather the rectangle in the center to form a bow tie. Using a short piece from remaining strip of fabric, make a center for the tie. (See fig. 2.) Baste center in place.

Attach the bow tie to the bunny figure with small overcast stitches.

Step 6:
Beginning at the bunny's right hand, pin-baste tape measure to the felt backing, ending at the bottom raw edge of the felt. The 50″ (127cm) mark should be in the bunny's right hand, and the marking for 18″ (45.7cm) should be at the bottom edge. Trim excess from top and bottom of tape measure.

Using a straight stitch, sew the tape measure to the felt along both edges.

Fold the bunny's right hand to cover the 50″ (127cm) mark. Appliqué the hand in place using the same zigzag stitches as in Step 3, and making sure to stitch the lines for the fingers.

Step 7:
Use embroidery floss or tapestry yarn to embroider the bunny eyes, nose, and mouth. (See fig. 1.)

Step 8:
Turn the top raw edge of the felt panel under 2″ (5cm). Stitch across the panel to form a rod casing.

Hold the completed wall hanging against the wall to measure the exact position for the dowel brackets. The brackets should be approximately 64″ (162.6cm) above the floor so that the bottom of the hanging is 18″ (45.7cm) above the floor.

Mount the dowel brackets following manufacturer's directions.

Slip dowel through rod casing and place in wall brackets.

Figure 1

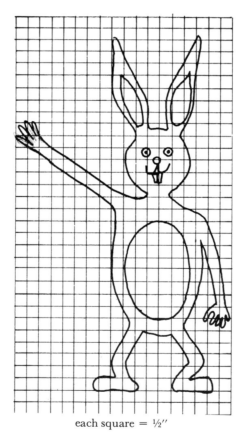

each square = ½″

Figure 2

Through-the-Looking-Glass Medicine Cabinet

Alice in Wonderland had a looking glass for day dreaming. Your little Miss can have her very own looking glass too. This is an easy way to dress up the bath eliminating the "sterile" appearance of a metal medicine cabinet.

If your medicine cabinet is recessed, simply fit an open-back picture frame around it, nail it in place, and paint it a bright accent color. If your medicine cabinet extends out from the wall, cut decorative molding to size with mitered corners, paint the molding, and glue it in place on top of the chrome frame. You might also try this technique to dress up a door or window frame.

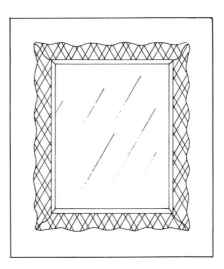

Little Boy's Bathroom

Little Boy's Bathroom

This is the ideal bath for any young lad who dreams of adventures on the high seas.

This room is not only striking in appearance but practical and easy to care for as well. The entire room is white—tub area, wall, and tiled floor—the perfect background for your sailor's favorite color combinations. White also tends to make a small space appear larger, and any colors used in this area will appear bright.

The shower curtain is the focal point of the room and being floor length heightens its drama, The washable sailboat motif is appliquéd onto the center of the washable fabric. A separate protective plastic liner is hung directly behind the outer curtain on the same hooks.

An inexpensive footlocker affords needed storage space for towels and treasures of the sea. Here the trunk is covered in practical, rugged terry cloth and embellished with a felt anchor design and braided cord trim. The trunk is a good step stool for reaching the sink, or it can serve as an excellent tub-side table or bench.

A miniature ship's ladder is the towel rack in the room—ideal in any area where towels must be hung. The sailboat motif of the shower curtain is extended and appliquéd onto the towels as well.

The once plain-looking medicine chest is embellished with the same rope that was used to make the towel rack. It is simply wrapped around the outside of the cabinet and glued in place, drawing the nautical motif around the room.

Of course every seafaring person needs a swag bag, and this one is of practical, heavy-duty washable fabric—ideal for soiled laundry and an easy way to cart it all to the washing machine.

Appliquéd Nautical Shower Curtain

The materials and directions given are for a 72″ (182.9cm) square appliquéd shower curtain. Without the appliqué, you have a plain, standard tub-size shower curtain.

Materials for Curtain
- 4½ yards (4.1m) light- to medium-weight solid color fabric, 42″ to 45″ (106.7cm to 114.3cm) wide
- tape measure
- tailor's chalk
- fabric shears
- dressmaker's pins
- 2 yards (1.8m) buckram, 4″ (10.2cm) wide
- thread to match
- grommeter and twelve large grommets
- shower curtain liner
- shower curtain hooks

Materials for Appliqué
- 2 yards (1.8m) lightweight canvas (may be interfacing canvas), 36″ (91.4cm) wide or wider
- ¾ yard (68.6cm) of each of two contrasting blue fabrics (ideally medium-blue denim and a print), 42″ to 45″ (106.7cm to 114.3cm) wide
- ½ yard (45.7cm) bright colored corduroy, 42″ to 45″ (106.7cm to 114.3cm) wide
- ¼ yard (22.9cm) dark percale or broadcloth, 42″ to 45″ (106.7cm to 114.3cm) wide
- ¼ yard (22.9cm) white dotted swiss, 36″ to 45″ (91.4cm to 114.3cm) wide
- 1 yard (91.4cm) tan or medium-brown grosgrain ribbon or braid, ½″ (1.3cm) wide
- 8 yards (7.3m) fusible bonding web, 18″ (45.7cm) wide

Method for Curtain
Step 1:
Press curtain fabric.

Measure, mark with tailor's chalk, and cut it into two equal lengths, each 81″ (205.7cm) long.

With right sides together, join two long sides together with a flat-felled seam. (See Techniques, Seams.) Trim excess fabric from each side to make curtain 76″ (193cm) wide by 81″ (205.7cm) long with the flat-felled seam running top to bottom in the exact center.

Step 2:
To make double hems along both side edges, turn edges under 1″ (2.5cm) and press. Turn under 1″ (2.5cm) again and press. Stitch hems in place and press again.

Step 3:
To make the heading, first measure, mark, and cut out a strip of buckram 2½″ (6.4cm) wide.

Measure, mark, and press top of curtain down 3″ (7.6cm) to form a 2½″ (6.4cm) hem with a ½″ (1.3cm) turn-under. Place buckram inside heading, wrapping raw edge of fabric around it. Stitch in place ⅛″ (3mm)

from each fold line along both lengthwise edges of the buckram; press. The heading is now 2½″ (6.4cm) wide.

Step 4:
To make the bottom hem, measure, mark, and turn up the bottom 6″ (15.2cm) to form a 5″ (12.7cm) hem with a 1″ (2.5cm) turn-under. Press, stitch in place, and press again.

Figure 1

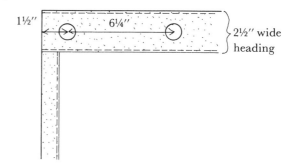

Step 5:
Using a grommeter, attach grommets to the heading, matching spacing of the holes in the shower curtain liner. If no liner is used, space grommets midway between stitching lines of heading. The two end grommets should be 1½" (3.8cm) in from the side edges; the remaining grommets should be evenly spaced across the curtain with their centers 6¼" (15.9cm) apart. (See fig. 1.)

Method for Appliqué
Step 6:
Enlarge and transfer appliqué design in fig. 2 onto desired fabrics. Cut out shapes.

Cut out corresponding shapes from the fusible bonding web.

Step 7:
Position and pin-baste all appliqué shapes onto right side of shower curtain with fusible bonding web in between.

Press to fuse design in place, following manufacturer's directions.

Using a narrow zigzag stitch, sew around all edges of the appliquéd pieces to prevent them from fraying.

Slip hooks through shower curtain and liner and hang.

Figure 2

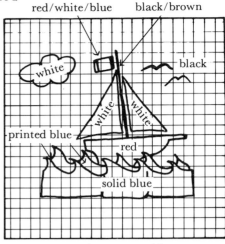

each square = 4"

Terry Covered Footlocker

Perfect for a bedroom or playroom as well as the bath, this nautical sea trunk is a great place to stow away extra towels and toys for your little sea captain.

Materials
- 1 footlocker, 32" x 13" x 16" (81.3cm x 33cm x 40.6cm)
- 1 quart (.95l) wall sizing
- paintbrush, 2" (5cm) wide
- 2½ yards (2.3m) terry cloth, 44" (111.8cm) wide
- tape measure
- fabric shears
- 1 quart (.95l) vinyl adhesive
- manicure scissors
- narrow wooden stick
- ½ yard (45.7cm) terry cloth in a contrasting color, 44" (111.8cm) wide
- ½ yard (45.7cm) small wale corduroy, 44" (111.8cm) wide
- 6 yards (5.5m) narrow, round military braid trim

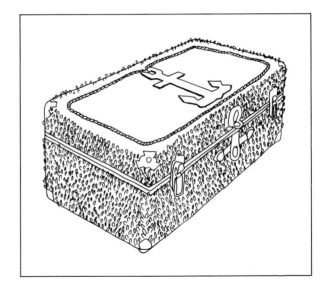

- white household glue
- small disposable container
- 4 yards (3.7m) ¼" (6mm) gingham, 44" (111.8cm) wide

(Continued)

Method

Step 1:
Prepare the outside of the footlocker by generously coating all nonmetal parts with wall sizing. Allow to dry thoroughly.

Step 2:
Press fabric.

Cut a section of terry cloth large enough to extend around the bottom, front, back and the one side which does not have a handle. (See fig. 1.)

Using a brush, coat the nonmetal surface of the bottom with vinyl adhesive. Apply enough adhesive so that the original color of the trunk is barely noticeable. Be careful not to drop vinyl adhesive on areas which will not be covered by fabric.

Position the terry cloth on the bottom and press firmly in place, smoothing it with your hands toward the outer edges of the footlocker.

Using manicure scissors, trim excess fabric from around the metal corners and edges. (See fig. 2.) To secure the fabric to the small areas surrounding the metal corners, apply vinyl adhesive with a narrow wooden stick. The terry fabric should extend to the edge of each metal part. If tiny spaces remain around the curves after you've trimmed and glued the fabric, cover these areas with bits of terry.

Step 3:
Once the bottom is thoroughly covered with terry cloth, brush vinyl adhesive onto the back of the footlocker. Smooth fabric into place, trimming and gluing around the metal corners and edges.

Repeat procedure on the front of the footlocker.

Fold the end fabric down over the side panel without the handle. Trim the triangles which form at the sides to remove excess fabric, allowing 1″ (2.5cm) overlaps from the bottom, back, and front sections. (See fig. 3.)

Glue overlap pieces to the side. Spread vinyl adhesive over the entire side surface and smooth fabric into place, trimming and gluing around the metal corners and edges.

Step 4:
To cover the opposite side, cut a section of fabric large enough to cover the entire area, including the handle. Spread vinyl adhesive onto the side panel, and begin attaching the fabric at the bottom, trimming around the metal corners and edges.

Cut fabric directly above the metal handle holders, using manicure scissors to trim around the handle. (See fig. 4.) Glue fabric under and around the handle. Trim along the top edge.

Step 5:
Measure, mark, and cut out a section of terry cloth large enough to cover the entire top and side of the lid.

Apply vinyl adhesive to the top. Smooth fabric into place, trimming and gluing around the metal corners and edges. Repeat procedure for the sides of the lid.

For a finished look, glue a small circle of fabric inside the lock.

Step 6:
Enlarge and transfer the anchor design in fig. 5 to tracing paper, and cut out shape to use as a pattern. Pin pattern to contrasting terry cloth, and cut out anchor. Cut out fusible bonding web in shape of the anchor.

Place anchor on right side of corduroy with fusible bonding web in between, and fuse the anchor to the corduroy, according to manufacturer's directions. Trim around the terry cloth anchor so that the corduroy extends out ⅛″ (3mm) from the terry cloth anchor. (See fig. 6.) Center the anchor on the

Figure 1

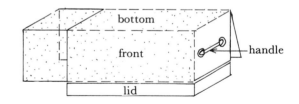

Figure 2

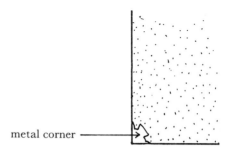

Figure 3

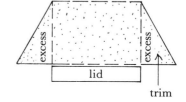

Figure 4

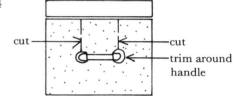

lid of the footlocker. Using undiluted glue, glue the anchor in place.

Cut military braid into two equal lengths. Twist the two lengths together to get an interesting effect.

Using vinyl adhesive to glue the braid in position, start at the top of the anchor, and extend the braid around the top of the footlocker 1½″ (3.8cm) inside the outer edge. Secure the ends of the braid inside the top of the anchor. (See fig. 7.)

Allow the footlocker to dry thoroughly before lining the inside.

Step 7:
To line the footlocker, cut pieces of gingham ½″ (1.3cm) larger than the dimensions of the inside sides of the trunk. Notch the corners of each fabric piece about ½″ (1.3cm) in from the points to prevent bulky overlaps. (See fig. 8.)

Pour glue into disposable container and dilute with water until it spreads evenly with a paintbrush—approximately two parts glue to one part water.

Working with one inside surface at a time, brush diluted glue generously over surface and smooth gingham pieces in place.

Cut a piece of gingham the exact dimensions of the inside bottom of the footlocker, and glue in place.

Cut a piece of gingham the exact dimensions of the inside lid, and glue in place.

Step 8:
Cover the storage tray of the footlocker by cutting a fabric section large enough to cover the outside of the tray and to extend at least ½″ (1.3cm) onto the inside. Brush with diluted glue and attach fabric, trimming as necessary for a smooth finish.

Cut pieces of gingham ½″ (1.3cm) larger than the dimensions of the inside side surfaces of the storage tray. Notch in the same way as you did the pieces of the trunk lining.

Brush diluted glue over inside surfaces, and attach gingham pieces one at a time.

Cut a piece of gingham the exact size of the inside bottom of the storage tray, and glue in place.

Allow all surfaces to dry thoroughly before using.

Figure 5

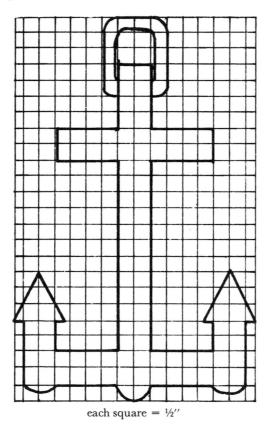

each square = ½″

Figure 6

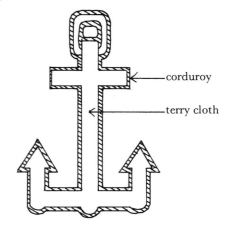

corduroy

terry cloth

Figure 7

Figure 8

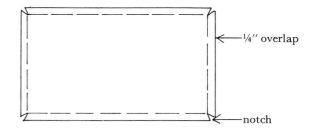

¼″ overlap

notch

Swag Bag Laundry Bag

This handy laundry bag can be made from many fabrics and may be enlarged for use as a carry-all for books, athletic gear, toys, packages, or as storage for seasonal wearing apparel.

Materials
- 1 yard medium-weight fabric, 45" (114.3cm) wide
- tape measure
- tailor's chalk
- fabric shears
- thread to match
- 2 yards (1.8m) cotton cord, ⅜" (9mm) thick
- medium-size safety pin

Method
Step 1:
Press fabric.

Measure, mark with tailor's chalk, and cut out two 31" x 19" (78.7cm x 48.3cm) rectangles of fabric.

Place right sides together. Using ½" (1.3cm) seams, pin-baste, then stitch around three sides, leaving one narrow end open.

Step 2:
Turn top edge of bag down ½" (1.3cm), right sides together, and press. Turn top edge down again to make a 5" (12.7cm) hem and press. Pin to hold in place.

Measure, mark, and stitch 3" (7.6cm) below top fold of bag. Turn bag right side out.

Step 3:
Just below the stitching line on outside of bag, make four vertical buttonholes through the top layer of fabric only, two buttonholes on either side of the two opposite seams. (See fig. 1.) (See Techniques, Hand-Bound Buttonholes.) Make sure the buttonholes go through the outside fabric only. Turn bag wrong side out.

To complete the casing, sew around bag 1" (2.5cm) below the first line of stitching and just below the buttonholes. (See fig. 1.) Drop down 1" (2.5cm), and stitch hem in place. Press and turn bag right side out.

Step 4:
Cut cotton cord into two equal lengths. Attach a safety pin to one end of one piece of cording, and run it through the casing, going in one buttonhole, all the way around the bag, and out of the adjacent buttonhole. (See fig. 2.) Tie ends together.

Repeat procedure for second piece of cord, beginning and ending at the two opposite buttonholes.

If you desire, finish the laundry bag with a giant initial transferred from the graph in the Country French Living room or a number cut out of felt and secured with overcast stitches.

Figure 1

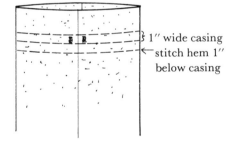

1" wide casing
stitch hem 1" below casing

Figure 2

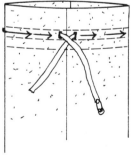

Ship's Ladder Towel Rack

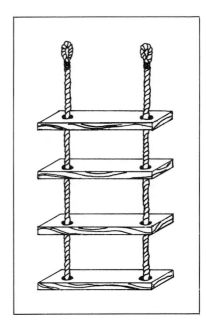

This clever rack is also an ideal way to display your pretty tea towels in the kitchen.

Materials
- 5 yards (4.6m) polished, braided cord #8 clothesline or hemp rope, ¼" (6mm) thick
- 4 wooden slats, 1" x ½" x 16" (2.5cm x 1.3cm x 40.6cm)
- lead pencil, #2
- ruler
- saw
- sandpaper, medium grade
- drill
- single-edge razor blade
- fishing twine
- upholstery needle
- nails or decorative hooks

Method

Step 1:
Have the local lumberyard cut four wooden slats from 1" x 2" (2.5cm x 5cm) wood (pine) to the exact size of 1" x ½" x 16" (2.5cm x 1.3cm x 40.6cm). Sand edges.

Drill ¼" (6mm) holes, the same diameter as the clothesline or rope, ¾" (1.9cm) in from each end of the slats and centered horizontally.

Step 2:
Thread clothesline or rope through the holes making sure both ends are pulled even. In each side of the clothesline, tie a single knot 7" (17.8cm) up from top of slat. Thread second slat onto clothesline. Make sure slat rests evenly on top of the knots. (See fig. 1.) Continue knotting and adding slats until all four are attached.

Step 3:
Allowing 11" (27.9cm) above the final slat, form 1½" (3.8cm) loops on each side. Cut off excess with razor blade and make sure cut ends of rope face in towards the center. (See fig. 2.)

Bind loops with fishing twine wrapped 1" (2.5cm) up from cut end. Secure twine ends by knotting or threading and drawing them through the center of the bound section with an upholstery needle. (See fig. 3.)

Hang finished ships ladder from nails or decorative hooks.

Figure 2

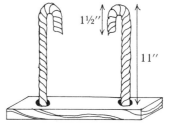

Figure 3

Figure 1

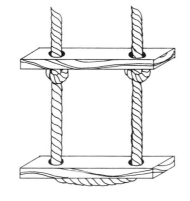

Guest Bathroom

Guest Bathroom

Blue is a cool and soothing color, and using it in this bathroom will make your guests feel pampered and totally relaxed.

The monochromatic color scheme takes its cue from the blue tiles around the tub area and extends to the floor which is covered with a thick, washable, wall-to-wall carpeting. The bright innocence of daisies printed on washable fabric lightens the atmosphere. Coordinating giant daisies are appliquéd onto the towels and terry stool cover to complete the theme.

Because the entire room is blue, it is an easy matter to change the accessories to brighten up the color scheme.

The gathered sink skirt is a good way to hide ugly pipes or an out of date pedestal. It is easily removed for laundering or changing completely. The covered cornice not only adds a decorator touch, creating a frame for the double shower curtains, but easily hides the shower curtain rod as well. You may wish the curtain panels to remain stationary while two separate shower curtain liners hang on a separate café curtain rod a few inches above or below the main shower curtain rod.

Shirred tiebacks are made from remaining scraps of fabric. Thick cord can be an alternate tieback and is an easy way to add accent color to the bath.

The café curtains at the window are eye-catchers for any room but are especially practical for a bathroom where both privacy and light are important.

Floor-Length Shower Curtains with Shirred Tiebacks

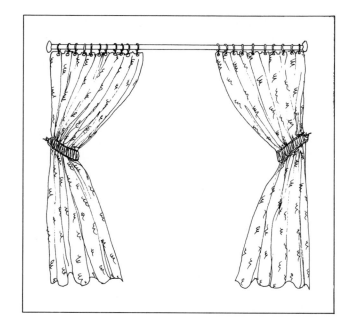

The materials and directions given are for two 72″ x 80″ (182.9cm x 203.2cm) standard-size curtain panels and two shirred tiebacks.

The shirred tiebacks are an elegant accent to any room of the house, whether used on shower curtains, draperies, or curtains.

Materials for Curtain
- 11 yards (10.1m) light- to medium-weight fabric, 42″ to 45″ (106.7cm to 114.3cm) wide
- tape measure
- tailor's chalk
- fabric shears
- dressmaker's pins
- 4 yards (3.6m) buckram, 4″ (10.2cm) wide
- thread to match
- grommeter and 24 large grommets
- two shower curtain liners
- 24 shower curtain hooks

Materials for Shirred Tiebacks
- 1 yard (91.4cm) light- to medium-weight fabric, 42″ to 45″ (106.7cm to 114.3cm) wide
- tape measure
- tailor's chalk
- fabric shears
- dressmaker's pins
- needle
- 1 package commercial piping in contrasting color

- thread to match
- 2 large cup hooks
- 4 small rings

Method for Curtain
Step 1:
Press fabric.

Measure, mark with tailor's chalk, and cut fabric into four sections, each the full width of the fabric and 89″ (226cm) long.

To make one shower curtain panel, place right sides of two fabric sections together and join long sides with a flat-felled seam. (See Techniques, Seam.) Repeat this procedure for remaining curtain panel.

Trim excess fabric from each side to make both curtain panels 76″ (193cm) wide by 89″ (226cm) long with the flat-felled

Figure 1

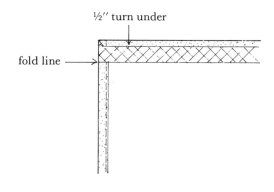

½″ turn under

fold line

seams running top to bottom in the exact center.

Step 2:
To make double hems along both side edges, turn raw edges under 1″ (2.5cm) and press. Turn under 1″ (2.5cm) again and press. Stitch hems in place and press again.

Step 3:
To make the heading, first measure, mark, and cut out a strip of buckram 72″ (182.9cm) long and 2½″ (6.4cm) wide.

Measure, mark, and press top of shower curtain panel down 3″ (7.6cm) to form a 2½″ (6.4) hem with a ½″ (1.3cm) turn-under. Place buckram inside heading wrapping raw edge of fabric around it. (See fig. 1.) Stitch buckram in place ⅛″ (3mm) from each fold line along both lengthwise edges of the buckram; press. The heading is now 2½″ (6.4cm) wide.

Step 4:
To make the bottom hem, measure, mark, and turn up the bottom 6″ (15.2cm) to form a 5″ (12.7cm) hem with a 1″ (2.5cm) turn-under. Press, stitch in place, and press again.

Step 5:
Using a grommeter, attach grommets to heading, matching spacing of holes in the shower curtain liner. If no liner is used, space grommets midway between stitching lines of heading. The two end grommets should be 1½″ (3.8cm) in from the side edges, the remaining grommets should be evenly spaced across the curtain with their centers 6¼″ (15.9cm) apart. (See fig. 2.)

Method for Shirred Tiebacks
Step 6:
Press fabric.

For one tieback, measure, mark with tailor's chalk, and cut out two strips of fabric, each 5″ (12.7cm) wide, and long enough to equal 75″ (190.5cm) when the strips are seamed together end to end using ½″ (1.3cm) seams. Press seams open.

Measure and press raw edges under ½″ (1.3cm) on long sides.

Step 7:
On each side of the fabric strip, run basting threads along each fold line and pull threads to gather fabric. (See fig. 3.) Distribute gathers evenly to make tieback 25″ (63.5cm) long.

Step 8:
From remaining fabric, measure and cut a strip 5″ (12.7cm) wide and 25″ (63.5cm) long.

Using a zipper foot attachment and ½″ (1.3cm) seams, pin-baste and stitch piping around all sides of right side of flat strip. The raw edges of the piping should face toward the outside edge of the fabric strip. (See fig. 4.)

Step 9:
Place right sides of gathered strip and piped strip together. Using ½″ (1.3cm) seams, pin-baste and stitch around all sides leaving a 3″ (7.6cm) opening for turning. Trim corners.

Turn tieback right side out and slip-stitch opening closed.

Repeat Steps 6 through 9 to make second tieback.

Tack rings in place on underside of tiebacks. (See fig. 5.)

Attach cup hooks 30″ to 35″ (76.2cm to 88.9cm) up from the floor to hold tiebacks in position.

Figure 2

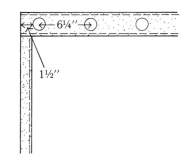

Figure 3

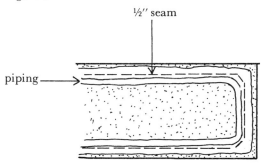

Figure 4

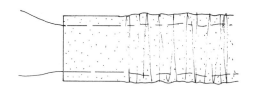

Figure 5

Bathtub Cornice

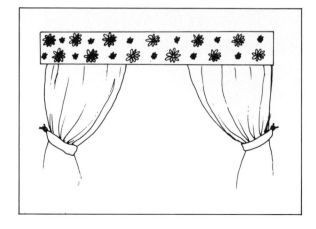

Consult your local building contractor before beginning this project to be sure your walls can support the weight of the finished cornice.

Materials
- 1¾ yards (1.6m) light- to medium-weight fabric, 42″ to 45″ (106.7cm to 114.3cm) wide
- tape measure
- lead pencil, #2
- ¾″ (1.9cm) plywood, approximately 18″ x 60″ (45.7cm x 152.4cm)
- saw
- polyester batting
- staple gun and staples
- 6 corner braces
- 24 toggle bolts
- 24 screws, ½″ (1.3cm)
- screwdriver

Method
Step 1:
To determine the length cornice needed, measure the distance between the walls at either end of the bathtub. To determine the cornice width, measure from the ceiling to 1″ (2.5cm) below the shower curtain rod. (See fig. 1.)

Do it yourself or have the local lumber-yard cut ¾″ (1.9cm) plywood to the exact width and length measurements.

Step 2:
Wrap plywood with a layer of polyester batting and staple in place.

Place padded plywood on fabric and wrap as you would a package. Trim excess and staple fabric in place, making sure staples only show on the edge of the plywood.

Step 3:
Attach three corner braces to each end of covered cornice. (See fig. 2.) Position cornice above the shower curtain rod, using toggle bolts to attach the braces to the walls.

Figure 2

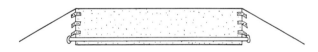

Figure 1

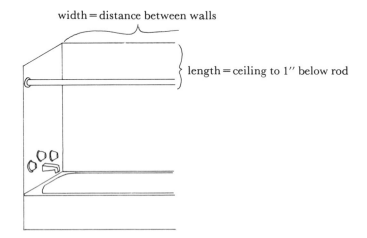

width = distance between walls

length = ceiling to 1″ below rod

Café Curtains

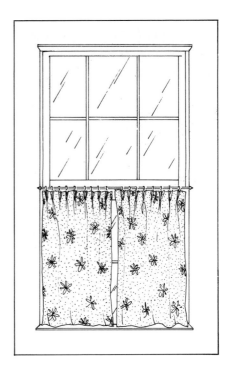

Café curtains may be made any length and are also quite effective when hung in overlapping tiers. Attractive accents for any room, the curtains may be as formal as you wish.

Before beginning this project, refer to Techniques, Window Treatments. For bathroom café curtains, follow the basic directions, minus the lining, for Lined Draperies on a Wooden Pole in the Early American Living Room, or the directions for Sheer Curtains in the Williamsburg Living Room. However, use 3″ (7.6cm) wide buckram or nonwoven interfacing for the heading.

Appliquéd Fingertip Towels

Appliquéing fingertip towels adds a touch of originality to the bath. Appliquéing is fun to do, does not take long, and your imagination may reign supreme. These make handsome, personalized hostess gifts as well.

Select pretty ribbons, braid, or rickrack, or cut out a design or initial from any small piece of decorative, washable fabric. Pin, then baste trim or design in place on top of towel. Attach by hand (see Techniques, Appliqué), or, using a narrow zigzag stitch and thread of the same or a contrasting color, stitch around the perimeter of the design. Broaden the zigzag stitch slightly and go over the outline again.

Gathered Sink Skirt

Materials and directions given are for a sink 55″ (139.7cm) around three sides and 28″ (71cm) from the floor. Since sinks vary in size, shape, and height, calculate the exact dimensions of your finished sink skirt before you begin. Be sure to select a fabric with a random print since in this project the selvages are treated as the top and bottom of the fabric.

Materials

- 4 yards (3.7m) lightweight fabric, 42″ to 45″ (106.7cm to 114.3cm) wide
- tape measure
- tailor's chalk
- fabric shears
- dressmaker's pins
- 2 yards (1.8m) cable cord, ¼″ (6mm) thick
- 2 yards (1.8m) nylon tape fastener
- 2 yards (1.8m) double-edge ruffle trim, 1¾″ (4.4cm) wide
- small safety pin
- thread to match
- non-water-soluble glue

Method

Step 1:
Measure around the base of the sink 1″ (2.5cm) above the lower edge. Measure the height of the sink from this point to 1″ (2.5cm) above the floor plus 6″ (15.2cm). (See fig. 1.)

Step 2:
Press fabric.

Using the selvage as the width, measure and cut a section of fabric 2½″ times wider than the distance around the sink, and 6″ (15.2cm) longer than the measured height.

Step 3:
Hem the short sides by turning under ½″ (1.3cm), then another ¾″ (1.9cm). Press and machine-stitch in place. (See fig. 2.)

Hem the bottom of the skirt (selvage) by turning under ½″ (1.3cm), then another 2½″ (6.4cm). Press and machine-stitch in place. (See fig. 2.)

Turn top of skirt (selvage) under 2″ (5cm) and press. Form a casing by stitching 1″ (2.5cm) below the fold line and stitching again ½″ (1.3cm) below the first stitching line. (See fig. 2.)

Step 4:
Attach cable cord to a safety pin and thread it through the casing. Pull to gather fabric to measured width. Secure ends temporarily with dressmaker's pins, and distribute gathers evenly.

With the hooked half of the nylon tape fastener up, pin-baste the tape to the wrong side of the sink skirt, covering the gathered casing. (See fig. 3.)

Figure 1

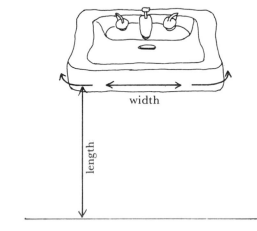

width

length

Step 5:
Pin-baste the double-edge ruffle trim to the right side of the sink skirt, centering it on top of the gathered casing. (See fig. 4.)

Using a large zigzag stitch, simultaneously attach both the nylon tape fastener and ruffle trim to the top of the sink skirt, sewing through the casing to secure the gathers. (See fig. 6.) Turn ends under.

Step 6:
Using a non-water-soluble glue, attach the looped half of the nylon tape fastener 1″ (2.5cm) above the bottom rim of the sink. Allow to dry thoroughly. Attach finished sink skirt by pressing the two halves of the nylon tape fastener together.

Figure 3

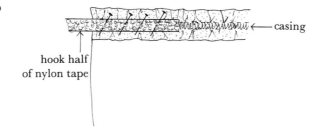

hook half of nylon tape

casing

Figure 5

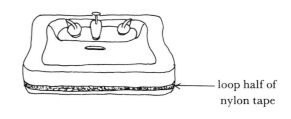

loop half of nylon tape

Figure 4

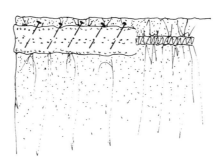

Figure 6

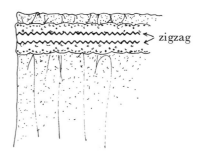

zigzag

Figure 2

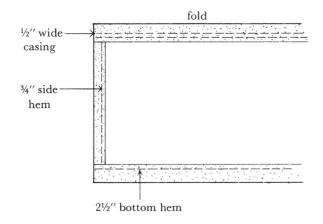

½″ wide casing

¾″ side hem

fold

2½″ bottom hem

Wicker Porch

Wicker Porch

Lush green tropical islands, bright, sun-drenched shores, and cool ocean breezes come to mind when relaxing in this dramatic setting. The wicker chairs add a regal accent to the porch and are remarkably comfortable to sit in.

The beautifully patterned sisal rug follows all of the circular design motions of the area as does the round wicker table, latticed planter, and rattan bench. Even the wind breaker/room divider in the background—canvas sheets (or you might like exotically printed fabric) laced to bamboo poles—is in a curved position. A shirred screen (Ms Bedroom) or a covered screen (Art Studio) might prove just as interesting.

The natural feeling in this airy porch is warmed and sparked by brightly colored chair and bench cushions with quilted boxings. The tablecloth and matching napkins also have quilted trims.

If you wish to increase the seating possibilities, how about a few turkish corner floor pillows (Eclectic Living Room) to toss around as the guests arrive?

Round Pillow with a Quilted Boxing

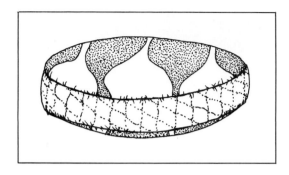

These attractive pillows are perfect as chair cushions or as accents on any sofa.

The materials and directions given are for one 16″ (40.6cm) round pillow with a quilted boxing.

Materials
- 1½ yards (1.4m) light- to medium-weight fabric, 42″ to 45″ (106.7cm to 114.3cm) wide
- tape measure
- tailor's chalk
- fabric shears
- dressmaker's pins
- ½ yard (45.7cm) polyester fleece padding
- polyester fiber fill
- thread to match

Method
Step 1:
Press fabric.

To locate the true bias, fold fabric on the diagonal so that the crosswise grain rests exactly on the lengthwise grain. (See Techniques, Bias Trim.)

Measure, mark with tailor's chalk, and cut a bias strip 4″ (10.2cm) wide by 54″ (137.2cm) long. (See fig. 1.)

Measure, mark with tailor's chalk, and cut two strips of fleece padding 4″ (10.2cm) wide by 55″ (139.7cm) long. Overlap two short ends 1″ (2.5cm) and zigzag stitch in place, making a single long strip 4″ wide and 109″ long (10.2cm x 276.9cm). Trim excess on either side of the stitching line.

Pin-baste fabric bias strip to the fleece padding strip and machine-quilt the piece by stitching horizontal and diagonal lines 1″ (2.5cm) apart. (See Techniques, Quilting.) (See fig. 2.)

Step 2:
From remaining fabric, measure, mark with tailor's chalk, and cut out two 19″ (48.3cm) squares. Fold each square into quarters and press.

Mark an arc 8½″ (21.6cm) from the folded center of each square. Cut along the markings to make a 17″ (43.2cm) circle from each square. (See fig. 3.)

Step 3:
Place right sides of one circle and quilted boxing together and stitch ½″ (1.3cm) in from the outer edge. (See fig. 4.) Repeat procedure to attach the remaining circle to quilted boxing, leaving a 4″ (10.2cm) opening for turning and stuffing. (See fig. 5.)

Trim gusset to ⅛″ (3mm). Notch seam allowances of pillow top and bottom.

Turn pillow right side out and stuff firmly with polyester fiber fill.

Turn in raw edges and slip-stitch opening closed.

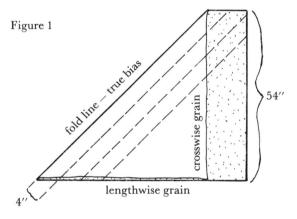

Figure 1

fold line – true bias

crosswise grain

lengthwise grain

54″

4″

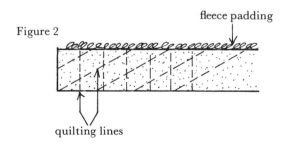

Figure 2

fleece padding

quilting lines

Figure 3

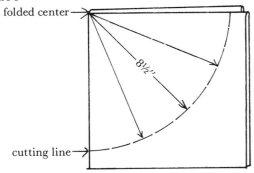

folded center

8½″

cutting line →

Figure 4

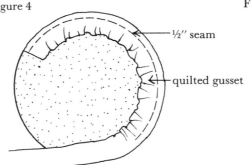

½″ seam

quilted gusset

Figure 5

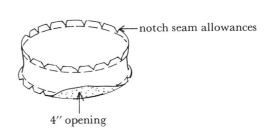

notch seam allowances

4″ opening

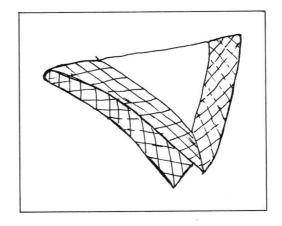

Quilted-Edge Napkins

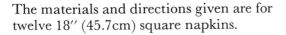

The materials and directions given are for twelve 18″ (45.7cm) square napkins.

Materials

- 1¾ yards (1.6m) light- to medium-weight washable fabric, 48″ to 52″ (121.9cm to 132cm) wide
- 4 yards (3.7m) contrasting printed light- to medium-weight washable fabric, 48″ to 52″ (121.9cm to 132cm) wide
- tape measure
- tailor's chalk
- fabric shears
- dressmaker's pins
- contrasting thread for quilting and sewing.

Method

Step 1:
Press fabric.

Measure, mark with tailor's chalk, and cut the 1¾ yard (1.6m) piece of fabric into twelve 14″ (35.6cm) squares.

Measure, mark, and cut the contrasting, printed fabric into twelve 24″ (61cm) squares.

Step 2:
Measure and mark, or use a quilter's guide bar on your sewing machine, and stitch diagonal parallel rows across each 24″ (61cm) square, making sure the lines are 2″ (5cm) apart. (See fig. 1.)

(Continued)

Figure 1

24″

24″

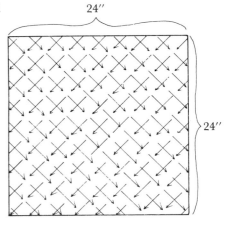

On each napkin, it is best to stitch the diagonal lines that run in one direction first, then stitch the diagonal lines that run in the opposite direction.

Step 3:
Placing right sides together, position the small squares in the exact center of the large, stitched squares. Fold over two opposite sides of large squares to meet sides of small squares. (See fig. 2.) Using ½″ (1.3cm) seams, pin-baste the sides of both squares together. Stitch in place and press seams open.

Turn squares right sides out and center the small squares so that the large squares form 2½″ (6.4cm) wide borders; press.

Step 4:
Turn remaining raw edges of large squares under ½″ (1.3cm) and press in place. (See fig. 3.)

Fold over remaining opposite sides of large squares to sides of small squares and pin-baste in position ½″ (1.3cm) inside raw edges of small squares, making 2½″ (6.4cm) wide borders. (See fig. 4.)

Fold under corners to miter them. Trim excess fabric from underneath, and pin-baste in position. (See fig. 5.)

Topstitch around all sides of napkins just inside the edges of the quilted border resting on top of the small squares. (See fig. 6.)

Figure 2

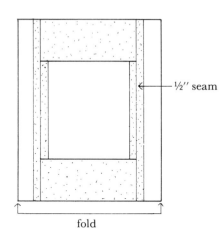

½″ seam

fold

Figure 4

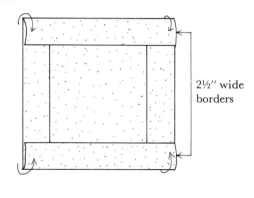

2½″ wide borders

Figure 3

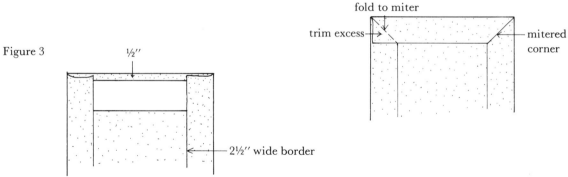

½″

2½″ wide border

Figure 5

fold to miter

trim excess

mitered corner

Figure 6

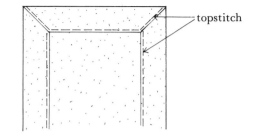

topstitch

Covered Bolster with Quilted Ends

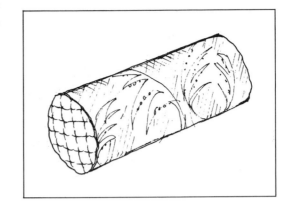

Follow instructions for the Round Covered Bolster in the Mr. Bedroom, but quilt the end circles before attaching them to the bolster. (See Techniques, Quilting.)

Clothesline Covered Planter

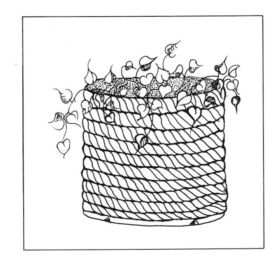

Do not use terra cotta containers for this project; moisture will eventually seep through the clay, weaken the glue, and all of your work may dissolve onto the floor. If you insist upon covering terra cotta, use a non-water-soluble glue to attach the clothesline. Make sure the planter is white or off-white. If it is not, spray paint it and allow to dry thoroughly before beginning. For a very attractive wastebasket, follow the same procedure using a #6 clothesline.

Materials
- round plastic or metal planter
- polished, braided cord clothesline, #8
- white household glue
- single-edge razor blade

Method
Step 1:
Beginning at the bottom center back just above the drainage holes, attach and wind clothesline around planter using undiluted glue applied directly from the bottle onto the container. (See fig. 1.)

Continue applying glue and winding clothesline around planter until container is completely covered. Cut off excess with a razor blade and glue in place.

Allow to dry thoroughly before using.

Figure 1

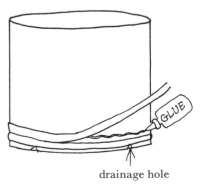

drainage hole

Redwood/Cedar Deck

Redwood/Cedar Deck

This beautiful, tree-top deck was designed to let you take full advantage of the seasons. The majestic tree in the center was not cut down, but instead became part of the living area, and serves as natural protection from the sun.

Popular wooden director's chairs are easy to store in case of stormy weather. One is covered with a very sturdy washable fabric. The other is refurbished with a terry cloth bath towel with a reinforced seat because the terry is not strong enough to hold up under continuous body weight. Terry cloth covered chairs are wonderful to sit in, especially if you're just up from a dip in the lake.

The bandana picnic cloth and napkins on the table are reversible. They are made out of inexpensive bandana scarves and can be as large or as small as you wish; just keep joining the squares together until you have the desired size. Additional napkins for this picnic are washcloths trimmed with bias strips—practical and very pretty.

The clever table weights are actually good-size rocks disguised in bandana scarves tied hobo fashion—a pretty way to keep the wind from whipping up the corners of the cloth, or use them as bookends.

Reversible Bandana Picnic Cloth and Napkins

The materials and directions given are for a 52″ (132cm) square cloth and nine 18″ (45.7cm) square napkins.

Materials
- 18 bandanas, 18″ (45.7cm) square, color A
- 18 bandanas, 18″ (45.7cm) square, color B
- scissors
- sewing needle
- thread to match

Method for Cloth
Step 1:
Press bandanas.

Arrange nine bandanas to form a 54″ (137.2cm) square, alternating colors.

With right sides together, join bandanas to form a large square, stitching as close to the rolled edges as possible.

Repeat procedure to make another large square.

Step 2:
Place right sides of two large pieced squares together. Pin-baste so that the seams of the individual squares on the top and bottom sections match.

Stitch around the large squares about ⅛″ (3mm) in from the outside edges, leaving a 10″ (25.4cm) opening in the center of one side. (See fig. 1.)

Step 3:
Turn cloth right side out, and press. Turn in edges, and slip-stitch opening closed.

Topstitch around reversible picnic cloth with regular thread ½″ (1.3cm) in from the outside edges.

Method for Napkins
Step 4:
To make each of the reversible matching napkins, pin-baste two contrasting bandanas together, wrong sides out. Stitch around squares ¼″ (6mm) in from the rolled edges, leaving a 5″ (12.7cm) opening in the center of one side.

Step 5:
Turn napkins right side out and press. Turn in edges, and slip-stitch opening closed.

Topstitch around reversible napkins with regular thread ¼″ (6mm) in from the outer edges.

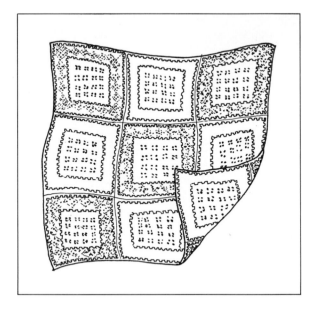

Figure 1

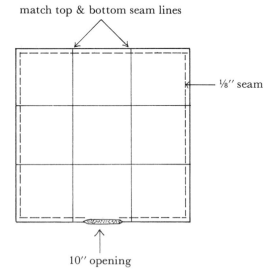

match top & bottom seam lines

⅛″ seam

10″ opening

Bandana Corner Weights

When not in use holding down the corners of a picnic cloth on a breezy summer day, these colorful weights double as bookends or paper-weights. Simply purchase brightly colored bandanas and tie each around a good solid rock, hobo fashion.

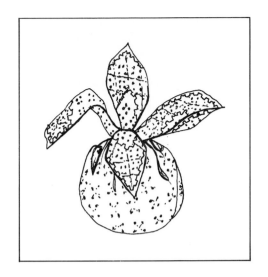

Washcloth Napkins

Stitch contrasting bias binding around brightly colored washcloths for a colorful aid to cleaning up after messy meals. Use them dry or wet.

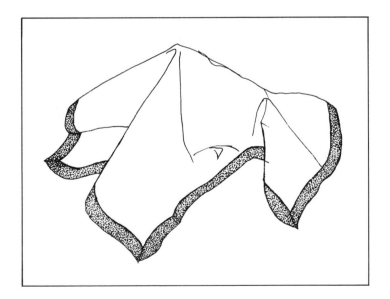

Director's Chair Cover

To ensure proper support, use fabric comparable to regular chair-weight canvas to make the director's chair cover.

Materials
- 1 yard (91.4cm) heavyweight fabric, 44" (111.8cm) wide
- tape measure
- tailor's chalk
- fabric shears
- dressmaker's pins
- heavy-duty thread to match

Method
Step 1:
Press fabric.

Measure, mark with tailor's chalk, and cut out a strip of fabric 44" (111.8cm) long and 8½" (21.6cm) wide for the back section of chair.

With right sides together and using ½" (1.3cm) seams, pin-baste, then stitch short ends of strip together, forming a tube. Press seams open.

Step 2:
Turn under top and bottom raw edges of tube 1" (2.5cm) to wrong side. Press and topstitch ¼" (6mm) in from the fold lines. (See fig. 1.)

Turn tube right side out. Fold tube and position seam 2½" (6.4cm) in from one side fold.

Topstitch through both layers of fabric and directly over seam to form a casing for

one side of the chair back. Topstitch 2½" (6.4cm) in from the opposite side fold. (See fig. 2.)

Topstitch the two layers of chair back cover together along the top and bottom edges. Do not stitch past the topstitching lines 2½" (6.4cm) in from either side fold. (See fig. 3.)

Step 3:
From remaining fabric, measure, mark with tailor's chalk, and cut out a section of fabric for the chair seat 39" (99cm) long and 18" (45.7cm) wide.

With right sides together and using ½" (1.3cm) seams, pin-baste, then stitch short ends together, forming a tube. Press seam open.

Figure 1

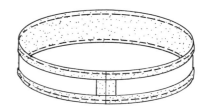

Step 4:
Turn under top and bottom raw edges of tube 1″ (2.5cm) to wrong side. Press and top-stitch ¼″ (6mm) in from fold lines.

Turn tube right side out. Fold tube and position seam in center of underside of seat.

Measure, pin-baste, and topstitch ¾″ (1.9cm) in from each side fold to make a casing for the dowels. (See fig. 4.)

Topstitch the two layers of chair seat cover together along the top and bottom edges. Do not stitch past the stitching lines for the casings ¾″ (1.9cm) in from either side fold. (See fig. 4.)

Slide dowels through chair seat casings, and place back and seat on chair.

Figure 4

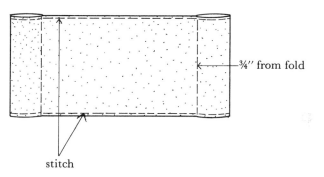

¾″ from fold

stitch

Figure 2

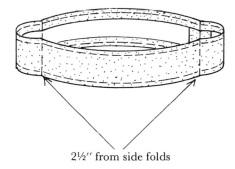

2½″ from side folds

Figure 3

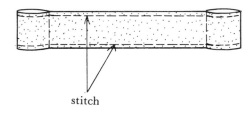

stitch

Wrought Iron Patio

Wrought Iron Patio

This very inviting extension of inside living would grace any home. The use of much fabric here achieves a softening effect against the hard textures of brick, wood, and wrought iron.

The cheerful, sunny yellow awning and matching side panel curtains should be constructed and installed by a professional awning contractor. When weather turns foul, simply untie each curtain panel and pull them closed as protection against wind and rain.

The bright, shirred flower pots and flower box covers are not waterproof but add a feminine elegance beside the natural brick flooring.

The good-size hassock can be left unadorned as pictured here, or you may wish to embellish it with a reverse appliqué design as described with the project. You might wish to carry the reverse appliqué motif to the love seats by repeating the design on accent pillows or cushions.

Shirred Flower Pot Cover

This is a clever way to disguise unattractive plastic pots. It also adds a decorative, personal touch to a plant you may be giving as a present. Do not cover terra cotta pots in this manner; fabric keeps them from "breathing."

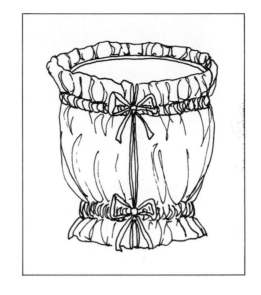

Materials
- light- to medium-weight fabric
- tape measure
- fabric shears
- tailor's chalk
- narrow ribbon
- safety pin

Method
Step 1:
To determine how much fabric you will need for any size pot, measure the height of your flower pot, multiply by two, add ½″ (1.3cm) at top and bottom, and 1″ (2.5cm) for seams. For instance, if your pot is 4½″ (11.4cm) tall, the resulting dimension would be 11″ (27.9cm).

Measure the top circumference of the flower pot, multiply by two and add 1″ (2.5cm). If your pot is 16″ (40.6cm) around the top, the resulting dimension would be 33″ (83.8cm).

Measure, mark with tailor's chalk, and cut out a strip of fabric equal to the above measurements.

Step 2:
Fold fabric strip in half lengthwise, wrong side out. Using ½″ (1.3cm) seams, stitch across the lengthwise edges of the strip to form a tube. Center seam and press open.

Turn tube right side out. Center seam again and press. Turn in raw edges at ends ½″ (1.3cm), press, and stitch in place.

Step 3:
Measure, mark, and stitch a ½″ (1.3cm) wide casing ½″ (1.3cm) in from each long side of the tube. (See fig. 1.)

Cut ribbon into two equal lengths, each 1½ times the length of the top circumference of the pot. Attach safety pin to ribbon and pull through casings to gather fabric. (See fig. 2.)

Wrap cover around flower pot, distribute gathers evenly and make sure top ruffle is above pot rim. Tie ribbon in bows and leave out or tuck in, as you desire.

Figure 1

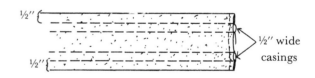

½″ wide casings

Figure 2

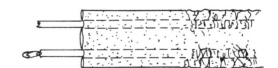

Shirred Window Box Cover

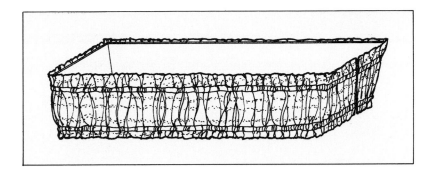

The materials given are for a 24″ x 6″ x 8″ (61cm x 15.2cm x 20.3cm) box.

Materials
- 1¼ yards (1.1m) light- to medium-weight fabric, 50″ (127cm) wide
- tape measure
- tailor's chalk
- fabric shears
- 5 yards (4.6m) cable cord, ¼″ (6mm) thick
- safety pin

Method

Step 1:
To determine how much fabric you will need for any size window box, measure the height of your window box, multiply by two, add 1″ (2.5cm) at top and bottom and 1″ (2.5cm) for seam. If your box is 6″ (15.2cm) tall, the resulting dimension would be 15″ (38cm).

Measure the top circumference of the window box, multiply by 2, and add 1″ (2.5cm). If your box is 67″ (1.7m) around the top, the resulting dimension would be 135″ (3.4m).

Step 2:
Measure, mark with tailor's chalk, and cut out a strip of fabric equal to the above measurements. If more than one strip is needed to obtain the correct length cut additional strips, adding 1″ (2.5cm) of fabric for each extra strip.

Step 3:
To obtain the correct length, place strips end to end, right sides together. Pin-baste, then stitch ends, using ½″ (1.3cm) seams. Press seams open.

Fold joined strips in half lengthwise, wrong sides out, and press. Using ½″ (1.3cm) seams, stitch across long side of strip to form a tube. Center seams and press.

Turn tube right side out. Center seam again and press. Turn in raw edges at ends ½″ (1.3cm), press, and stitch in place.

Step 4:
Measure, mark, and stitch a ½″ (1.3cm) wide casing ½″ (1.3cm) in from each long side of the tube. (See fig. 1.)

Cut cable cord into two equal lengths. Attach safety pin to cord and pull through casings to gather fabric. (See fig. 2.)

Turn empty window box upside down and wrap cover around it. Tie bottom cord into a bow first, then tie top cord. Tuck ends in. Distribute gathers evenly and make sure top ruffle is above window box rim. Return window box to upright position and fill with your favorite plants.

Figure 1

½″ wide casing
½″
seam

Figure 2

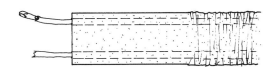

Reverse Appliqué Hassock

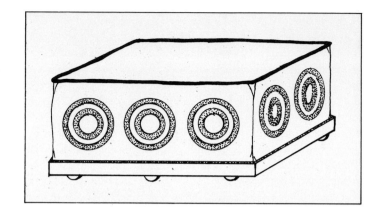

The materials and directions given are for a 42" x 16" x 6" (106.7cm x 40.6cm x 15.2cm) hassock.

You may wish to forego the appliquéd design and simply construct a solid color hassock as shown in the patio setting.

Materials
- 2¼ yards (2.1m) lightweight fabric, 44" (111.8cm) wide for top, bottom, and reverse appliqué design
- ¾ yard (68.6cm) lightweight fabric, 44" (111.8cm) wide in contrasting color or pattern for reverse appliqué design
- ¾ yard (68.6cm) lightweight fabric, 44" (111.8cm) wide in another contrasting color or pattern for reverse appliqué design
- 7 yards (6.4m) cable cord, ¼" (6mm) thick
- fabric shears
- polyurethane foam, 42" x 16" x 4" (106.7cm x 40.6cm x 10.2cm)
- polyurethane foam, 42" x 16" x 2" (106.7cm x 40.6cm x 5cm)
- tape measure
- tailor's chalk
- compass with pencil
- serrated knife (optional)
- thread to match

Method for Cover
Step 1:
Press all fabric.

Measure, mark with tailor's chalk, and cut off ½ yard (45.7cm) from the large piece of fabric. From this ½-yard (45.7cm) piece, prepare continuous bias 1½" (3.8cm) wide. (See Techniques, Bias Trim.) Cover cable cord with the bias strip as directed to make piping.

Measure, mark, and cut out two sections of fabric for hassock top and bottom, each 44" x 17" (111.8cm x 43.2cm).

Step 2:
From remaining length of same fabric, measure, mark, and cut out three strips, each 44" x 7" (111.8cm x 17.8cm).

Measure, mark, and cut out three more 44" x 7" (111.8cm x 17.8cm) strips from each of the two contrasting fabrics. Using ½" (1.3cm) seams, pin-baste, then stitch matching strips together to make three long strips, each approximately 130" x 7" (330.2cm x 17.8cm). Press seams open, and trim each strip to 117" (297.2cm).

Step 3:
Using large basting stitches, sew two fabric strips together, one on top of the other, with right sides facing up.

At regular intervals along the strip, draw 4" (10.2cm) diameter circles with their

Figure 1

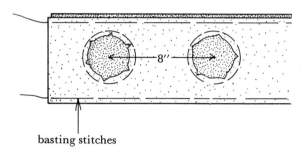

basting stitches

Figure 2

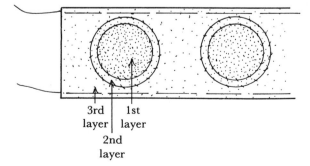

3rd layer | 1st layer
2nd layer

centers 8″ (20.3cm) apart. (See fig. 1.) Mark around outer edge of all circles with tailor's chalk. Beginning at the center of the circles, trim away top layer of fabric to within ¼″ (6mm) of the outlines. Clip to the edge of the circles. (See fig. 1.) Turn under edges and using very small stitches, whipstitch in place. (See Techniques, Hand Stitches.)

Step 4:
Using large basting stitches, sew the remaining fabric strip on top of the other two, right side facing up.

Using the same center point, mark off 5″ (12.7cm) diameter circles, the edges of which appear outside the edges of each of the 4″ (10.2cm) diameter circles just completed. Beginning at the center of the circles, trim away the top layer of fabric to within ¼″ (6mm) of the outlines. Clip to the edge of the circles. Turn under edges and using very small stitches, whipstitch in place. (See fig. 2.)

Step 5:
From same fabric as the third layer, measure, mark, and cut out 3″ (7.6cm) diameter circles. Turn edges under ¼″ (6mm) and press. Center these 2 ½″ (6.4cm) circles in the exact center of the design and whipstitch in place.

From the same fabric as the second layer, measure, mark, and cut out 2 ½″ (6.4cm) diameter circles. Turn edges under ¼″ (6mm) and press. Center these 2″ (5cm) circles in the very center of the design and whipstitch in place. (See fig. 3.)

Method for Hassock
Step 6:
If necessary, cut polyurethane foam to the correct size with a sawing motion using a serrated knife. Make sure the edges are straight.

Place the 2″ (5cm) thick piece of polyurethane foam on top of the 4″ (10.2cm) thick piece.

Center one 44″ x 17″ (111.8cm x 43.2cm) fabric section, right side up, on top of the foam. Pin-baste the piping prepared in Step 1 to the fabric, rounded edge facing in toward the center, so that the stitching line rests exactly on the edge of the foam. (See fig. 4.)

For a smooth finish where ends of the piping overlap, pull cord out of covering and clip it so the cut ends of both sides meet. Stitch ends in place.

Remove hassock top with piping pin-basted in place. Using a zipper foot attachment, stitch exactly on top of the piping stitching line.

Repeat this procedure to attach piping to the bottom piece of fabric.

Step 7:
With right sides together and using ¾″ (1.9cm) seams, pin-baste the reverse appliquéd strip to the top and bottom fabric sections, leaving a large opening in the center of one side for turning and stuffing. This will make the finished cover approximately 5 ½″ (13.7cm) deep for a snug fit.

Try cover on hassock and make adjustments as necessary.

Using a zipper foot attachment, stitch reverse appliqué strip in place.

Trim seam allowances as necessary. Turn cover right side out and slip over polyurethane foam hassock pieces. The two pieces of foam will not shift.

Slip-stitch opening closed to complete cover.

Figure 3

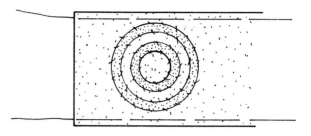

Figure 4

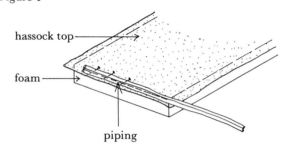

hassock top

foam

piping

Oriental Porch

Oriental Porch

Simplicity speaks its own beautiful language in this open, easy-to-care-for porch. The accent here is on space, light, and beautiful woods. Furniture is kept to a minimum and what there is of it depicts the stark elegance and functional simplicity of the Far East.

The floor cushions positioned around the low parson's table are actually made of tea towels and filled with thin foam cushions. They are lightweight and extremely totable—ideal for use inside or out.

The stacked, three-cushion benches are elegant in any room of your home. Executed on a smaller scale they can embellish a small footstool. The low floor couch is composed of three foam mattresses, each individually covered, then stacked and bound with wide ribbons. These separate easily to offer extra sleeping space for weekend guests.

The couch is accented with an elegantly covered bolster, and for an additional accent, the window shades are trimmed with coordinating bands of color.

To cover the shades with fabric, adapt the directions appearing in the Mr. Bedroom.

Three-Cushion Footstool

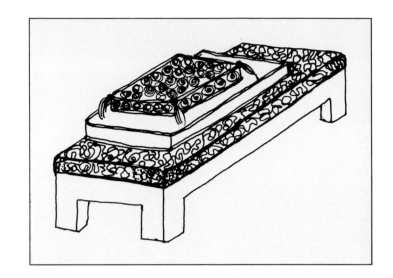

An effective way to make a low stool higher and add a touch of elegance to any room is shown by these footstools, which are simple to make and are the perfect solution to extra seating problems.

If you have a footstool with a slip seat, follow the directions for Fabric Covered Slip Seats in the Williamsburg Dining Room.

To make cushions to stack on top of any bench or stool, follow the directions for making the rectangular pillow with boxing in the Mr. Bedroom.

As an added accent, make tassels, and attach them to all four corners of each pillow or attach tassels to the top pillow only. (See Techniques, Tassels).

Floor Couch

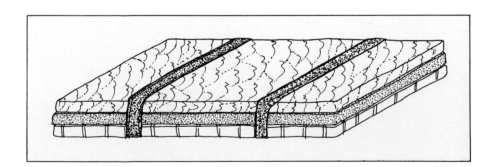

Twin-size polyurethane mattresses make decorative floor couches, and they are practical to have on hand for extra guests. Cover in assorted colors, and stack as many as you wish.

To make the versatile mattresses, follow directions for Rectangular Pillow with Boxing in the Mr. Bedroom. Work with twin-size polyurethane mattress forms, adjust yardage requirements, and omit the piping.

Quilted Bolster Cover

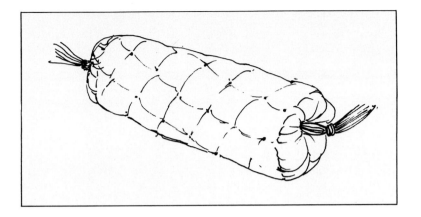

An attractive accent to any bed or seating arrangement, this quilted bolster is a simple version of the one found in the Mr. Bedroom.

The materials and directions given are for a 36″ x 8″ (91.4cm x 20.3cm) bolster.

Materials
- 2 yards (1.8m) lightweight fabric, 42″ to 45″ (106.7cm to 114.3cm) wide
- 1 yard (91.4cm) polyester batting
- 1 polyurethane foam bolster, 36″ x 8″ (91.4cm x 20.3cm)
- fabric shears
- dental floss
- thread to match

Method
Step 1:
Press fabric.

Measure and cut fabric into two 1-yard (91.4cm) pieces. Layer the two pieces of fabric, right sides out, with polyester batting in the middle.

Quilt the layers. (See Techniques, Quilting.)

Step 2:
Wrap quilted fabric, wrong sides out, around bolster form as if you were creating a giant firecracker. (See fig. 1.)

Measure ½″ (1.3cm) seams, and stitch one-third of the way in from each end, leaving a 12″ (30.5cm) opening in the center.

Tie each end very tightly with dental floss. (See fig. 1.)

Step 3:
Remove cover from bolster form, and trim seam allowances. Turn cover right side out, and press gently.

Reinsert bolster form, and slip-stitch opening closed.

Add a tassel to each end, if desired. (See Techniques, Tassels.)

Figure 1

Fabric Covered Parson's Table

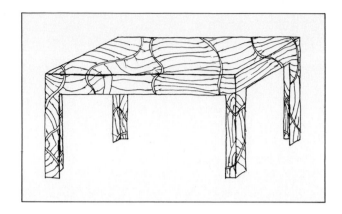

Two methods of covering a parson's table are included here: Method I works with one large piece of fabric whereas Method II suggests cutting individual pieces for the top and legs of the table. Either method will apply to any size square or rectangular parson's table.

If the table's overall dimensions are larger than the width of the fabric you plan to use, join as many equal lengths of fabric together as you need to create the necessary width, using ¼″ (6mm) seams. The materials and directions given are for a 16″ (40.6cm) square.

Materials
- 1½ yards (1.4m) fabric, 54″ (137.2cm) wide
- tape measure
- fabric shears
- white household glue
- small disposable container
- paintbrush, 2″ (5cm) wide
- dressmaker's pins

Method I
Step 1:
Press fabric.

To determine the amount of fabric needed for a size other than a 16″ (40.6cm) square table, measure the distance from the floor to the top of the table, across the top, and down to the floor. (See fig. 1.) Add 2″ (5cm) to the figure and cut out a square of fabric using that distance as the length of the sides.

For a rectangular table, measure up, across, and down the width and length of the table. (See fig. 2.) Add 2″ (5cm) to each figure, and cut out a rectangle of fabric using those dimensions.

Step 2:
Pour glue into disposable container and dilute with water until it spreads evenly with a paintbrush—approximately two parts glue to one part water.

Using long even strokes, brush diluted glue onto table top. Center fabric on top, and smooth in place. Brush glue onto one apron (side) of the table (longest sides on a rectangular table), and smooth fabric in place. Repeat on opposite apron.

Step 3:
Miter remaining sides of table (short sides on rectangular table) by forming a diagonal fold and pinning excess fabric up against itself. (See fig. 3.) Return to glued sides, and

trim excess fabric ½″ (1.3cm) from leg edges and 1½″ (3.8cm) from bottom of apron. (See fig. 4.) Wrap and glue fabric to underside of table. Wrap and glue fabric to back side of legs.

Figure 1

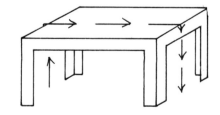

Figure 2

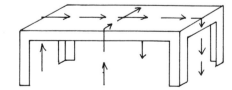

Step 4:

Unpin excess fabric on remaining opposite sides. Hold fabric out straight from un-glued sides of table. Cut along fold lines. (See fig. 5.)

Let center part fall naturally, and trim it 1½″ (3.8cm) from bottom of apron. Repeat procedure on opposite side.

Slash fabric to corner where table top meets leg. Cut ½″ (1.3cm) toward outside of leg, and trim toward corner allowing ¼″ (6mm) to extend beyond natural diagonal. (See fig. 6.) Repeat procedure on opposite side.

Brush diluted glue onto apron, and smooth fabric in place. Wrap and glue excess to underside of table. Repeat procedure on opposite side.

Step 5:

Fold remaining loose fabric on the diagonal to form mitered corners; then press to get the perfect lines you need. (See fig. 7.)

Working with one side at a time, open up diagonal fold, and hold flat against side of table. Cut out triangle of fabric on upper corner by cutting straight down to the inside corner where leg meets table. Then cut diagonally up to outside corner, ¼″ (6mm) inside fold line. (See fig. 8.)

Step 6:

Brush diluted glue onto table leg, and wrap fabric around it smoothing out all wrinkles. To trim excess fabric, fold fabric back on itself and cut ¼″ (6mm) in from edge of leg. (See fig. 9.) Repeat procedure on remaining legs.

To cover bottoms of legs, clip each corner in a V-shape. Turn excess under and glue in place. (See fig. 10.)

To protect top of table, cover it with a sheet of glass secured in place with a dot of epoxy at each corner.

(Continued)

Figure 3

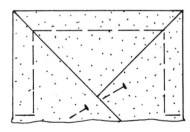

Figure 4

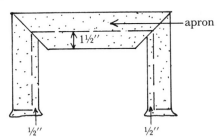

Figure 5

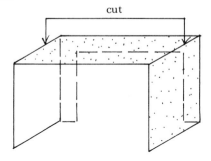

Figure 6

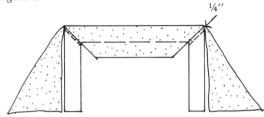

Figure 7

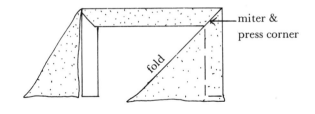

Figure 8

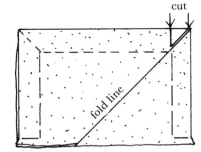

Figure 9

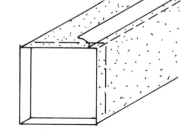

Figure 10

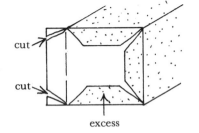

Method II

Step 1:

Cut out a piece of fabric equal to the dimensions of the table top and the aprons (sides) plus 1″ (2.5cm) on all sides. (See fig. 11.)

Brush diluted glue onto the top and aprons, center fabric, and glue in place. Miter corners, using a steel ruler and a single-edge razor blade. (See fig. 11.) Wrap and glue the extra 1″ (2.5cm) of fabric to the underside of the table.

Step 2:

Measure and cut rectangles of fabric equal to the dimensions of each leg plus a ½″

(1.3cm) overlap. Glue fabric to outer sides of legs. Trim to miter top corners to match first miters. Wrap and glue fabric to undersides of legs, overlapping seams. Miter fabric at underside of each leg, and glue in place.

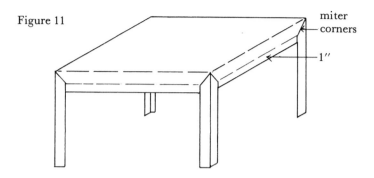

Figure 11

miter corners

1″

Floor Mats

Practical as well as pretty, floor mats add the perfect touch to any picnic or party where ground or floor seating is required.

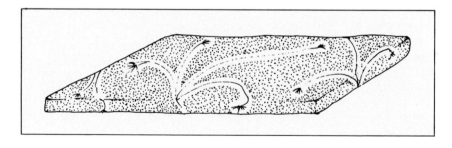

Materials

- 2 tea towels
- one 16″ (40.6cm) zipper
- dressmaker's pins
- thread to match
- fabric shears
- 1″ (2.5cm) thick polyurethane foam

Method

Step 1:

Press tea towels.

Place tea towels right sides out, end to end, and attach zipper according to manufacturer's directions along one end.

Step 2:

Fold tea towels with right sides together. Using ¼″ (6mm) seams, pin-baste, then stitch around three open sides. Trim excess fabric from corners. Turn right side out and press.

Step 3:

Cut a section of polyurethane foam ½″ (1.3cm) larger on all sides than the finished floor mat cover. Insert foam and zip cover closed.

Techniques

Appliqué

Appliqué is simply various shaped pieces of fabric placed on top of a background fabric and stitched in place.

Cut out one pattern piece from cardboard or heavy paper for each piece in the design. Place each pattern piece on the right side of the fabric to be the appliqué, using only one fabric thickness.

Trace around the pattern pieces with a soft pencil or tailor's chalk. This is the pattern outline. For seam allowance mark another line ¼″ (6mm) outside the pattern outline. This is the cutting line. (See fig. 1.)

For a smooth turning edge, stitch around the pattern outline. (See fig. 2.)

Cut out design pieces along the cutting line. (See fig. 3.)

Clip all corners and curves, and turn seam allowance in toward the wrong side of fabric to just inside the stitching line. (See fig. 4.) Gently press flat.

Place cardboard pattern pieces on background. Lightly trace around each piece to insure accurate placement. Pin and baste fabric design pieces in position on background fabric. Using very small stitches, slip-stitch design in place. (See Techniques, Hand Stitches.) (See fig. 5.)

For appliquéd pieces that touch each other, use only one row of stitching to catch both design pieces to the background fabric.

Figure 1

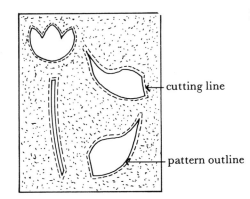

cutting line

pattern outline

Figure 2

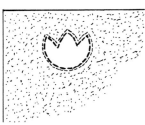

Figure 3

Figure 4

Figure 5

Bias Trim

Bias trim adds a professional finishing touch to any project. It conceals and strengthens raw edges, and, because of its unique ability to turn over edges smoothly and evenly without twisting or puckering, it is ideal to use to cover cable cord to make piping or larger welting for seams on pillows, bedspreads, and slipcovers. Bias trim may be made of matching or contrasting fabric, depending upon the effect you wish to achieve.

Bias describes direction. It is any diagonal which intersects the crosswise and lengthwise threads on a piece of fabric. Fabric cut on the bias displays much greater elasticity than a cut on either the crosswise or lengthwise grain.

True bias is the diagonal obtained by folding on-grain fabric diagonally so that the crosswise threads run in the same direction as the lengthwise threads. Maximum elasticity occurs on the true bias. True bias should always be used for piping or welting because it readily conforms to the cable cord it covers.

Ideally, bias strips are cut from a single piece of fabric long enough to fit the desired area. However, this method is not the most economical, so pieced bias strips are necessary. There are two types of pieced bias strips:
1. *Continuous, pieced strips,* recommended when many yards are needed, and 2. *Individual, pieced strips,* which tend to be more time-consuming to make than continuous pieced strips, but which are recommended when short lengths are called for.

The width of a bias strip depends on the specific project requirements. For binding raw edges, 1″ to 1¼″ (2.5cm to 3.2cm) is usually sufficient. For covering cable cord, 1″ (2.5cm) plus three times the diameter of the cable cord is generally sufficient.

Ready-made bias strips are available in a variety of colors and a choice of varying widths. They come packaged in single or double-fold, with the edges pressed under for convenience. In this way, the folds may be pressed open to the full width of the bias strip, depending upon your particular needs.

Whether you are using commercial bias strips or strips you have made yourself, the techniques outlined for applying or piecing the strips are identical.

Individual, Pieced Bias Strips
To find the true bias of a rectangular piece of fabric, fold the crosswise edge of the fabric down, and align it perfectly with the lengthwise threads, or the selvage. (See fig. 1.) Press the fold.

Using tailor's chalk, draw lines parallel to the true bias fold line and the width bias strip needed. Measure and mark as many strips as are needed to cover the length of cable cord required. (See fig. 2.) Cut along the fold; then cut along the chalk lines.

Bias strips should always be joined on the lengthwise grain, which creates a flat, less noticeable diagonal seam across the strip. If the ends of any strips have been cut on the crosswise grain, fold those ends on the lengthwise grain, and cut off the triangle that forms.

With right sides together, lap the ends so that the points extend ½″ (1.3cm) and the strips are at right angles to each other. Using ½″ (1.3cm) seams, stitch ends of strips together. (See fig. 3.) Press seams open and trim to ¼″ (6mm).

Continuous, Pieced Bias Strips
Find the true bias of a rectangular piece of fabric as outlined for individually pieced bias strips. Cut along the true bias fold line and discard the triangle.

Figure 1

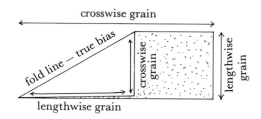

Figure 2

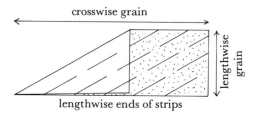

Figure 3

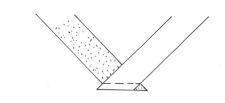

Figure 4

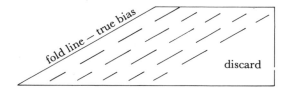

Using tailor's chalk, draw lines parallel to the true bias fold line marking off the width bias strip needed. Measure and mark as many strips as are needed to cover the cable cord. Label opposite ends of each strip with corresponding letters. (See fig. 4.) Each line must begin and end on a side edge of the rectangle of fabric. Discard the excess corner triangle.

Form a tube by bringing right sides together so that A meets A, B meets B, etc. The lines should meet exactly to form one continuous line. Stitch a ¼″ (6mm) seam and press open. (See fig. 5.)

Begin cutting along line A and continue in a spiral fashion to the end.

Covered Cable Cord
To make welting or piping, cover cable cord by wrapping the bias strip around it, right sides out. Make sure the raw edges are even. (See fig. 6.)

Using a zipper foot attachment, stitch the bias strip in place close to the cable cord, but be careful not to crowd the cord too tightly. (See fig. 7.) Gently pull the bias strip in front and in back of the needle as you stitch.

To determine the width bias strip needed to cover a particular cable cord diameter, wrap a tape measure loosely around the cable cord to determine its circumference; then add 1¼″ (3.2cm) for seam allowances.

Figure 5

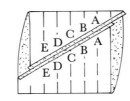

Figure 6

Figure 7

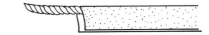

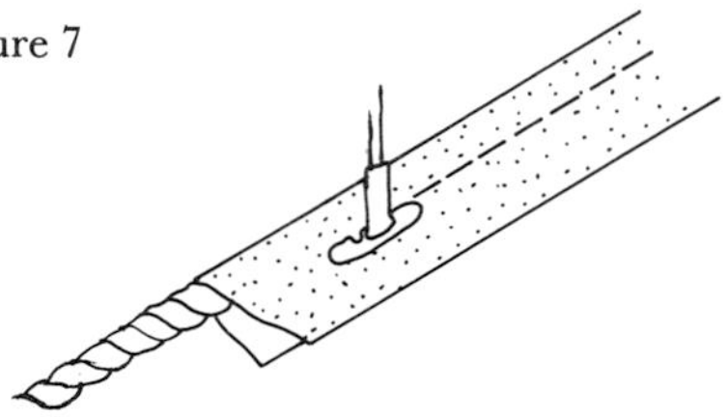

Fabric Covered Walls

Covering walls with fabric is not new, and as a decorating technique, it is both attractive and functional in any room of the house. With fabric, you have the added advantage of working with widths wider than wallpaper, thus giving you fewer seams to contend with.

There is no "easiest" or "best" way to cover a wall with fabric. Only by trying different techniques in different situations will you be able to determine the method most convenient for you and best suited to your abilities. *Fabric Decorating for the Home* includes five different methods of covering walls with fabric: shirred walls in the Country French Living Room, fiberboard technique in the Music Room, double-faced carpet tape method in the Study, pasted fabric walls in the Mr. & Mrs. Bedroom, and

stapled fabric walls in the Mrs. Bathroom. A discussion of the advantages of each method appears along with the specific measuring instructions included in each project.

Before beginning any wall covering project, make sure that your walls are clean and white or off-white in color. If the walls are colored, the fabric will appear tinted, especially if it is a sheer or light- to medium-weight fabric. If your walls have obvious bumps, lumps, or cracks, make the necessary repairs before covering the walls with fabric.

Always use new fabric, whether it is sheeting or yard goods from the local fabric store. When selecting printed fabrics for wall coverings, try to choose a small allover design, a random print, or a stripe. However, should you fall in love with a repeating pat-

(Continued)

Figure 1

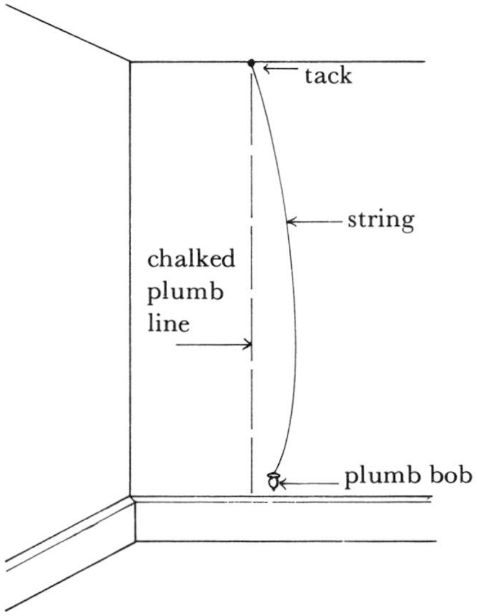

tern, be sure to add an extra repeating length to your calculations for necessary pattern match ups. Specific instructions for measuring and yardage requirements appear with each project.

Many fabrics are printed slightly off grain. Therefore, never pretrim fabric to fit your wall area. To compensate for off-grain fabric, allow at least 2″ (5cm) extra fabric at the top and bottom of the wall area for pattern alignment.

Your walls may also be a bit "off grain" due to settling. Always establish a plumb line on your wall so that the fabric may be positioned correctly. (See fig. 1.) To determine the true vertical line of your wall, tack a length of chalked string to the place where the ceiling meets the wall and wherever you will place your first length of fabric (usually in a corner). Tie a heavy weight such as a plumb bob or rock to the end of the string near the floor. This holds the string taut. While holding the weight in place, snap the string against the wall. The chalked line which appears is the true vertical of the wall and will serve as a guide in positioning the fabric.

To cover a ceiling with fabric, follow the same procedures as for applying fabric to walls. Simply treat the ceiling as a wall on the horizontal. Two people are really needed to do a ceiling. Should you decide to use the pasting method, reinforce the fabric with staples while the paste dries. If you are working on a bathroom ceiling, be especially careful not to hang yourself on the shower curtain rod or to crack your skull open on the bathtub or sink; bathroom ceilings are not one of the easiest areas to cover with fabric.

You may wish to trim a fabric covered wall to hide the raw edges or seam lines. Braid, grosgrain ribbon, or self welting can be easily applied with undiluted white household glue. Painted or fabric covered moldings can also be attached with headless nails. These border trims create a more finished and sometimes a more formal effect.

To clean fabric covered walls, vacuum them. New fabric is coated with a resin finish which protects against soot and dirt penetration. Therefore, any soil that may accumulate just sits on top waiting to be vacuumed off. If a really bad stain occurs, clean it as quickly as possible with a liquid, spray, or paste dry cleaning agent. For extra protection against soiling, apply a clear acrylic spray to the wall fabric. This is a particu-

larly good idea if you have small children with sticky fingers.

Removing fabric from walls is actually much easier than you may imagine. To remove stapled fabric, protect your eyes, and use a staple remover to pull the staples from the wall. Be prepared to spackle an occasional hole or two after the wood stripping has been removed.

To remove pasted fabric, saturate it using a rented steamer, hot water in a plant sprayer, or a hot, wet sponge. Gently peel fabric off the wall; then wash down the wall with hot water to remove any excess paste.

To remove shirred fabric, remove the café curtain rods and unthread the fabric from the rods. Remove cable cord from casings.

To remove carpet taped fabric, peel fabric off tape, then carefully peel tape off wall. Wash taped areas with a solvent.

To remove fabric covered fiberboards, pry boards away from the wall with a screwdriver. Be prepared to spackle an occasional hole or two.

Fabric from all methods except pasted walls can be recycled into small projects once it is removed and cleaned. Fabric that has been pasted to walls cannot be used again.

Hand-Bound Buttonholes

Generally, buttonholes are ⅛″ (3mm) longer than the diameter of the button. However, when very small buttons are used, the difference should be slightly less than ⅛″ (3mm), and if you are using a very thick fabric and the button is covered or has a high domed design, the difference should be slightly greater than the ⅛″ (3mm) difference.

Depending upon the fabric, use either

regular thread, heavy-duty thread, or buttonhole twist. Always use a single thread.

Mark the length of the buttonhole needed. Stitch around hole for reinforcement, 1/16″ (1.5mm) away from the marking.

Cut the buttonhole open between the two lines of stitching.

Working on the right side of the fabric, make a bar tack across the one end of the

Figure 1

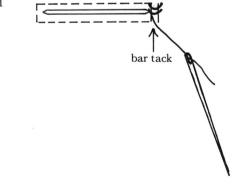

bar tack

hole to fasten your thread in place (do not knot it). Then work across the bar tack with tiny perpendicular stitches through the fabric and over the bar. (See fig. 1.)

Working from right to left, bring thread to the left, then down, around, and up to the right forming a loop. Push the needle down through the fabric just outside the reinforcement stitching, up through the slit, and through the center of the thread loop. (See fig. 2.) Pull thread through carefully to place the "purl" of the stitch along the raw edge of the buttonhole slit. Do not pull thread tightly.

Work across one side of the buttonhole in the same manner. (See fig. 3.) Bar tack the opposite end, and work up the remaining side of the buttonhole slit. (See fig. 4.) Fasten thread in place on the underside with two back stitches.

Figure 2

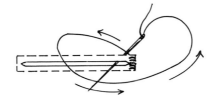

Figure 3

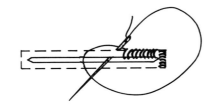

Figure 4

Hand-Rolled Hem

Hand-rolled hems are an elegant finish for table linens or any item requiring a small, delicate hem.

Mark the fabric with tailor's chalk where the hemline is to be, and stitch ¼″ (6mm) below the mark. Trim excess hem allowance ⅛″ (3mm) below the stitching line. Press stitching. (See fig. 1.)

Fold stitched edge to wrong side of fabric, making sure the stitching line is just below the folded hem allowance. (See fig. 2.)

Working from right to left and using a fine needle with thread to match, take a small stitch through the fold. Then, diagonally ⅛″ (3mm) below and beyond the stitch, pick up a few threads of the main fabric. (See fig. 3.)

After several loose stitches, carefully pull thread to roll hem to wrong side of fabric. (See fig. 4.)

Figure 1

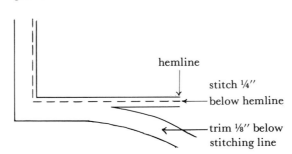

hemline

stitch ¼″ below hemline

trim ⅛″ below stitching line

Figure 2

Figure 3

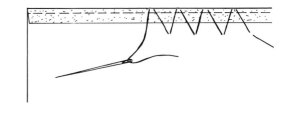

Figure 4

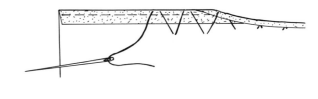

Hand Stitches

Although most of the projects in *Fabric Decorating for the Home* are designed to be stitched on the sewing machine, there often are some details that are best done by hand. The four basic stitches explained here are techniques used throughout the book to give items a neat, finished appearance.

Slant Hemming Stitch
A very popular and basic technique, the hemming stitch is similar to the slip stitch but is considered stronger. It is practically invisible on the right side of the fabric, while long slanting stitches are visible on the wrong side. Always match the thread color to the fabric and use one thread.

Baste hem in place. Thread needle and knot long end of the thread.

Hold hem edge between thumb and index finger of the left hand. Left-handed people work in opposite direction, holding hem with the right hand.

Fasten thread on the wrong side of the hem. Working from right to left, bring the needle up through the hem edge, then diagonally down over the hem edge catching only a single thread of the main fabric. Bring needle back up and out of the hem edge. (See fig. 1.) Each stitch should be ¼" (6mm) to ⅜" (9mm) to the left of the preceding stitch.

When finished, fasten thread securely with three tiny backstitches in the hem edge. (See fig. 2.)

Slip stitch
The slip stitch is a practically invisible stitch used to join two folded edges or one folded edge to a flat surface, as for hems or appliquéing. It is also ideal for closing pillow openings after stuffing.

Fasten thread on the wrong side of the fabric. Working from right to left, bring needle up through one folded edge. Slip needle through fold of opposite edge, bring needle out, and pull thread through. (See fig. 3.) Each stitch should be ¼" (6mm) to ½" (1.3cm) to the left of the preceding stitch and fairly loose.

Topstitch
Topstitching is not only decorative but practical as well. Single or multiple rows of parallel stitching add importance and stability to finished edges on such items as napkins, placemats, tablecloths, and pillows.

Either regular thread or buttonhole twist may be used for topstitching. When using buttonhole twist in your sewing machine, use it for the needle thread, and use regular thread for the bobbin. Use a size 18 needle and a slightly longer stitch than for regular stitching. It is usually necessary to increase needle thread tension when stitching with buttonhole twist. Always test your topstitching on a piece of scrap fabric before stitching directly on the item you plan to accent.

Whipstitch
The whipstitch is usually favored for joining two finished edges, but it is often used to hold raw edges neatly to a flat surface.

Fasten thread on the wrong side of the fabric. Insert needle close to and at right angles to the fabric edge, picking up only a few threads. (See fig. 4.) Repeat, working from right to left. The distance between the stitches will vary according to the project.

Figure 1
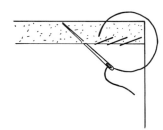

Figure 2
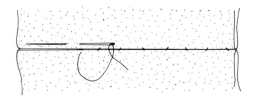

Figure 3

Figure 4
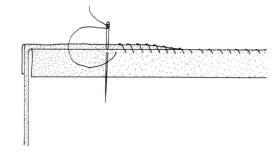

Mitered Corners

Mitering is a common method of removing bulk at corners of napkins, tablecloths, or any other items requiring neat, square corners.

Turn seam or hem allowances to the inside and press in place. (See fig. 1.) If working with a hem allowance, fold raw edge under ¼″ (6mm) and press in place.

At the corners, open up the seam or hem allowances (not the ¼″ [6mm] fold). Turn the corner down so that the diagonal fold crosses exactly at the junction of the lengthwise and crosswise folds of the hem. (See fig. 2.) Press in place.

With right sides together, fold corner in half. Pin-baste along diagonal fold line; then stitch in place. (See fig. 3.)

Trim excess fabric to within ⅜″ (9mm), and clip corners. Press seam open. (See fig. 4.)

Turn corner right side out. Pin-baste edges, and stitch in place. (See fig. 5.)

Figure 1

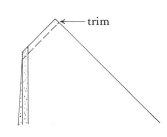
folds
raw edges

Figure 4
trim

Figure 2
diagonal fold
¼″ fold for hem
fold lines

Figure 5
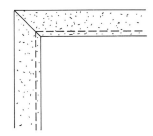

Figure 3
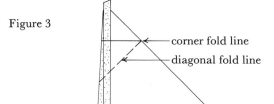
corner fold line
diagonal fold line

Quilting

Since each project includes the materials and specific instructions necessary, this section does not deal with all the facets of quilt making. Rather, the emphasis is on the very basic technique of hand or machine stitching a padding between two layers of fabric. Quilting stitches are usually executed in a planned design. For beginners, and for purposes of the projects in this book, only two elementary quilting patterns are suggested here: horizontal/vertical lines, and diagonal lines.

Select a light- to medium-weight fabric for quilting. The lighter the fabric the easier it is to quilt. The fabric should be firmly woven with a soft texture, and should not ravel freely. Cottons and cotton synthetic blends are excellent choices because they wear so well. Use a "glazed" cotton thread (size 40) for both hand and machine quilting.

Press the fabric. Measure and cut out fabric pieces to be quilted, each a bit larger than you need because the fabric tends to draw up and become smaller as it is quilted.

Place the top layer of fabric right side up on top of a flat working surface. Using a ruler and tailor's chalk, measure and draw horizontal and vertical lines across the fabric to be quilted. (See fig. 1.) Spacing of the lines would naturally depend upon the size of the item to be quilted.

(Continued)

Figure 1
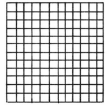

Figure 2
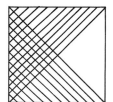

For diagonal quilting, draw an X connecting opposite corners of the fabric to be quilted and continue marking lines parallel to each line of the X. (See fig. 2.)

Place polyester or cotton batting or other filling between the top and bottom fabric layers, right sides out. (See fig. 3.) Working from the center out, pin, then baste along all quilting lines to hold fabric in place.

Again working from the center out, stitch along all quilting lines, beginning with the center vertical, then the center horizontal lines. Eight to ten stitches per inch is recommended for machine quilting.

A quilter's guide bar greatly simplifies quilting; its adjustable spacer guides your stitching lines.

Figure 3

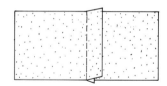

top fabric
← batting
← bottom fabric

Seams

There are a myriad of types of seams in sewing, each with specific advantages. For purposes of the projects found in this book, two popular and versatile seam techniques are given here.

Flat-Felled Seams

This technique gives seams a very tailored appearance and conceals raw edges. Since it is formed on the right side of the fabric, a flat-felled seam may also be very decorative. In addition, flat-felled seams are particularly sturdy and are therefore favored for use on heavyweight fabrics.

Using a ⅝″ (1.5cm) seam allowance, pin-baste wrong sides of fabric together; then stitch in place. (See fig. 1.)

Trim edge of one seam allowance to one-half its width. (See fig. 2.) With a press cloth between iron and fabric to protect against shine, press seam open.

Using a press cloth again, press both seam edges to one side with the wider edge on top. (See fig. 3.)

Turn the wide edge under, catching up trimmed edge. Topstitch in place. (See fig. 4.)

Using a press cloth, press seam on wrong side of fabric.

French Seams

A French seam is a seam within a seam and is used to conceal raw edges. It is stitched twice, once from the wrong side and again from the right side of the fabric. French seams are particularly popular on sheer or lightweight fabrics.

Pin-baste wrong sides of fabric together. Stitch in place using ¼″ (6mm) seams.

With a press cloth between the iron and the fabric to protect against shine, press seam to one side. Then carefully press seam open with point of iron. Trim seam allowance to ⅛″ (3mm).

Fold right sides of fabric together so that the stitching line lies directly on the folded edge; press. Using ½″ (1.3cm) seams, stitch in place enclosing the raw edges of the first seam. (See fig. 5.) Press the seam to one side.

Figure 1

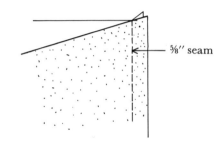

← ⅝″ seam

Figure 2

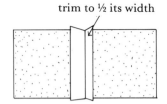

trim to ½ its width

Figure 3

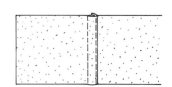

Figure 4

Figure 5

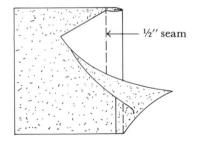

← ½″ seam

Slipcovers

The secret of professional slipcovers is cutting the fabric to the exact size and shape of the furniture to be covered. It is not difficult but does require an understanding of fabric grain.

If you are making your first slipcovers, begin on an item with straight lines, such as an ottoman. Once you understand the principles of placing and cutting the fabric, you will be able to cover almost any type of furniture.

Select slipcover fabric carefully. Your best choice is a tightly woven fabric manufactured especially for upholstery such as chintz, velveteen, lightweight denim, duck, sailcloth, broadcloth, brocade, and jacquard weaves. Purchase light- or medium-weight fabric that is sturdy enough to withstand the wear you expect to give it. Remember, in making slipcovers you often have to stitch through several layers of fabric when attaching welting and adjoining sections. Most heavyweight fabrics are too thick to be stitched through easily with a home sewing machine, especially if you are working with six or eight layers.

Test the fabric for wrinkling by crushing a small piece in the palm of your hand. Choose fabric that does not wrinkle easily.

Avoid fabrics that ravel freely. Pull a few threads along a cut edge to be certain that the fabric does not fray any more than is normal.

If you plan to wash your slipcovers instead of dry cleaning them, test-launder a swatch of fabric before making the covers. You may find that the finished covers will remain bright longer by cleaning them in a coin operated dry cleaning machine.

For items that will be near a window or in bright sunlight, test the fabric for sunfastness by placing a small swatch in direct sunlight for several hours and comparing the swatch to the original fabric.

Some fabrics have a stain resistant finish which helps extend the life of the slipcover. If the fabric you select does not have such a finish, sprays are available at most hardware stores.

Fabrics with a small, all-over design which do not require matching are the easiest to work with. If you select a print with a large motif, or one that needs matching, be sure to buy enough fabric to allow for matching. Directional prints or napped fabrics should be positioned so that the design is centered on each large section of the furniture—inside and outside back, cushions top and bottom, (inside arm pieces should match each other)—and so that the lengthwise grain runs from the top of the furniture toward the floor.

Striped patterns should be matched to form a continuous line from the top of the back down the back across the seat, down the apron and skirt to the floor. Arm stripes should be continuous, starting at the seat, up over the arm, and down to the floor.

Always work with the right side of your fabric facing up when positioning and cutting. Keep in mind that upholstery fabric is designed to be viewed at a distance and that at close range you cannot always appreciate the impact of the print in relation to the lines of the furniture. When positioning fabric on each section of the furniture, secure it with T-pins; then step back at least six feet to check overall appearance.

The amount of fabric needed will depend upon the style of the item you plan to cover. A salesperson will assist you if you bring a simple sketch of the item to be covered along with its basic dimensions.

If you do not wish to follow a fabric guide, determine your own yardage: measure all the chair sections as shown in figure 1.

Figure 1

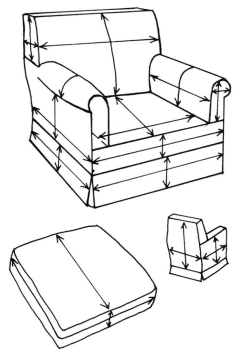

Total all the lenthwise measurements; then add tuck-in allowances (10″ [25.4cm] where the seat and inside back meet, and 5″ [12.7cm] where the seat and each inside arm meet). Add 2″ (5cm) for every seam crossed on the original cover. Allow 2 yards (1.8m) for welting. Divide the total number of inches by 36 to determine the number of yards you will need. If the item you are measuring is wider than 48″ (121.9cm), which is the standard width of upholstery fabric, multiply by two or three to be certain you have enough fabric to cover the complete width.

It is wise to have several sewing machine needles on hand since it is not uncommon to break or bend them as you stitch through several layers of fabric. For most slipcover fabrics, size 16 (heavy-duty) sewing machine needles are your best choice.

(Continued)

Before you begin making slipcovers, plan carefully and assemble all the necessary equipment.

- T-pins and dressmaker's pins for attaching the fabric to the piece of furniture and for pin-basting.
- upholstery zippers, depending upon the piece of furniture
- heavy-duty thread
- fabric shears
- tape measure and a small gauge or ruler
- tailor's chalk
- zipper foot sewing machine attachment

Be sure the piece of furniture to be covered is clean. Repair any tears or sagging springs. Fill in any flattened or hollowed out areas with new padding covered with a heavyweight fabric patch sewn directly to the old cover.

For beginners it is wise to construct a muslin pattern before working with the slipcover fabric. The procedure is identical as for the finished slipcover, plus you have the advantage of working out any problems on the muslin. Then use the muslin as the pattern for the actual slipcover.

If your chair already has a well-fitting slipcover, you can take it apart and use the pieces as a pattern, adding for seam allowances.

For a neat, tailored appearance, use welting or cording of either contrasting or matching color in the major seams of the slipcover.

Prepare as much covered cable cord (welting) as you will need. Estimate the amount by measuring around all the areas of the furniture piece that are to be edged with the welting, including the outer back, arms, seat, pillow edges, etc. In general, you will need about 15 to 20 yards (13.7m to 18.3m) of welting to cover a standard size upholstered chair. Since the amount of welting used for a sofa can vary greatly, it is best to determine how much you need by measuring each welted seam and adding all measurements together. (To make welting, see Techniques, Bias Trim, and follow directions for covering cable cord.)

Place fabric on the most prominent section of the piece of furniture first. On a chair or sofa begin by placing the fabric on the inside back panel; on an ottoman, begin by placing the fabric on the top. Cut the slipcover fabric about 3″ (7.6cm) larger on all sides than the area to be covered. The excess fabric can be trimmed off after the welting has been attached and the adjoining sections are stitched in place.

Pin-baste welting to the fabric section so that it rests exactly on top of the seam lines of the piece of furniture being covered. The

rounded part of the welting should be facing toward the center of the piece of furniture so that the raw edges of the welting extend as seam allowances.

Remove the fabric section with welting pin-basted in position and stitch welting in place using a zipper foot attachment.

Pin the fabric back onto the piece of furniture to be certain that the welting is attached correctly. Pin-baste the adjoining fabric sections to the cover. Remove the pinned section, stitch together. If necessary, clip curved seams to allow the fabric to fit smoothly. Be careful not to clip closer than ¼″ (6mm) from the stitching line. Trim excess fabric to within 1″ (2.5cm) of the stitching line.

Continue pinning one fabric section at a time to construct the cover piece by piece. Remember that a slipcover must fit as snugly as possible, so do not allow any "ease" as you place, pin, and cut each section.

Most slipcovers have snap tape strips or heavy-duty zippers to facilitate removal. Snap tape strips can be cut to any length. Heavy-duty zippers, designed especially for slipcovers, come in 24-, 27-, 30-, and 36-inch lengths. Slipcovers should have a snap tape or zipper closing along one side of the outside back of the chair. Each cushion should also have an opening along the back and around one corner.

Tablecloths

Besides helping to save household dollars, designing and making a varied wardrobe for your table is a wonderful outlet for your individual creativity. Many of the room projects include table linens. Interchange the ideas to suit your life-style, or whip up several to make your dining an experience in fashion.

As a general rule, purchase fabric as wide as possible when making a tablecloth, and plan any necessary piecing to avoid a seam in the center of the cloth. If using a large print or a stripe, be sure to match the design at the seams.

Measure your table accurately before purchasing fabric. The amount needed will depend on the style tablecloth desired, fabric

Figure 1

short cloth

floor-length cloth

pattern, and length of the drop. For a formal cloth, the drop is usually 16″ to 24″ (40.6cm to 61cm). Never let the tablecloth drag the floor. A short cloth usually has a drop of 10″ to 14″ (25.4cm to 35.6cm). Never have less than a 10″ (25.4cm) drop or the cloth will appear skimpy.

Be certain the fabric is preshrunk, or preshrink it yourself before measuring the fabric for the tablecloth. Be sure the fabric is on grain before cutting.

Allow ½″ (1.3cm) for hems and ½″ (1.3cm) for all seams.

Round Tablecloths
Estimate the diameter of the finished table-cloth. Round cloths are usually 52″ (132cm), 70″ (177.8cm), 90″ (228.6cm), or 108″ (274.3cm) in diameter.

For a short cloth, measure the diameter of the table top; then add 10″ to 14″ (25.4cm to 35.6cm) to each side to provide for a suitable drop. (See fig. 1.)

For a floor-length cloth, measure the diameter of the table top; then add two times the height of the table. (See fig. 1.)

If the finished tablecloth is to measure less than 90″ (228.6cm) in diameter, and your fabric is not wide enough, divide one width of fabric in half lengthwise. Using ½″ (1.3cm) seams, stitch the selvage edge of each half width to the selvages of the center full width. (See fig. 2.)

If the finished tablecloth is to measure more than 90″ (228.6cm) in diameter and your fabric is not wide enough, stitch three full widths of fabric together along the selvages.

Press seams open and fold the fabric into quarters. Pin to hold in place and press.

Using a yardstick and tailor's chalk, measure from the folded point to one half the diameter of the finished cloth plus ½″ (1.3cm) for the hem. For example, if the finished round tablecloth is to measure 90″ (228.6cm) in diameter, measure 45½″ from

the folded point. Mark with tailor's chalk and cut along the arc. (See fig. 3.)

Whether hemming by hand or by machine, first stitch around the circle ¼″ (6mm) in from the outer edge. Trim to ⅛″ (3mm).

Turn the fabric under along the stitching line, and turn under again to form a finished hem. Topstitch ¼″ (6mm) in from the folded edge or slip-stitch by hand to finish.

Oval Tablecloths
To estimate the amount of fabric needed for a short cloth, measure across the width and length of the table top; then add 10″ to 14″ (25.4cm to 35.6cm) to each side to provide for a suitable drop. (See fig. 4.)

For a floor-length cloth, measure across the width and length of the table top; then add two times the height to each figure. (See fig. 4.)

If your fabric is not wide enough, piece equal lengths of fabric together along the selvages using ½″ (1.3cm) seams.

Center the fabric, right side up on top of the oval table. The large middle fabric section should be centered across the widest part of the table so that the seams run along the sides. (See fig. 5.)

Place weights such as books on top of the fabric in the center and evenly around the edge of the table to hold the tablecloth in place while measuring and cutting.

For a short tablecloth, measure around the fabric and place pins 10″ to 14″ (25.4cm to 35.6cm) plus ½″ (1.3cm) hem allowance below the table edge at 3″ (7.6cm) intervals. (See fig. 5.)

For a floor-length cloth, place pins 1″ (2.5cm) above the floor at 3″ (7.6cm) intervals. Cut along the pinned line.

Remove cloth from table and stitch around the outside of the oval ¼″ (6mm) in from the outer edge. Trim to ⅛″ (3mm). Hem by hand or by machine using the same techniques as for a round tablecloth.

Figure 2

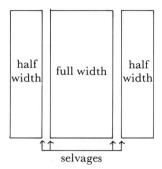

selvages

Figure 3

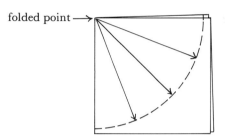

folded point →

Figure 4

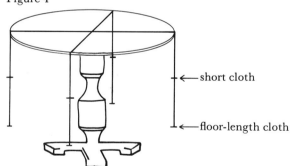

← short cloth

← floor-length cloth

Figure 5

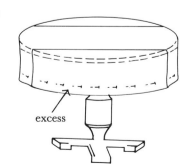

excess

Tassels

Whether made of matching or contrasting colors, tassels add an exotic accent to many pillow shapes.

Cut a rectangle of cardboard to the desired length of the tassel. Wind yarn or embroidery floss around the cardboard twenty or more times, depending upon the thickness desired for the tassel. (See fig. 1.) It is best to position threads next to each other rather than "stacking."

Thread a large-eyed needle with 8″ (20.3cm) of yarn or embroidery floss. Slide needle under top of tassel strands and tie strands together tightly. (See fig. 2.) Clip untied ends of yarn or embroidery floss, and remove from cardboard.

Tightly wrap a piece of yarn or floss several times around the tied strands, one-third of the way down from the top. Knot firmly and trim. (See fig. 3.)

Trim ends of finished tassel evenly.

To sew tassel to an item, thread needle with loose yarn from the top knot of the tassel.

Figure 1

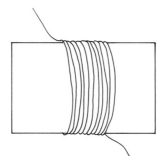

Figure 2

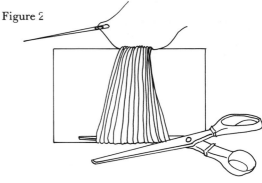

Figure 3

Window Treatments

Windows are special areas of a home which can either enhance or detract from the desired finished appearance of your decor. It takes special care and planning to create a functional, as well as attractive, window treatment. The correct window wardrobe can cut fuel bills by reducing the amount of heat or air conditioning escaping from your home. Some other window fashions offer screening from bright headlights or traffic noises. Or a very stylish window treatment may simply be a pleasure to look at.

Besides being functional, a window treatment can work decorating miracles by making the window look wider, narrower, shorter, or longer. There are many types of window styles—double hung, casement, corner, ranch, bay, picture, and French doors—and an even greater number of fashions for each style. Appropriately dressed, a window's problems are camouflaged and its best qualities are enhanced.

Use your windows to help create a mood in the room; it is a great opportunity to tie textures and colors together to give a finished, polished look to your decor. Or, instead of a background role, let your windows be true showstoppers. Experiment with different window styles—do the unexpected. You are limited only by your imagination.

Many fabrics are suitable for draperies or curtains. But, before investing money and time in a pretty fabric that may turn out to be totally "wrong," do a little experimenting at the store. Gather the fabric into folds and

Figure 1

Figure 2

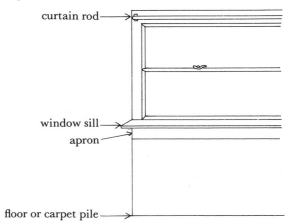

curtain rod

window sill

apron

floor or carpet pile

check the way it drapes. Is it stiff and angular or does it hang naturally and gracefully?

Is the fabric durable, or will repeated washings make it appear limp and old? What effect will the humidity have on the fabric's fiber, weave, and texture? Will the sun fade the colors in a few month's time?

This last question can be solved quite simply by lining your draperies or curtains. Lining can protect the drapery fabric from the sun's rays, but it must be of a quality that will last the life of the drapery fabric. An alternative is sun-resistant sheers placed between the window and the draperies to prevent fading.

Before measuring for your draperies or curtains, decide on the window treatment you wish to use. *Then install the appropriate rods and hardware.* Rods may be placed at the ceiling, above the window frame, or directly on the frame. Expansion rods for café curtains go within the window jamb.

Always measure each window separately; those that appear to be identical may not be. There are three standard lengths for draperies or curtains: to the window sill, to the bottom of the apron, or 1″ (2.5cm) above the floor or carpet pile. (If the room has baseboard heating, the draperies may have to stop just above the baseboard.) If you plan to hang sheers behind the draperies, their length should be 1″ (2.5cm) shorter at the bottom, and ½″ (1.3cm) shorter at the top than the draperies they are to hang behind.

Complete construction of your draperies or curtains up to hemming; then let them hang for at least a few hours before final hemming. By doing this you will be able to determine if the length needs adjusting beyond what you planned. The standard hem allowance for full-length draperies is 5″ (12.7cm), or 3″ (7.6cm) for café curtains.

Measuring for Draperies or Curtains
Finished width of each panel: 2½ to 3 times the width of the curtain rod from its outer corner to the center, plus the return. (See fig. 1.) For traverse rods, measure each half separately from the wall bracket, including the return, to the end of the center master slider.

Total width of each panel before sewing: Finished width plus ½″ (1.3cm) seam allowances if more than one fabric width is required, plus 1″ (2.5cm) side hems.

Finished length of each panel: Distance from the top of the curtain rod to the window sill, bottom of the apron, or to the floor or carpet pile. If the hooks you plan to use will cause the drapery to extend above the curtain rod, add that amount to the length. (See fig. 2.)

Total length of each panel before sewing: Finished length plus top heading and turn-under, and bottom hem allowances. (See fig. 3.)

Measuring for Casement Curtains
Finished width of each panel: 2 times the width of the curtain rod from end to end. (See fig. 4.)

Total width of each panel before sewing: Finished width plus ½″ (1.3cm) seam allowances on each side of the pieced panel, plus 1″ (2.5cm) side hems.

Finished length of each panel: Distance from top of upper curtain rod to bottom of lower curtain rod. (See fig. 5.)

(Continued)

Figure 3   Draperies or Curtains

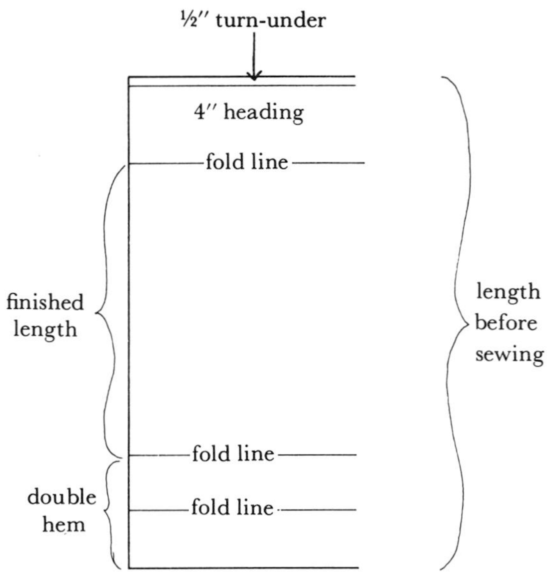

½″ turn-under

4″ heading

fold line

finished length

length before sewing

fold line

double hem

fold line

Figure 4

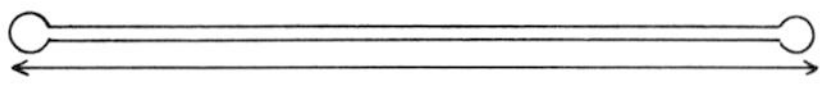

Figure 5

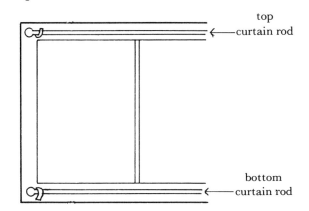

top
curtain rod

bottom
curtain rod

Total length of each panel before sewing: Finished length plus top and bottom rod casings, and headings, and turn-under. (See fig. 6.)

Measuring for Café Curtains
Finished width of each panel: 2½ to 3 times the width of the curtain rod from its outer corner to the center. (See fig. 7.)

Total width of each panel before sewing: Finished width plus ½″ (1.3cm) seam allowances on each side of the pieced panel, plus 1″ (2.5cm) side hems.

Finished length of each panel: Distance from bottom of curtain rod to the window sill, bottom of the apron, or to the floor or carpet pile. (See fig. 8.)

Total length of each panel before sewing: Finished length plus top heading, plus top and bottom hem allowances. (See fig. 9.)

Figure 6   Casement Curtains

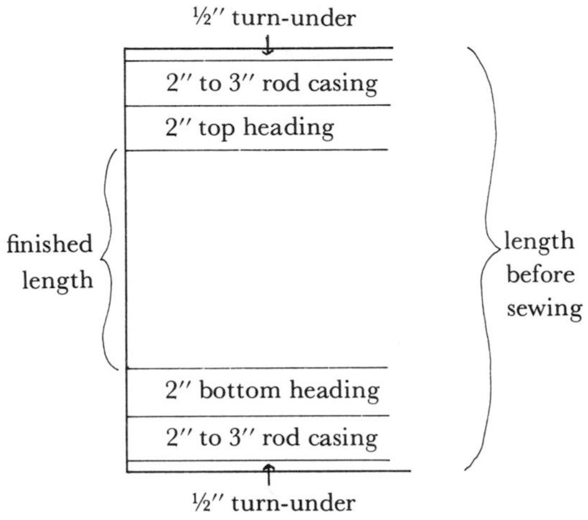

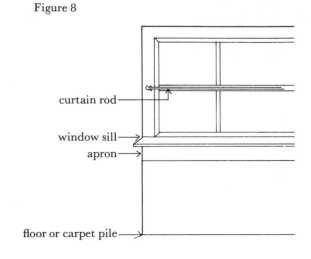

½″ turn-under

2″ to 3″ rod casing

2″ top heading

finished length

length before sewing

2″ bottom heading

2″ to 3″ rod casing

½″ turn-under

Figure 8

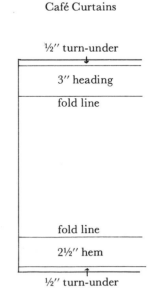

curtain rod

window sill

apron

floor or carpet pile

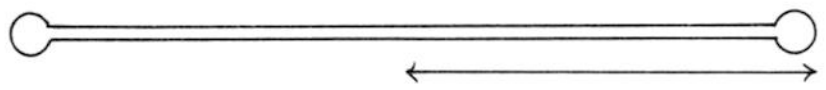

Figure 9   Café Curtains

½″ turn-under

3″ heading

fold line

fold line

2½″ hem

½″ turn-under

Figure 7